D0587015

Creating an
Outstanding
College

Creating an Outstanding College

Sir Bernard O'Connell

Published in 2005 by:
Nelson Thornes Ltd
Delta Place
27 Bath Road
CHELTENHAM
GL53 7TH
United Kingdom

05 06 07 08 09 / 10 9 8 7 6 5 4 3 2 1

A catalogue record for this book is available from the British Library

ISBN 0-7487-9603-7

Page make-up by Northern Phototypesetting Co. Ltd, Bolton

Printed and bound in Spain by GraphyCems

To my role model and wife, Jane,
and to the staff of Runshaw College.

CONTENTS

FOREWORD

The task of leading and transforming a tertiary college into an outstanding college is a formidable and complex challenge. This book is a fascinating account of the journey of a college principal who has led a genuine transformation. In sharing his journey he provides a guide to others who face or choose a similar path of leadership and transformation. Sir Bernard O'Connell's book about co-creating an outstanding transformation of Runshaw College with his staff is a description of transformational leadership in action. It begins with a situation that is common to many colleges and takes the reader through the process involved step by step, sharing the pitfalls and difficulties which have to be overcome as well as the successes and joys.

At the heart of this transformation is total dedication to the success of learners aligned with the building of an effective management team. What unites the team is its commitment to learners and a values-driven approach to leadership with a culture built around the concept of a professional learning community. This requires significant effort and time to discuss shared purpose and meaning, the staff competencies required, appropriate leadership styles, and the development and training of staff.

I hope that the sharing of this honest, stretching and hugely rewarding journey gives readers confidence that such changes can be carried out successfully and provides the inspiration to begin (or continue) on their own leadership journey of transformation. We can all learn from the experience of Runshaw College.

This personal and professional leadership journey undertaken so powerfully by Sir Bernard illustrates the lived reality of the Centre for Excellence in Leadership's vision of developing world-class educational leadership for every learner through a student-led culture and inspiring values.

We hope that this book will inspire all who read it, particularly those who lead colleges and other kinds of organisations. Within these pages lies a valuable framework that leaders at all levels can use to generate new ideas and actions to improve the quality, quantity, diversity and performance of leaders.

I have the greatest admiration for Sir Bernard and am delighted to support and endorse his book.

Lynne Sedgmore

Chief Executive
Centre for Excellence in Leadership
10 Greycoat Place
London
SW1P 1SB

ACKNOWLEDGEMENTS

Since 1993 I have received support from two mentors, John Oliver OBE and Stewart Pierce. Throughout the 1990s they were respectively the Chief Executive Officer and Director of Human Relations at Leyland Trucks. They were also respectively Chair and Deputy Chair of the governors at Runshaw: John was Chair from 1993 to 2003 and Stewart was Deputy Chair from 1991 until 1993 and then a governor and Chair of a governor's committee on organisational development from 1993 to 2004. I cannot express how much I owe to both of them, firstly for their professional mentoring and for inspiring the whole culture-change approach described in this book; secondly for their friendship, personal support, patience and tolerance; and thirdly for role modelling how senior managers can be value driven, honourable, decent and committed to supporting others.

This book makes constant reference to individual staff at Runshaw who acted as 'champions' of the new value-driven culture. I found many of them inspirational and supportive. They include the current principal at Runshaw, Mike Sheehan, and the deputy-principal, John Morrison, two of the people who came to the fore in 1995 and displayed the new form of moral leadership. In writing this book I have also received guidance and support from Professor John Mackness at Lancaster University and the Centre for Excellence in Leadership, and from my publisher, Claire Hart. I have drawn inspiration, too, from many academic books, most notably the work of Professor David Hopkins and David Jackson in the schools sector and from Professor Jackie Lumby and Dr Ann Briggs in the college sector. I owe a tremendous debt of gratitude to the many staff and managers at Runshaw with whom I have debated all the issues described in this book. The process of writing this book has been very cathartic for me because it has allowed me the opportunity to reflect not only on all the approaches that we used at Runshaw but also on all the happy memories of warm relationships, friendships and support that I received from so many people. I am grateful to them all.

Sir Bernard O'Connell
oconnellbernard@yahoo.co.uk

1 INTRODUCTION

In a remarkably short time of 18 months, between the summer of 1993 and the end of 1994, Runshaw College was transformed from a 'good' college into an 'outstanding' one as the direct result of a culture-change programme. By 1996 it achieved grade 1 for four of the five cross-college elements in its government inspection and over the next few years it achieved further dramatic improvements in student success rates, recruitment and staff morale to achieve seven grade 1s in its 2001 inspection. This made it the joint best performing further-education college in that four-year inspection cycle. It then developed the goal of achieving 'a grade 1 in everything' in its next inspection. In the event it achieved grade 1 in everything except two curriculum areas (for which it was graded 2) in its February 2005 inspection. On the basis of this success, this book seeks to answer three questions:

- How did it make the breakthrough between 1993 to 1995?
- How did it sustain and improve on its level of excellence over the next decade?
- Is whatever it did transferable to other colleges?

The idea behind this book is the same as that behind an approach used at Runshaw College called 'best in class'. We constantly encouraged all staff to identify examples of best practice elsewhere and to find out what they could about them, particularly about whether their approaches were transferable to Runshaw. If we had come across a book by the former principal of an outstanding college, which gave his or her account of how that college had become outstanding, we would have read it very carefully.

With regard to the three questions listed above, this book argues that the answer to the third question is 'yes' and it seeks to show how the approaches used at Runshaw can work elsewhere. The 'Runshaw way' is proposed as a generally applicable approach to college improvement. In fact, as is explained in Chapter 2, 'the Runshaw way' did not originate at Runshaw. We borrowed it from the private sector, from Leyland Trucks to be specific, and we have seen it being introduced successfully elsewhere with rapid and significant results.

In 1999, for example, the deputy-principal at Runshaw became principal at another college in a deprived inner-city area. The college had just received a poor inspection report with, for example, grade 4 for quality assurance. On his first day as principal he introduced a raft of initiatives drawn from 'the Runshaw way'. The impact was immediate and dramatic. Four years later, the college received a grade 1 for leadership and management. In April 2004, another senior manager left Runshaw to become principal of a college elsewhere, which was in severe financial difficulties, and in May 2005 it similarly achieved a profile of inspection rates predominantly at grade 1.

Saying that Runshaw's approaches are transferable seems to fly in the face of the prevailing 'common-sense' view that all colleges are different, that they are at different stages of development, that they have different environments and different priorities, so what works in one college will not necessarily work in another. Of course I agree with this but this book argues that there is a core approach, involving forms of 'transformational' and 'instructional' leadership, which can be adapted to the circumstances of any organisation and can succeed in building the capacity for all colleges to succeed. Moreover, this book argues that traditional approaches to leadership – 'transactional' leadership – are bound to fail in the world of further education, faced as it is with constant change and complexity.

In reflecting on Runshaw's experiences, I have tried to make sense of all the various developments and initiatives by relating them to the world of educational theory. The problem with this is that there has been very little research or development of such theory for colleges. Two of the leading authorities on college research are Professor Jackie Lumby and Professor Tim Simkins, they report:

> *The worldwide industry of research on schools feeds an international fascination with leadership in education. No such equivalent body of research exists to support our under-standing of leadership in (the) colleges . . . there is a need to use existing research (in schools) to inform reflection on and development of leadership and management in colleges. (Simkins and Lumby, 2002)*

As a result of this paucity of theory on colleges, I turned to the 'existing research' on schools in both the British and North American context to find that there has been considerable development of theoretical models for the kind of dramatic improvements that was achieved at college-level in Runshaw. In particular, Leithwood *et al.* (1999) constructed a fictional case study of a school in Ontario. This sought to illustrate the key components of successful schools. When I read this book, I was struck by the similarities between the case study and Runshaw College, and it occurred to me that a book that contained a real case study rather a fictional one about a British college rather than a Canadian school could be a powerful tool to aid improvement in colleges in the UK.

Within the UK, one of the leading authorities on existing research is Professor David Hopkins – until 2005 the Director of the Standards and Effectiveness Unit at the Department for Education and Skills and formerly Dean at the University of Nottingham. He concentrated on developments for school improvement by the Organisation for Economic Co-operation and Development (OECD) through its Centre for Educational Research and Development (CERI), which, between 1982 and 1986, sponsored an International School Improvement Project to identify best practice in educational research. He went on to report on more recent developments, specifically those by the National College for School Leadership (NCSL) in England, which initiated a research programme in 2000 entitled 'Building capacity for school improvement'. It drew from theory and practice in successful schools to develop a model for capacity that could have practical and applied utility for schools. No such equivalent exists for colleges in the UK or, it seems, in any other country.

This book, therefore, begins to develop such a model. It borrows theory from the schools sector and applies it to the college sector. It uses the models, definitions and concepts developed by Leithwood and Hopkins and others to try to make sense out of what happened at Runshaw and to analyse the processes that built the conditions which underpinned Runshaw's success. As such, it shares the aim of the NCSL project 'to translate theory and research into active tools and models they will support (college) leaders with the process of improvement in raising student achievement' (Hopkins and Jackson, 2003).

So, in summary, what happened at Runshaw?

Runshaw was created as a sixth-form college in 1974. In 1984 I was appointed as principal to lead its transformation into a tertiary college. At that time it was a poor college in terms of quality, achieving 40% success rates (with a pass rate of about 68% at A-level and a retention rate of about 60% to 65%) and it enrolled about 900 students. Between 1984 and 1987 quality improved significantly and, by 1987, the college was formally congratulated in a government inspection. Then it plateaued in performance until 1990, at which time it began to suffer 'incoherence', faced by the external changes driven by the government's reform agenda and by the enactment of the Education Reform Act (1988). Runshaw did not have the capacity to cope with the multiple changes it faced and, by 1993, it began a spiral of decline.

It was then that a culture-change programme was introduced, bringing about a rapid and dramatic improvement in every key performance indicator, including staff morale. It changed Runshaw completely, leading to the introduction of what theorists term 'transformational leadership', 'moral leadership', 'dispersed leadership', 'instructional leadership', a new culture of 'high performance expectations' and a multidimensional range of new processes, structures and approaches that created a 'professional learning community' and, with it, the 'capacity' to improve itself continuously.

Hence, Runshaw can be seen as a case study that illustrates the application of educational theories about what makes some educational institutions outstandingly successful. It demonstrates the reality of what is meant by 'transactional' and 'transformational' leadership, the 'before' and 'after' of a culture-change programme. It shows how the theory of 'transformational leadership' can be translated into practice. It offers an account of how any college could develop a coherent, focused and long-term strategy for improvement using approaches that could be transferred elsewhere to achieve similar success. Hopefully, people can take from this account an understanding of the importance of 'culture' in the strategic management of colleges.

The next section of this chapter explains educational theories in more depth, setting the framework for theoretical reflections in later chapters, which tell the story of Runshaw's approaches. The third section of this chapter provides background information about Runshaw, substantiating its description as 'outstanding' and the assertion that Runshaw was a 'typical' college, hopefully thereby countering any temptation to dismiss its success as due to contextualised and therefore non-transferable advantages. The fourth section of this chapter explains the context of change for colleges since 1990 and how these changes have produced significant problems for most colleges, making it more important that colleges address those problems with approaches similar to those adopted at Runshaw.

A THEORETICAL FRAMEWORK

Each of the chapters in this book describes specific approaches used at Runshaw to make it successful. This section provides an overview of educational theory and explains – necessarily relatively briefly – the concepts used by academics in analysing what makes some educational organisations outstandingly successful. The concluding section of each subsequent chapter will relate the practice explained in that chapter to this theory, showing how the practice illustrates the theory and how it operates in synergy and alignment with other practices. So what kind of leadership do theorists advocate?

Transformational leadership

The first and most important debate within educational theory since the mid-1990s is about the importance of 'transformational leadership'. As Hopkins (2003) says, 'During the past decade the debate about educational leadership has been dominated by a contrast between the so-called "transactional" and "transformational" approaches.' Harris *et al*. (2003) defines the former in terms of a 'leader-follower dichotomy in which leaders are superior to followers and followers depend on leaders . . . leadership consists of doing something for, to and on behalf of others . . . an exchange of services for various kinds of rewards that the leader controls.' She adds that most leaders in education are transactional.

She quotes Burns (1978) as providing a 'competing and compelling alternative theory of transformational leadership' in which there is an increasing emphasis on the links between leadership and culture, 'having the potential to alter the cultural context in which people work . . . by focusing on the moral values and value-laden activities of a leader and how these are disclosed to other colleagues . . . they purposely impact upon the culture in order to change it . . . It is concerned with relationships and engagement of individuals.'

Leithwood *et al*. (1999) say that transformational leadership may be identified by several core leadership activities. These include setting direction, developing people, culture-building, and building relationships. They argue that research demonstrates that there is a strong correlation between this form of leadership and school improvement.

The definition of transformational leadership that I will use throughout this book is:

> *Transformational leadership is concerned with engaging the hearts and minds of others. It works to help all parties achieve greater motivation, satisfaction and a greater sense of achievement. It requires trust, concern and facilitation rather than direct control. The skills required are concerned with establishing a long-term vision, empowering people to control themselves, coaching, and developing others and challenging the culture to change. In transformational leadership, the power of the leader comes from creating understanding and trust. In contrast, in transactional leadership power is based on the notion of hierarchy and position. (Professor John Mackness, personal correspondence)*

In 1993 Runshaw introduced a culture-change programme – explained in the next chapter – and it was this that that 'transformed' Runshaw. We then built upon the processes that underpinned it and embedded them in our new approach to 'transformational leadership'. So in 1993 Runshaw adopted the overarching leadership approach that theorists align with successful educational organisations.

Moral leadership

It is not just this concept that explains the success. Harris *et al.* (2003) goes on to report that 'most recently, leadership studies have focused upon values and moral purpose . . . the moral craft of leadership.' 'Moral leadership', she concludes, is a particular kind of transformational leadership, one that involves creating a sense of moral purpose and about creating powerful learning communities which 'integrate the intellectual, emotional and spiritual'. Moral leaders, she says, 'recognise the importance of core values and that organisational performance is largely dependent on the beliefs people hold and how they work together.'

Chapter 3 of this book explains how Runshaw's culture-change programme identified a range of barriers to staff commitment and how Runshaw's primary response was to focus on defining its core values and explicitly translating them into behaviours, policies, strategies and role models. Our entire culture-change process was dominated by perceptions and debates about what was 'right' and 'wrong', about values and beliefs and about how people should behave. We had never heard of terms like 'transformational' or 'moral' leadership then, but we unknowingly adopted these new forms of leadership and new ways of working in the college, and it was these that created rapid and significant improvement.

Dispersed leadership

The introduction of transformational and moral leadership was the key to rapid improvement in the period from 1993 to 1995, but a further variation on 'transformational leadership' was the key to enabling us to sustain that improvement and to go on to build upon it with repeated quantum-leap improvements over subsequent years. That is, we developed a model of what is termed 'dispersed' (or 'distributed') leadership. Putting it perhaps simplistically, between 1984 and 1993 the assumption at Runshaw was that senior managers should provide most aspects of leadership: after 1993, that assumption changed completely as we increasingly 'dispersed' leadership first to middle managers and then to all staff. We came to believe that, as Hopkins (2003) explained it, leadership 'resides in the potential available to be released within an organisation, residing (sometimes dormant or unexpressed) within its members . . . the role of the leader is to harness, focus, liberate, empower and align that leadership towards common purposes and, by so doing, build and release capacity.'

This meant that we had to reconceptualise the meaning of leadership and the role of leaders. Our efforts to do this are explained throughout this book but particularly in Chapter 4.

Instructional leadership

Both 'moral' and 'dispersed' leadership approaches belong to the concept of 'transformational' leadership but Hopkins argues that, while he considers these approaches as 'necessary', he also believes them to be 'insufficient' because they lack 'a specific orientation towards student learning . . . in line with many other educational reforms, transformational leadership simply focuses on the wrong variables.' Hence, he advocates the concept of 'instructional leadership': he argues that success in educational institutions needs to include a focus on teaching and learning and the organisational conditions of the school (or college), particularly the approach taken to staff development and planning. He says that 'instructional leadership is actively and visibly involved in the planning and implementation of change, but encourages collaboration and working in teams. It emphasises the quality of teaching and learning with high expectations of all staff and all pupils . . .'

As later chapters will show, the culture-change programme at Runshaw in 1993 and 1994 led to a reassertion of the importance of teaching and learning as our top priority and a rejection of many of the values associated with 'managerialism'. Leadership was reconceptualised to be about roles associated with being 'leading professional teachers'. This approach was fundamental to Runshaw's success, as Chapter 3 explains more fully.

The concept of 'capacity'

The introduction and development of 'instructional' and 'transformational' leadership – including those forms of it described as 'moral' and 'dispersed' leadership – were the essential building blocks for Runshaw's rapid and significant improvement in 1995, but what was essential to sustaining it over the next decade was the theoretical concept of 'capacity', the outcome of these forms of leadership. As Hopkins (2003) said, 'Contemporary discussions are focusing far more on the concept of "capacity" . . . the key construct in creating the conditions within the (college) to enhance both leading and learning.' He argues that, without a clear focus on capacity, the organisation will be unable to sustain continuous improvement efforts or to manage change effectively. He says that 'it is therefore critical to be able to explore, explain and illustrate the concept of "capacity" in operational terms – and this is more complex and elusive than it might seem.'

The Hopkins and Jackson (2003) model for capacity has two key components. They are the concept of a 'professional learning community' and the idea of leadership capacity as the 'route to generating the moral purpose, shared values, social cohesion and trust to make this happen and to create impetus and alignment.'

Professional learning community

Hopkins and Jackson believe that it is essential first to establish what they call the 'foundation conditions' – that is, creating a sense of order, stability, safety and security, without which capacity cannot start to be built.

Then it is possible to start to develop the 'heart of capacity', that is, the 'professional learning community'. This depends upon implementing the concept of 'dispersed leadership', developing relationships and trust (termed 'social capital and cohesion'), developing shared beliefs and the urgency to act together to achieve 'higher order purposes' (called 'values coherence and moral agency') and the creation, transfer and utilisation of knowledge (called 'intellectual capital'). These add a concept called 'external opportunities' – the capacity to use external forces that often paralyse, destabilise or debilitate schools and colleges to work in creative, resourceful and entrepreneurial ways for internal purposes. In our context, they would argue that we should have used all that followed as an opportunity to do the things that we believed in – student success, increased participation rates, better quality – and to do it by harnessing staff commitment.

So how did Runshaw apply these theories?

One of the immediate outcomes of the culture-change programme at Runshaw was the creation of 'the New Beginning', an entirely new approach to managing staff–student relationships and student performance – our case of establishing the 'foundation conditions'. We then introduced a range of multidimensional structures, processes and strategies to develop individual staff, teams and whole-college learning and development opportunities, our equivalent of a 'professional learning community'. These approaches are described in subsequent chapters. They included an approach that we termed 'values-driven behaviours' (Chapter 3), another that redefined the role of leadership, management style and core competencies (Chapter 4), another that created one united management team and changed roles and structures, especially those of middle managers (Chapter 5), to develop a shared sense of direction and purpose (Chapter 6). There was another that introduced best practice human relations processes for communications, listening, recognition and reduced workloads (Chapter 7), another that created a staff development infrastructure (Chapter 8) and another that introduced new approaches to quality management and continuous improvement, using the business excellence model (Chapter 9). The following chapters explain Runshaw's multidimensional and overlapping approaches to creating a new culture based on the notion of creating a 'professional learning community' and deploying a new model of leadership. In short, they tell the story of how Runshaw built the 'capacity' to become an outstanding college and then to sustain and improve its high standards.

RUNSHAW'S CONTEXT AND TRACK RECORD

This section seeks to do three things:

- to provide background information about Runshaw College
- to substantiate the claim that it was 'outstanding'
- to argue that Runshaw was a 'typical' college and that, therefore, its success should not be dismissed as being due to any particular contextual situation.

Background information

Runshaw College was created in 1974 as a sixth-form college to serve 350 A-level students attending the sixth forms of two local grammar schools, one in Leyland and one in Chorley, Lancashire. The college was built on Runshaw Moor on the rural outskirts of Leyland. Originally, it was intended that Lancashire New Town would be built on the green belt between Leyland and Chorley, putting Runshaw in the middle of the new town, but this plan was subsequently scrapped, leaving Runshaw 'in the middle of nowhere', remote and difficult to access via country lanes on one side and suburban streets on the other.

Nevertheless, in the 10 years after its creation the student numbers grew from 350 to 900 and it was at that point, in 1983/4, that it became a tertiary college. This is worth noting because what little research has been done on our sector (see, for example, Simkins and Lumby, 2002) seems to suggest that a distinction should be made between what has happened to sixth-form colleges and what has happened to general further education colleges since 1990. That is, the evidence seems to suggest that the former have coped with the traumas of incorporation better than the latter. However, there is, as far as I am aware, no research on what has happened to tertiary colleges like Runshaw, which are often a mixture of sixth-form college and general further education colleges. Indeed, one could go much further by distinguishing between colleges that originated as sixth-form colleges, like Runshaw, and tertiary colleges that originated as general further education colleges like, for example, Blackburn College. Those inside the world of further education could add all sorts of other classifications – for example, agricultural colleges, other specialist colleges, rural colleges, London colleges and so on.

I was appointed as principal at Runshaw in 1984, with a background in further education, and my brief was to widen access at Runshaw for school leavers of all abilities, to make it accessible for people other than A-level students, and to develop adult education. The result was that, by the time I left in 2004, Runshaw was recruiting 3700 students aged 16 to 19 each year, 1800 of whom were A-level students and 1900 of whom were vocational or pre-vocational students, with over 600 of these enrolled on pre-entry, entry and foundation courses. These were all accommodated on the original site of the sixth-form college although, of course, the number of rooms had increased fourfold. Moreover, over 10 000 adult students were accommodated on two separate sites in Chorley and in a range of outreach centres. They were enrolled on courses at many different levels, including basic skills, full-time access programmes, higher education courses and part-time vocational courses. We also provided the education services for Wymott and Garth prisons. All of these programmes were offered by Runshaw's 'adult college', a substructure that was deliberately separated from that of the 'sixth-form centre' on the original site. In Chorley we also accommodated Runshaw Business Centre, which focused on the needs of employers. It generated over £1 000 000 per year and enrolled over 2000 students. It included Runshaw Training for work-based learners.

Substantiating the claim that Runshaw was 'outstanding'

First, Runshaw was 'outstanding' in terms of the phenomenal growth record described above. In 1984 Runshaw had been a relatively small sixth-form college 'in the middle of nowhere'. By 2005 it had become a large and complex tertiary college.

Secondly, Runshaw was described as 'outstanding' in the three outstanding inspection reports of 1996, 2001 and 2005. We have seen that in 2001 it achieved the joint highest number of grade 1s for general further education colleges over the previous five-year inspection cycle. These were for management, quality assurance, student support, resources and three curriculum areas.

The third claim is the college's 'outstanding' student achievement and retention, with success rates of at least 10% above national benchmarks at all levels and for both age groups in, for example, 2003–4. The results for 16- to 19-year-old students on full-time A-level courses in 2004 were 335 average points earned per student and the average points per entry were 86. Its A-level results placed it within the top 10% of sixth-form colleges, even though it was classified as a general further education college. There is a view in this country that only sixth-form colleges 'work' and that general further education colleges should not try to be 'all things to all people'. Runshaw College demonstrated that this could be wrong. It showed that it was possible to match the best of the top 10% of sixth-form colleges and, at the same time, offer a comprehensive portfolio that achieved equally exceptional standards for those on vocational and pre-vocational courses at all levels and to both age groups.

By 2004 it had also earned a national and international reputation for excellence. For example, in 2001 it became a Beacon College; in 2002 it won the UK Business Excellence Award; in 2003 it won the equivalent European Foundation for Quality Management (EFQM) Award as well as the European Special Prize for Leadership and Constancy of Purpose. Its chief of governors has received an OBE and its principal received a knighthood for services to education.

Moreover, its growth and success made Runshaw a relatively prosperous college with grade A financial status, despite spending over £10 million transforming it into a 'showpiece' in terms of its physical resources.

On the basis that Runshaw College was regarded as 'outstanding' in the ways described above, between 2001 and 2004 the Learning Skills Council provided nearly £500 000 to disseminate Runshaw College's approach to leadership to the rest of the college sector. This included the production of two manuals, *The Runshaw Way: Values Drive Behaviours* and *Leadership and Management in Colleges using the Business Excellence Model*. These were distributed to 350 representatives of colleges who attended six national conferences. In addition, Runshaw became a Beacon College and used its Beacon funds to provide six two-day workshops for the management teams of six colleges. This book seeks to build on these initiatives.

Was it 'easier' for Runshaw to succeed?

When discussing the question of how Runshaw became 'outstanding', there is always a danger that people will dismiss what happened by suggesting that Runshaw had some particular advantage that explains its success and that it is 'impossible' for others to do what Runshaw did. In exploring this suggestion – and hopefully countering it – it is useful to consider the five variables that are often used to explain differences between colleges other than the way they are run. These are the social background of students, the staff profile, the size of a college, its competitive environment and the coherence of its curriculum.

In terms of the social background of its students, it is true that Runshaw did recruit 1800 A-level students and these did set a generally diligent tone (although some of them lacked high levels of motivation or high standards of behaviour) but Runshaw also recruited 1900 other full-time students aged 16 to 19, many of whom had less diligent attitudes, to put it mildly. The same was true of adult education: there was a mixture of, for example, very diligent higher education students, cake decorators and so on, as well as significant numbers of others who had difficulties in coping with college life. For example, we operated a programme for over 700 students who were recovering from mental illness and many of these were integrated into mainstream courses. All of this, of course, is standard for most further education colleges but the point here is that Runshaw shared these difficulties. It was not 'easier' for Runshaw; indeed, it was a great deal harder for Runshaw than for the 100+ sixth-form colleges that did not have such a mixture of students and yet Runshaw matched the top 10% of these colleges in A-level results.

Nor did the demography of Runshaw's catchment area make it 'easier' for it to succeed. In Leyland, the largest employer, Leyland Trucks, reduced its workforce from over 13 000 to 800. In Chorley, the largest employer, Royal Ordnance with over 14 000 employees, closed altogether. The average income in Chorley was significantly below that of the rest of the UK. And both Leyland and Chorley had many pockets of severe social deprivation. When the government introduced incorporation in 1993 it asked colleges to widen participation. Runshaw did so quite dramatically, increasing, for example, level 1 and level 2 student recruitment from 200 to over 600. This changed the social mix of the college significantly and it changed the college's ethos, making it very necessary for us to re-establish our 'foundation conditions'.

With regard to the staff profile, the debate here usually focuses on the use of part-time staff. Sixth-form colleges, for example, usually have a relatively smaller ratio of full-time to part-time staff, so creating greater social cohesion, easier communication and better quality assurance. In Runshaw's case, we employed over 300 part-time staff, so there is no basis for suggesting that, in this respect, it was 'easier' for us; we had the staff profile of a typical further education college.

The competitive environment in which Runshaw existed could hardly have been worse. Runshaw was based in Leyland, a small town of only 30 000, and had a catchment area of 200 000 scattered over a vast area between Wigan, Blackburn, Preston and Southport. Each had a general further education college and each regarded Runshaw's catchment area, especially the town of Chorley, as 'fair game' for competitive marketing and recruitment. In addition, Runshaw was surrounded by four sixth-form colleges, two of which provided free transport from Leyland and Chorley and targeted the most able school leavers, promoting themselves as colleges for the 'most able'. A local grammar school that had retained its sixth form also actively marketed itself in the same way.

A particularly thorny issue in competing with sixth-form colleges was that of 'size'. Runshaw had become the largest sixth-form centre in the UK with over 3700 16–19 year olds on one single site. This gave our competitors ammunition to promote themselves as 'smaller' than 'other' local colleges and to suggest that 'small' equated with 'caring', 'individual support' and 'knowing the individual', whereas 'large' equated to 'uncaring', 'cold', 'impersonal' and lack of focus on the 'individual'. We developed many strategies to combat such suggestions, one of which was to assert very strongly that they were not true and that a college which had earned a grade 1 in student support in all of its inspections – like Runshaw – could hardly fit such descriptors. Nevertheless, it was a constant battle. More than that, we had to make sure that there really was no truth in the allegations – and that was difficult. The fact was that Runshaw was very big, especially its sixth-form centre, and this did create all sorts of difficulties. So, if anything, in this respect it was more difficult for Runshaw to succeed, not 'easier'.

The issue of size was related to the coherence of the curriculum. As the college expanded, we introduced a wide range of additional courses, new vocational areas, different levels of provision and we extended the scope of specialist student support. This affected both the 16–19 and post-19 age groups and it included new provision for employers, for local community groups and for business agencies. In short, Runshaw became very complex as well as very large.

Our responses to some of these issues are described in later chapters, especially Chapter 6, but it is important to establish here that, although every college is different, Runshaw was not 'different' to the extent that it was 'easier' for it to succeed. In fact, Runshaw was fairly typical and, if there was anything particularly unusual about it, it was the fact that it could act as a role model for sixth-form colleges and further education colleges. For example, it compared its performance with sixth-form colleges for A-level results as well as with general further education colleges for all its other areas of provision. In many ways, it bridged approaches in sixth-form colleges with those in general further education colleges; it could relate to both worlds.

THE CONTEXT OF GOVERNMENT REFORM

This section seeks to outline the context of change to colleges – primarily the government's reforms – and to consider whether these have been responsible for the difficulties that colleges have faced in achieving improvement of standards, financial stability and a workforce characterised by high morale and commitment to change. It seeks to answer six questions:

- Where did the drive for government reforms come from? What was the 'case for change'?
- What were the government's key strategies for reform?
- Was the traditional culture of teacher 'professionalism' the root of the problem?
- Did 'managerialism' make matters worse?
- What challenges did the 'new realities' present?
- What happened to colleges?

Where did the drive for reform come from?

In 1988, when the government passed the Education Reform Act (ERA), it began the process of transformation of post-16 education that still preoccupies us today. The Act represented a determined challenge by the government to the prevailing culture of further education. It stemmed from the pent-up frustrations that produced the 'great debate', begun in 1976 by the Prime Minister, James Callaghan, in a speech at Ruskin College, in which, in effect, Callaghan said 'enough is enough'. Rightly or wrongly he represented the views of many who saw the post-war period of educational development as a disaster in terms of lowering standards. The final straw may have been the headline-grabbing events at William Tyndale Primary School in 1976 where staff there asserted that the logic of the deschooling movement should be taken to its extremes. It was reported that teachers there did not teach and pupils did not learn and that teachers claimed that this situation was intellectually and ideologically justifiable. The Prime Minister did not agree and, in starting the 'great debate', it was said that he wedged open the door to the 'secret garden' of teacher professionalism.

In the 1980s the Conservative government developed this debate further. It created the Audit Commission in 1983 to enable it to explore ways of obtaining better 'value for money', especially from local authorities. In 1985, the Audit Commission produced a seminal report called *Obtaining Better Value from Further Education*. It asserted that at least £50 million per year was being wasted and that this meant that 75 000 more students could have been taught with no significant additional expenditure. It specifically criticised inadequacies in marketing, financial management and management information systems and it claimed that there was considerable waste in the way that accommodation was managed. With regard to the management of the curriculum, it claimed that there was overteaching on many courses, that many lecturers did not teach sufficient hours and that many class sizes were far too low. All in all, it amounted to a devastating critique of further education and, at the time, there was no coherent response to it by colleges in defence of these practices. Indeed, everything that the report criticised was instantly recognisable in most colleges. Over the following years, the Audit Commission kept up its criticisms and produced a second seminal report in 1993, which claimed that 150 000 16–19 year olds either failed or dropped out of courses each year in colleges and that this amounted to a waste that cost £330 million per year.

Meanwhile, by the end of the 1980s, the Confederation of British Industry and the Trade Union Congress had jointly condemned low skill levels in the UK as one of the causes of low productivity, low wages and unemployment. Subsequently, the Organisation for Economic Co-operation and Development (OECD) has repeatedly produced overwhelming evidence that Britain is relatively weak in skill development. There is, therefore, a consensus that post-16 skill levels in the UK are far too low.

What were the government's key strategies for reform?

The outcomes were the 1988 Education Reform Act, enacted in 1990, and then incorporated in 1993. 'Incorporation' was the change of legal status that occurred in 1993 to colleges when responsibility for them was transferred from local government to independent, autonomous corporations composed largely of private sector representatives. They were intended to transfer responsibility for the financial management, staffing and strategic planning of colleges from the local authority to the newly created individual corporation for each college. They gave colleges autonomy and, with it, the 'freedom to manage' and the 'freedom to go bust'. Incorporation gave responsibility for pay, conditions of service and all employment matters to a new set of employers. These were the new governing bodies composed largely of representatives from the private sector. Effectively, the government handed over the problem of managing what it saw as the relatively ill-disciplined teaching culture of colleges to those whom, it believed, would introduce the more disciplined and customer-oriented culture of the private sector.

On the other hand, in 1993, the government also created the Further Education Funding Council (FEFC) (replaced by the Learning Skills Council (LSC) in 2001) to regulate colleges in a number a ways. These included the new inspection regime, the publication of examination results and league tables, the introduction of target setting, benchmarking and the national measurement of performance data, which for the first time included the concept of retention. Colleges were also subjected to the 'carrot and stick' treatment meted out by the new funding body. The 'carrot' was to be the incentive of additional funds for growth. This would represent 'success' in the new world of market forces where an environment of competition was deliberately created. The 'stick' was the fact that 2.5% of a college's income was withheld each year until the respective college met that year's annual requirements to implement government policies. For example, colleges were required to try to introduce new contracts for staff, which, in the case of teachers, meant that their holidays were reduced, their working week increased and their teaching loads increased, all without any salary compensation.

All these initiatives fit within the context of what the government now calls 'public sector reform', a programme that is driven by the need for public sector organisations to serve the different needs of individuals as consumers. The focus is on the 'customer' as opposed to the 'supplier'. In the case of colleges, the government was saying very clearly that it was primarily concerned with the student and not with the college or its staff. If the college could not achieve student success and student satisfaction then it would not recruit successfully and would, therefore, not generate income. In short, the money would follow the student, not the institution. This represented an attempt to shift the balance that had existed in many colleges from serving the needs of staff as the priority to serving the needs of the student. The 'new realities', as the new era was often described by government ministers, would quickly bring higher standards. Or, at least, that was the theory.

The government's reform programme did not stop with incorporation in 1993. Since incorporation there has been a constant stream of new initiatives, all trying to achieve one or more of three key goals. These are:

- increased growth, especially targeting low-achievers in an ongoing campaign to 'widen participation'
- higher standards
- increased efficiency.

In short, the government has wanted 'more, better and for less money'.

Was the traditional culture of teacher 'professionalism' at the root of the problem?

One of the central conclusions that emerged from the debate that Callaghan initiated was that the culture of 'professional autonomy' was at the root of the problems with education. This was illustrated at the extreme by the attitudes of teachers at William Tyndale School. This culture was seen as one of unaccountability in which the concept of 'professionalism' had been defined by many in terms of 'individual autonomy'. The outcome, it was argued, was low standards and an unmanaged culture in which overteaching, small classes, underutilisation of teachers' contracted hours and poor teaching were widespread.

Whatever the theoretical or ideological position that one chooses to adopt about the concept of professionalism, the reality of college life in the 1970s and 1980s seemed to depend upon the culture of the particular college in which one worked. In my first 11 years in further education I had worked in a very successful college in Liverpool and, looking back, I can now see that I thrived in what I still think of as a very 'professional' culture. Staff were generally very student centred, very well organised, punctual, set regular coursework and marked it thoroughly, took enormous pride in their students' achievements, especially when those students were engaged in 'second chance' opportunities, and they worked effectively in teams, standardising, sharing resources, spreading good practice and collaborating in a friendly team spirit. These were the characteristics that I thought defined 'professionalism'.

During my time there I was surprised when, in 1973, I became an exchange-teacher in a community college in St Louis, in the US. There I found what I consider to be a completely 'unprofessional' set of practices. For example, many lecturers behaved pompously, believing they had a superiority over others. Each decided independently what to teach, how to teach it and how to – or even whether to – assess students. In practice, what was taught (I taught political science) would be described in the UK as 'social slops', a peculiar mixture of 'issues' taught without much reference to academic literature or any knowledge base. I attended several of my colleagues' classes to observe their teaching and frequently found them attended by three or four students instead of the 120 who were supposed to be there. Assessments were generally not set and, when they were, they consisted of multiple-choice tests that were 'marked' by a secretary. There were no team meetings of any sort. Every decision seemed to be made by staff for staff, geared to minimise their workload. The standards of students' work were, not surprisingly, appallingly low. Despite this, there was an obsession with concepts like 'academic freedom', 'tenure' and 'professionalism'. I thought it was all simply absurd and disgraceful. I had left England regarding myself as a radical thinker who enjoyed challenging the status quo – I even had a beard, long hair and never wore a tie! I returned a year later with firm beliefs in the virtues of high standards, rigour, structured approaches and the realisation that I was, after all, much more 'conservative' than I had thought.

So when I went to Runshaw as principal in 1984, after working in another college that was very similar to the St Louis college, I believed that truly 'professional' approaches should include concepts and practices like student centredness, teamwork, standardisation, rigour, high standards and high expectations for both students and staff, staff development, sharing and collaboration. I believed that we needed processes, systems and structures to make these concepts work and that, if we believed that we should do something in a certain way, then we should all act consistently: agreed college policy, college processes and procedures should be adhered to by all, so compliance was a 'professional' requirement. I believed that 'accountability' was truly 'professional', that we should not waste money, that we should take pride in working hard and that we were there primarily to serve the student. This is what I meant by 'professionalism'.

What I found at Runshaw when I arrived there in 1984 was quite the opposite. That is, I found that the traditional concept of 'professionalism' had been interpreted to mean complete individual autonomy. For example, many teachers went to class only if they felt like it. Many declared to me that they did not believe that it was their job to motivate students who did not want to learn. They saw themselves as 'academics' who were 'fountains of knowledge', dispensing their expertise on a take-it-or-leave-it basis. They did not want to teach low achievers, describing them as 'dross', and they certainly did not want to provide what some called 'Mickey Mouse' post-19 provision. There were no schemes of work, no assessment plans, no teamwork, no staff development (they were affronted by the presumption that they could improve!) and very little pastoral support.

Hierarchy was very strong, with the longest serving occupying the senior posts. The latter regarded themselves as 'superior' to those whom they described as 'junior' staff. The ethos was similar to that of an 'officers' mess'. The idea of lesson observation was simply not mentioned, nor was that of seeking the views of students about their needs or levels of satisfaction. Although there was a dominant veneer of 'intellectualism', with status determined by expertise in one's subject, there was no intellectual rigour in reviewing 'teaching and learning', nor was there any rigour in reviewing results. Non-compliance was rife: individual autonomy was taken to mean that each individual could decide for himself or herself whether to comply with the rules of the college, including the completion of registers.

This set of rules and cultural context quite simply did not work. The college produced appalling results. For example, of the 453 students who enrolled for the first-year A-level course in 1982, over 100 dropped out by 1984 and another 100 achieved no passes. Only 193 of the original 453 students who enrolled in 1982 achieved two grade Es or more in 1984, a 'success' rate of about 40%. When I produced and published these data on my arrival in 1984 I was regarded by many as 'unprofessional'. It was the kind of situation that had sparked off Prime Minister Callaghan's frustrations.

Moreover, it was typical nationally. The national pass rate at A level was then about 67%. This was bad but the real situation was much worse because retention was not then included in the concept of 'success rates'. Nor was Runshaw regarded as especially bad. In fact it was featured in 1983 on BBC's *Panorama* as a success story – one of the first of a new breed of successful 'sixth-form colleges'; but to me, in 1984, it had all the faults of a very bad grammar school. It had the elitist values of a grammar school but it had none of the rigour, standards and what I would describe as truly 'professional' approaches that probably existed in the best grammar schools.

If, in 1984, one wanted to challenge a culture like that at Runshaw, one was effectively 'on one's own'. There was no external source of authority saying what was right or wrong. Inspections occurred infrequently, were clothed in mystique and were secretive, there were no grades and there was no public set of criteria defining 'excellence' or anything else. Nor were there any national benchmarks regarding the publication and review of data about educational institutions. It was virtually impossible to hold an individual accountable, no matter how poor his or her performance. There was no appraisal system, no performance management or performance measurement. Even if evidence of extreme misbehaviour by an individual emerged, the local authority was the employer and both it and the governing body were highly political. In reality they rarely dismissed anybody and were very reluctant to engage in disciplinary matters.

In such circumstances, it was probably foolish for an individual principal to challenge a staff culture like that at Runshaw. Nevertheless, I did impose my version of 'professionalism'. This included a requirement for teamwork, compulsory staff development, a new system of performance management, required documentation on schemes of work and assessment plans, a new structure for pastoral support with new roles for all teachers and a focus on teaching and learning as an intellectually worthy subject for research and development. I also challenged individuals' misbehaviour and tried to change the worst examples of staff-student relationships. It was extremely difficult and I felt completely unsupported by the world outside the college. On reflection, I wish that I had the support then of the reform strategies that the government produced post-1990.

Did 'managerialism' make matters worse?

The debate in academic research over the last decade has focused on an assumed contest between the concepts of 'professionalism' and 'managerialism'. It seems to be an assumption in some writings that the former belongs to a 'golden age' (Elliott and Hall, 1994; Ainley and Bailey, 1997; Randle and Brady, 1997), suggesting that the position before incorporation was that the culture in colleges was firmly focused on the needs of the learner and on teaching and learning and that, afterwards, 'managerialism' replaced this focus with one that was described as 'businesslike'.

In my first 11 years in further education, the culture of the college in which I worked was focused on teaching and learning and the needs of learners, but in the examples of my experiences in a US community college and at Runshaw in 1984, 'professionalism' was defined in a completely different way. Its approach was much nearer to what Burton (1994) and Gorringe (1994) described as 'complacency' and 'staff focused'. Although this debate was supposedly 'academic', it seems to be characterised by emotive arguments and ideological posturing in a power contest for the moral high ground with the interests of the learner being claimed as the primary interest of the person presenting the argument. Simkins and Lumby (2002), for example, make a telling comment when they say: 'The language used, for example, that managers have been "tempted", "seduced" into "hard" variants of management activity (Elliott and Hall, 1994) or that staff were not "realistic" or "open-minded" due to a previously "emasculated college management" (Lewis, 1994) indicate, particularly in the sexual metaphors, a power contest fuelled by ideology.'

My view of 'professionalism' at Runshaw in the post-1990 period was essentially the same as that which I held in the 1960s, 1970s and 1980s. I would define it in the terms that I have used above – a belief in high standards, rigour, accountability, consistent application of the agreed rules and processes by all staff, compliance to rules and procedures, teamwork and continuous improvement through staff development and constant evaluation.

The Education Reform Act and incorporation provided the opportunity to implement this definition of 'professionalism'. It also changed the culture of further education by creating imperatives to become more efficient, to become more effective by improving standards, and to compete successfully. Overall, the culture became significantly more accountable. Managers no longer had the option of indulging in the kind of laid-back, *laissez-faire* and generally unmanaged cultures that I had found in St Louis or at Runshaw in 1984. If senior managers did take such an option, then the college would become financially unstable, lose out in recruitment to other colleges and enter a cycle of decline, with job losses, low morale and management restructuring the order of the day. What the government wanted was, in my view, reasonable. The problem arose when colleges, like Runshaw, found that they lacked the capacity to organise themselves successfully to deliver the required outcomes. This was due to the fact that colleges practised 'transactional' leadership rather than 'transformational' leadership.

What challenges did the 'new realities' present?

The challenges facing colleges were threefold:

- They had to expand, widening participation by recruiting a new cohort of students who had not previously considered college as an option that might be suitable for them.
- They had to do so at the lowest cost, with colleges being run as efficient businesses.
- The quality and effectiveness of provision had to improve.

To achieve all three successfully they had to obtain the commitment of staff.

Most of these changes – like reduction of course hours, the increase in class sizes and the increase in lectures teaching loads – were extremely unpopular with staff. So how should colleges have introduced the required efficiencies in such a way that staff would be committed to make these changes work?

How should colleges have introduced new quality assurance processes – like performance management, appraisal, lesson observation, 'mock' inspections, detailed scrutiny of data (on student achievement, added-value, retention, attendance, progression), student satisfaction surveys, compulsory staff development, self-assessment and mandatory teamwork – in such a way that staff supported them fully and thereby increased accountability and improved standards?

How should colleges have coped with all the strains and pressures of, for example, rapid expansion, new student groups who brought with them behavioural problems, and the new and diverse curriculum developments, in such a way that staff retained or developed dedication to student success?

These were the challenges for leaders of colleges. So what happened?

What happened to colleges?

What happened obviously depended upon the college in which one worked, but research does indicate that several significant patterns of change occurred in colleges.

The first is that the nature of the culture of most colleges changed significantly, with an increased focus on marketing, competition, financial management, efficiencies, management information and quality. Curriculum hours for courses were cut, lecturers' teaching hours were increased and class sizes also increased.

Many senior managers interpreted 'businesslike' behaviours to mean 'macho' behaviours and appeared to relish the new powers to sack staff, to make many of them redundant, to adopt an attitude that one principal called 'my way or the highway'. Some principals saw themselves as 'captains of industry', mistakenly believing that best practice in the world of the private sector was about being 'ruthless'. It is described by Simkins and Lumby (2002) in the following terms:

> *A dominant picture of leadership in further education has emerged through the literature to date. It has been argued that since incorporation in 1993, principals and those in senior management positions have adopted a role which is invested with greater power than previously, distant from other staff, focused on external relations and the systems supporting activities other than teaching and learning.*

College management structures changed significantly and the roles of senior managers changed with them, often becoming 'corporate'. Managers looked to the private sector to identify 'best practice' in such managerial approaches as strategic planning, human resource management and the management of performance indicators. Senior management teams appeared to become smaller and more cohesive, acting as corporate teams to oversee the conduct of colleges (Harper, 2000). New posts were created at a senior level in finance, quality, marketing and management information systems. The activities of senior managers appeared to become primarily focused on planning, funding and external relations, at the expense of pedagogical issues (Lumby and Tomlinson, 2000). Restructuring of senior management teams reduced the presence in them of those who directly manage teaching staff, students and teaching and learning. It was partly these responses that generated the academic debate about the emergence of 'managerialism'.

For middle managers the situation seemed to be complex and confused. Middle managers often felt disorientated, 'caught in the middle', trying to mediate change between senior managers and staff in coping with the new culture. Many were torn between their traditional roles as curriculum leaders and the newer roles in managing processes, performance and budgets. Gleeson and Shain (1999a) identify three new categories of middle manager:

- 'willing compliers', fully committed to the new approaches
- 'unwilling compliers', disenchanted with the new culture
- 'strategic compliers', retaining their commitment to colleagues and students whilst adapting to the new agenda.

Most middle managers appear to fall into the latter category, which defines their role primarily in terms of mediation, persuading staff of the need to change whilst at the same time filtering communications from above.

It is clear from the literature that there is a growing diversity of middle-management roles and that middle managers are key players in determining the way that culture change occurs. Gleeson and Shain (1999a) write of the 'reconstruction of professional and managerial cultures in this volatile sector'. Briggs (2003) talks about the emergence of a 'new professional' role for middle managers and suggests that 'the era of conflict and crisis in defining and enacting manager roles may be reaching some kind of resolution'. She suggests that there may be 'new definitions of professionalism within the sector, particularly for middle managers' and she suggests five aspects of the role of middle managers:

- corporate agent
- implementer
- staff manager
- liaison, and
- leader.

These are explored further in Chapter 4 in the context of Runshaw's reconceptualisation of roles.

The post-incorporation period also saw a massive growth in the number of support staff posts. Many of these new posts performed duties that had traditionally been associated with the roles of lecturers. This exacerbated concerns by the latter about the changing culture as they perceived the creation of new support posts as quasi-lecturers, doing a similar job to lecturers but on less pay.

The question that arises is 'has it all worked?' There is no doubt that there has been significant expansion, increased efficiency and improve effectiveness. But the fact is that after more than 10 years of independence at least 25% of colleges are still in real difficulty and at least another 25% are constantly on the brink of a similar situation. The decade following the mid-1990s was a turbulent time for further education. Academic writers describe it in terms of a 'crisis' (see, for example, Elliott, 1996a) and there is a focus on what Gleeson and Shain (1999a) call 'managing ambiguity' rather than on the kind of debate about 'transformational' leadership that occupies the attention of academics writing about the schools sector. But things do seem to be improving. For example, Briggs (2003) concluded that the 'schismatic' view of college management 'is being replaced by a holistic one, where professionalism is seen to encompass both client-centred, learning-based values and the principles of funding-based business efficiency.'

All of these sector-wide developments were reflected in developments at Runshaw between 1990 and 1993. Relationships between senior managers and staff deteriorated, senior management roles changed to focus on new corporate responsibilities, teaching and learning seemed less important for senior managers, middle managers were asked to take over the curriculum management and staff management roles previously performed by senior managers, and many new 'business support' specialists were appointed. Staff morale dropped and we began to realise that our approach to leadership was simply inadequate. We were perceived as having become 'managerial'. Hence, in 1993 we introduced a culture-change programme borrowed from best practice in the private sector, and it transformed Runshaw.

On the whole, the government reforms did appear, on the surface, to have made things worse for us. Quality did not improve, we wasted increasing sums of money by trying to become 'businesslike', and we lost the staff's commitment to change. On the face of it, one could argue that we had made a significant mistake in replacing a 'professional' culture with that of 'managerialism' and that this happened as the inevitable consequence of the government reform. But it is not as simple as that.

First, this argument appears to make assumptions about the nature of 'professionalism' before 1990 that do not accord with my experience or the views of those who criticised the culture of colleges at that time. It seems to assume that teachers worked together in collaboration and in teams, that they had an intellectual concern with the craft of teaching and learning, that they consistently implemented approaches based upon consensus and collegiality, that they were primarily student focused rather than staff focused, and that they were accountable to high standards established by their peers. All this was true in the college in which I spent my first 11 years but it was certainly not true of the three colleges – including Runshaw – in which I later worked.

Secondly, there seems to be an assumption that competition, efficiency and the drive for higher standards were introduced in 1990 as 'new' elements of government reform. Such an assumption is wrong. These were not new concepts. Most colleges were already extremely competitive and many senior managers like myself 'lived and breathed' concepts like quality and efficiency in the 1970s and 1980s. What the ERA and incorporation did was to give us the opportunity to achieve, in particular, higher standards.

Nor was it 'inevitable' that staff morale should suffer as a result of government reforms. To use the concept of 'external opportunities', incorporation gave managers the opportunity to introduce more collaborative, collegial, 'transformational', 'moral', 'dispersed' and 'instructional' forms of leadership – as we did eventually at Runshaw. It was our choice. But we could have chosen differently. We could have behaved in a 'macho' way, as many did, or, in contrast, we had the opportunity to explore what was truly regarded as 'best practice' by many leading organisations in the private sector. 'Best practice' and 'businesslike' practice were interpreted by the College Employers Forum and its keenest followers in the period from 1990 to 1996 as being about macho management despite the fact that, in 1989, 14 of the most successful 20 European companies had come together to define what they considered to be 'best practice' by articulating the eight fundamental concepts of the Business Excellence Model. These concepts included the belief that best practice was the opposite of macho management and that it was about caring, supporting, communicating with and developing one's workforce. It was about what is now called 'transformational' leadership.

CONCLUSION

What Runshaw did in 1993 was to learn from such best practice in the private sector and, thanks to the support of two enlightened and public-spirited senior managers from Leyland Trucks who acted as mentors to me, it transformed itself into an organisation that developed a powerful form of moral value-driven leadership – a form of 'dispersed leadership' that involved all staff in developing a shared vision and a strong consensus of goals, and a new focus on teaching and learning – 'instructional' leadership – as our first priority. By developing such leadership approaches, we created a 'professional learning community' and thereby developed the capacity for sustained and significant improvement in our college over the long term.

When I first began to write this book I scanned the academic literature on colleges over the previous 15 years and found that the debate about 'managerialism' and 'professionalism' had a sense of despair about it, a feeling that market forces, competition, a new focus on financial management and the introduction of multiple new forms of external accountabilities made it 'inevitable' that colleges would fail and that there was really nothing much that they could do about it. Yet when I reviewed the educational theory on schools I found that the Education Reform Act of 1988 – the legislation that introduced what was later labelled as 'managerialism' in colleges – affected both schools and colleges but that academic research on school improvement hardly mentions 'managerialism'. It is, by contrast, optimistic and aspirational and focuses constructively on creating transferable models for school improvement.

It is not the aim of this book to present a critique of the debate about 'professionalism' versus 'managerialism' in the college sector but, in telling this story about Runshaw, it is important to assert that we did not take the view that it was 'inevitable' that we should fail and that 'there was nothing that we could do about it'. At the same time, we did not accept the view articulated by some government reformers that 'the root of the problem was teacher autonomy'. We did not regard the concept of 'professionalism' as some kind of absolute concept; it was just about the way that respective colleges were led and the consequent cultures – their norms, values, beliefs, attitudes and behaviours. And 'managerialism' did not describe some kind of new phenomenon created after 1990. What was fundamentally different after 1993 was the 30% cut in government resources between 1993 and 1997 and, with it, changes to staff pay rates and conditions of service and mass redundancies. It was, in my view, the funding reduction that created a crisis, not 'managerialism', although it is fair to say that the post-incorporation 'freedom to manage' did give managers the licence for macho behaviours, just as it gave them a licence to act in precisely the opposite way.

It is possible, therefore, that much academic research on colleges in the since the mid-1990s has wasted a great deal of time and energy focusing on false premises and, as a result, we have failed to develop the kind of useful models produced in the schools sector. As Schon (1993) expresses it:

> *in dealing with many social problems, such as how to improve schools and pupil achievement, a great deal of effort is wasted and ineffective because we operate with the wrong kind of stories or 'generative metaphors' which leads us to set wrong problems and hence develop wrong solutions.*

The theme of this book is that the real problem was transactional leadership, that it created a paradigm that made it very difficult to produce high standards, growth and value for money, that external pressures put too great a strain on it and thereby destabilised and debilitated colleges, and that it led to short-term and very limited 'efficiency' strategies. For example, in the period between 1990 and 1993, Runshaw really struggled to cope with the external pressures created by government reforms. The drive for increased accountability, the creation of an even more competitive environment, the difficulties of managing the behaviours of large numbers of new cohorts of students as we 'widened participation', and the financial cuts that resulted in the worsening of staff's conditions of service all combined to create a sense of incoherence. Nor had we then articulated our values or created a unity of purpose built around shared beliefs, as we did later. Leadership was in the hands of the few, transactional in nature, and unable to generate the combined capacity to overcome our problems. We were 'paralysed, destabilised and debilitated' by external pressures. We simply could not keep all these balls juggling in the air at the same time.

During those difficult years we tried a range of short-term remedies like 'tightening the screws', 'maximising effort', and 'focusing energies' but it became patently clear that such approaches were very limited. What was needed was what happened at Runshaw: a frank admission by 1993 that things were not working, that transactional leadership had not motivated staff, that they were not committed to change or improvement, and that we simply lacked the capacity to cope, let alone become 'outstanding'. We needed a new form of leadership – transformational leadership – which engaged all staff in working together to identify the problems and to solve them. The result was the introduction of a culture-change programme in the summer of 1993.

It was, to put it simply, an appeal to staff that 'we are all in this together'. We needed to do something more than 'harnessing' our current limited capacity: we needed to 'grow' our capacity to unlimited horizons to meet the ever-changing demands for higher quality. And we had to create the conditions in which people took control and ownership for this growth. We had to change the paradigm of leadership so that, instead of people at the top 'dispensing' opportunities to 'followers' down below, everybody would share leadership by collectively achieving and sustaining standards of excellence and operating through peer accountabilities. We would have agreed with the view that:

> *The only way to beat the complexity, uncertainty and continued change that [colleges] face and still maintain order is by creating local communities of responsibility that are able to motivate higher levels of disciplined self-management among students, teachers, heads, parents and other members of the local [college] community. (Sergiovanni, 2001)*

This was the start of 'dispersed' leadership. A new focus on values – 'moral' leadership – grew quickly within it together with a reassertion that teaching and learning should be our main priority. Managers refocused on teacher and learning, a form of 'instructional' leadership was recreated, and a 'professional learning community' was established.

This became a self-sustaining force that drove up standards, made Runshaw an increasingly attractive place for students and thereby generated financial success. Transformational leadership created a virtuous circle with Runshaw simply becoming better and better, growing its intellectual capital – that is, the knowledge, skills and capabilities of staff as individuals and collectively – enabling it to take external initiatives 'in its stride', and using them to further the interests of its own vision and goals. The whole approach simply worked. Runshaw's growth, success rates, inspection reports, accolades and relative prosperity were testimony to that, and the real winners were the students and staff who worked there and the community served by it.

SUMMARY

- Runshaw college was 'transformed' in a remarkably short period from 1993 to 1994 as a result of a culture-change programme.
- This chapter explained how that happened and how the college sustained its high standards. It explored whether what happened at Runshaw suggests a transferable model for college improvement.
- There is a paucity of academic literature on college improvements so this book draws from theory about school improvement.
- This theory suggests that transformational leadership is essential and that its focus on managing the culture offers the only way to cope with the increasing level of complexity and the increasing pace of change.
- Two specific forms of transformational leadership are 'moral' leadership and 'dispersed' leadership. This book will illustrate how both were deployed at Runshaw.
- Theorists argue that transformational leadership is insufficient and that there must additionally the 'instructional' leadership – leadership that focuses on teaching and learning and the conditions that support it.
- These kinds of leadership collectively build capacity for improvement and support the creation of a professional learning community.
- The claim that Runshaw was 'outstanding' was substantiated with reference to its track record for growth, success rates, inspection grades and financial success.
- This chapter sought to counter any suggestion that success was 'easier' for Runshaw and that its approaches are therefore not transferable. It did this by exploring five variables: the social background of students, the staff profile, the size of the college, its competitive environment and the coherence of its curriculum.
- The context of government reform is outlined – specifically, the changes that took place and the government's key strategies for reform.

- The chapter briefly reviewed the debate about 'professionalism' versus 'managerialism', contesting definitions that have been used in academic debate and suggesting that the focus on this debate ignores the real problem – the limitations of transactional leadership and the need for solutions that address this.

2 THE STORY OF CULTURE CHANGE AT RUNSHAW

FIRST STEPS IN TRYING TO BECOME 'BUSINESSLIKE'

The attitude of Runshaw's management in 1990 was one of willingness to explore the new opportunities that the Education Reform Act 1990 and then incorporation (in 1993) seemed to offer. We were stimulated by the idea of working with employers and we felt that we had something to learn from them. However, not all principals felt this way. Some set about complying with the new requirement that one-third of members of governing bodies be composed of employers by recruiting employers like local builders who would pose no 'threat' and who would be 'out of their depth' with the scale and complexity of colleges, unable to contribute much to policy and strategy or to challenge the authority of the principal.

We took the opposite view and set out to attract the leading employers in the area, people at chief executive or director level. In the event, from 1990 to 1993 seven leading figures from the local business community came forward and formed a new finance and general purposes committee, which effectively acted as a kind of 'cabinet' in governing the college. Interestingly, despite being senior figures in the local employer community, not all them were able to contribute effectively and they were all initially reluctant to take a real lead in reshaping policy or strategy or to identifying 'best practice' businesslike approaches.

In the event, it was left to the college's senior management team to find out what 'businesslike' meant, what 'best practice' businesslike approaches looked like, and how they could be applied to our college environment.

Our first step on this new path occurred in the summer of 1990. The college had been relatively successful in terms of growth, having increased recruitment by 17% per annum for the previous six years. We had been inspected in 1987 and had been 'formally congratulated' in the Inspectorate's report to the local authority. Examination results had made a remarkable improvement. For example, A-level pass rates had quickly risen from 67% in 1984 to plateau at about 88% in 1987 and each year thereafter, at that time about 10% above the national figure.

By 1990, however, problems seemed to outweigh successes. In particular, the accommodation situation was in crisis. The college was extremely overcrowded and this restricted future developments. Our funding was also very poor: following incorporation in 1993, the new Further Education Funding Council published the Average Level of Funding (ALF) for each college and we then found out that, of the 463 colleges, we were the tenth worst funded.

Our worst problem was undoubtedly low staff morale. The overcrowding, initiative overload, rapid expansion, increased workloads, pressure to raise standards, the introduction of 'efficiencies' like larger class sizes and reduced curriculum hours for particular courses and inadequate funding were taking their toll. I was keen to find out how the private sector coped with such pressures and whether there was some magical formula that could create a breakthrough in terms of our performance, our marketing, our financial wellbeing and especially our staff morale.

In the summer of 1990 I came across Tom Peters's book, *Thriving on Chaos,* and it impressed me enormously. I began to find out as much as I could about successful organisations and what could be transferred from them to a college environment. Consequently, I attended conferences, read books and talked to people about total quality management (TQM).

At the beginning of 1991 I attended a Department of Trade and Industry conference at which I was particularly impressed by a presentation given by Professor John Oakland, the Head of the European Centre for TQM at Bradford University. One of his remarks made particularly good sense: 'Why start a journey – a quality journey – without a map and a guide?'

With this in mind I employed a consultant to provide a map and to act as our guide. He focused on introducing a process management model linked to BS5750 (now ISO 9000), on strategic planning and on developing an elaborate structure of process review teams. I now believe that there was a great deal of sense in what he told us and that what he recommended is essential. However, none of it worked for us at that time.

One explanation for this is that we did not really understand it. But the real explanation is that it did not seem relevant to our needs. It seemed to be based on the premise that management was all about systems, that it was a pseudoscience and a purely mechanistic activity. In short, it did not engage us because it did not appear to add any value to what we perceived to be our real problems. For example, it did not address staff morale issues. Indeed, it appeared to make them worse by increasing workloads and introducing us to a world of alien business jargon, drawing us further away from educational values. In short, it struck the wrong note with our culture.

By 1993, having tried our very best to become 'businesslike', we were suffering what we recognised as 'death by 1000 management initiatives'. There had been no significant improvement to any of our key performance indicators. There was certainly no breakthrough. If anything, we were worse off than we had been in 1990.

On top of all that, incorporation brought new staff contracts and with them the lowest staff morale that I had ever encountered; 1993 was without a doubt the low point of my career, as it was for other principals. Little wonder that about a third of principals left that year.

CHANGING DIRECTION: A NEW FOCUS ON CULTURE CHANGE

It was at that point that, perhaps foolishly, I introduced yet another management initiative. I kept coming across articles about something called 'culture' and I became increasingly intrigued by it. I heard about something called 'employee surveys' and how it was important to measure staff satisfaction and to identify the issues that were creating barriers to staff's effectiveness. I was at the end of my tether. Realising that things were getting worse rather than better I decided that I had to plunge into an engagement with staff that might act as a catalyst in identifying and confronting our problems together.

In July 1993, therefore, I introduced a staff survey at Runshaw in the midst of attempts to introduce new contracts. One could take the view that it was an inopportune time to ask people if they were satisfied but I had the feeling that one could make the excuse that there was never a good time to ask such a question. In the event, about 35% of staff expressed satisfaction with the way that the college was being run and about 65% expressed strong dissatisfaction, particularly with such aspects as communications, 'feeling valued', involvement in decision making and management style. I have since learned that such a low rating is 'normal' when one first conducts an employee survey but nevertheless it still came as quite a shock.

The methodology for the particular employee survey that I employed had two ground rules. The first was that I would give completely honest feedback to staff about what they had said. The second was that I would tell them what I intended to do in response to it. Hence, I convened a staff meeting and told them the results of the survey. When it came to explaining what I would do about these results I could only say that I would take on board the criticisms made and would consider how I could respond in a constructive and positive way. The problem was that I did not really know how to respond or how to make any progress.

A white knight to the rescue

Almost in despair I turned to one of my governors for advice: Stewart Pierce, the Director of Human Relations at Leyland Trucks, a local company that had seen its workforce shrink from 13 500 to 800. He told me the story of how his company had faced a crisis in industrial relations with appallingly low staff morale in 1990 and how it had addressed these issues, achieving in the process a 'breakthrough' that transformed human relations, created a committed workforce, achieved a remarkable improvement in productivity, quality and profits and improved staff morale to levels rarely seen in any private sector company in this country. What had produced such a turnaround?

The answer is that in 1990, on behalf of his board, he had headhunted a new chief executive, John Oliver, to lead a transformation of the company. Although an engineer by training and experience, John had immediately focused on the quality of relationships between managers and the workforce. He found that traditional management approaches dominated, with 'bosses' and 'workers', 'them' and 'us', 'leaders' and 'followers' – all fixed in roles and structures where status and hierarchy determined authority.

Many of the shopfloor workers confessed that they took their greatest work satisfaction from frustrating the wishes of the 'bosses'. They felt alienated, excluded, insecure, angry and contemptuous of the values of the company's leaders. John Oliver swiftly concluded that Leyland Trucks was doomed unless these feelings, emotions and attitudes were transformed.

Consequently, he employed a consultant to lead a 'culture change' programme in the period between 1991 and 1993, by which time Leyland Trucks had been transformed. John Oliver could point to a £10 million improvement in the 'bottom-line' profits and to employee satisfaction levels that had risen to unprecedented heights.

So when I asked Stewart Pierce for advice in 1993, he advised me to begin a 'culture-change' programme. He suggested that I employ the same consultant that his company had used and, between us, we persuaded John Oliver to become chair of the governors at Runshaw College, a role that he filled for the next 10 years and for which he was recognised with an OBE.

With the support of John Oliver, Stewart Pierce and the consultant, we began the start of Runshaw's transformation.

Where had we been going wrong?

The consultant started by explaining to the management team that we had made a typical and classic mistake by focusing, from 1990 to 1993, on systems, strategy and structures – the 'hard Ss' as they are called. He acknowledged that our mistake was typical and understandable because managers are almost always attracted to tangible, concrete, technical, observable tools, techniques and methodologies in the belief that management is a kind of science.

However, he explained that none of these would have any impact unless the four 'soft Ss' were first addressed. That is, there had to be the right climate based on a culture of 'shared values' and high 'staff morale'. People needed to have the appropriate 'skills' and managers needed to deploy the appropriate management 'style'. So, in summary, shared values, staff morale, skills and management style make up the 'soft Ss'. These are about being creative, intuitive and about using the 'hard Ss' to implement an appropriate culture.

In plain English, he was saying that the traditional management model used in Leyland Trucks and in Runshaw was fundamentally flawed. It was what management theorists call 'transactional leadership'. It was a model of leadership based on the concept of 'command and control', on the idea that roles divide 'leaders' who are 'superior' from 'followers' who are 'dependent' and on relationships that are based on the transaction of services for rewards, which are controlled by the leader. It emphasises the management of systems rather than people and focuses on structural change rather than cultural change.

There is nothing intrinsically wrong with this model. It simply does not equip an organisation to be capable of coping with rapid and significant change and complexity. Colleges face constant and massive changes and are extraordinarily complex. John Oliver often said to me that Leyland Trucks was relatively static compared with Runshaw. For example, he could barely believe the extent to which the government moved the goalposts or constantly produced new initiatives, or the way that other factors like the curriculum changed significantly. More important than any of these examples, however, was the way in which the entire context of further education was changing, with a relentless movement towards expansion, increased efficiency and improved standards.

The consultant argued that colleges needed to develop the capacity to cope with constant pressure. They needed to be dynamic. They could only succeed if they had a highly motivated workforce with the commitment and ability to engage collectively in continuous improvement, always proactively seeking new opportunities to develop, to raise standards and to innovate. A culture based on 'us' and 'them', 'command and control' or 'superiors' and 'dependants' could not produce such capacity. In a context of change, such a culture would be far more likely to demotivate people, to create cynicism and, with it, resistance to change.

So what kind of culture did we want to create?

We wanted to create a climate of trust and mutual respect, one in which positive, collaborative, friendly attitudes prevailed. We also wanted to create a strong sense of commitment based on the 'right spirit' and strong motivation that sprang from the shared belief that, ultimately, we were doing something very worthwhile. We thought that it was important to create a sense of belonging that would stimulate people to engage fully in forging a shared sense of direction and in taking ownership of the development of the college. In summary, we wanted to create a sense of pride and excitement in achieving shared success.

Most of all, we wanted staff to develop the collective competence, the confidence and the capacity to manage the constant changes, complexities, problems and difficulties that we faced. We also wanted to provide the students with an excellent learning experience and outstanding results.

This placed culture change at the forefront. Our assumption was that we would expand, improve quality and achieve increased efficiencies if the whole staff acted together to achieve these shared goals. If staff morale remained low, with cynicism, withdrawal of commitment, resistance to change and people keeping their heads down at best, at worst acting in a hostile, aggressive manner, then we had little or no chance of making the required transformation in our culture or a breakthrough in our results.

Culture change, for us, was about focusing on relationships, transforming feelings, attitudes and beliefs. Theorists would describe this as 'transformational leadership'. It was about recognising that only a committed workforce will deliver outstanding results and that the way to achieve commitment was by transforming relationships, feelings, attitudes and beliefs. The focus had to be primarily on the management of people and the culture. In this context, we defined 'culture' as follows:

> *Intangible characteristics, the value system, the general tone, the standards that are recognised and rewarded, the ingrained working habits, the conduct of staff and students, the 'unwritten rules', the quality of personal and professional relationships and the overall educational ethos by which everyone 'recognises this place'.*

The basic premise behind this approach is that culture change is the most effective form of strategic management and that the most important thing that a leader can do is to manage the culture. Similarly, it is believed that the prevailing culture has a profound impact on how people respond to change. People may pay lip service to reforms and comply with changes but there will be no sustained improvement unless there is also real commitment. We also recognise that the prevailing culture can act as a strong conservative force.

So the first step in our culture-change programme was recognising the importance of culture. We had to take it very seriously. It could not be 'just another management initiative'. It had to be something that we would focus on above all else, committing energy, time, funds and enthusiasm to culture change as the priority in our strategic plan. We had many problems, not least of which was that we were in grave financial difficulties with category C financial status. Nevertheless, intellectually and emotionally, we were determined to adopt a suitable culture and to try to create a sense in which the whole college would work together as one community, with shared values, in recognising, understanding and solving the problems that we all faced.

THE CULTURE-CHANGE PROCESS

The process for changing the culture consisted of two main elements:

- surveying staff perceptions and 'unpacking' the outcome of these surveys in staff focus groups, thereby identifying the real meaning behind the data
- feeding back the perceptions of staff to managers and management groups so that they could formulate solutions.

The consultant conducted a series of interviews with groups of staff, identifying their concerns, their priorities and their levels of dissatisfaction. He then provided feedback to both staff and managers. As part of this process he also facilitated the creation of practical action plans that addressed the real issues.

The interviews began with the consultant explaining his purpose to the staff. This was not initially received with any real enthusiasm. It was perceived as 'yet another' initiative and there was scepticism about whether there would at any meaningful outcome.

Over a period of several months he interviewed virtually all full-time staff in small groups. He encouraged them to be completely honest and open and he promised them that what they said would not be reported back to managers in a way that could be attributed to any individuals.

A month after this, when he had identified their key concerns, he returned to the staff for a second round of meetings. This time he asked them to prioritise those concerns, firstly in terms of their importance and secondly in terms of the level of existing dissatisfaction or satisfaction. A particular issue might have been very important but if everyone was reasonably satisfied with the way in which it was being handled it did not need to feature in the list of things that had to be addressed. At the end of this stage in the process, 70 issues had been prioritised and the consultant said that the management team should try to tackle half of these, the top 35.

The 'perception gap'

While surveying staff views, the consultant began regular workshops with the senior management team. Initially these focused on engaging their commitment. One of the first things that the consultant did here was to explain that, in almost all organisations, there is a 'perception gap' between what the senior managers believe the staff will identify as the real issues and what the staff themselves actually say. He asked us what we thought staff would identify as their priorities and we responded with great conviction and certainty that staff would focus on the new contracts, the increased efficiencies, the new quality assurance processes and pay. In fact, we thought that this part of the process was a waste of time, so certain were we that we knew what staff would say. We did not believe in his 'perception gap'.

In the event, as will be seen later in this chapter, we were completely wrong. This was worrying because, had we not gone through the full process we might have wasted our energies and time addressing the wrong issues. Had it not been for the consultant's successful experience at Leyland Trucks we might have even objected to his wish to interview all staff. In the event, we agreed for this to go ahead but only with much scepticism.

The feedback stage

The next stage was the feedback stage. The consultant provided feedback to me separately and then to the senior management team without my presence. At this latter workshop, he began to reinforce some of the messages that were emerging from the staff about management style and teamwork by asking each senior manager to write down, in confidence, how each of the other senior managers could improve themselves. This apparently proved to be very effective in ensuring that the staff's concerns were recognised as valid. Senior managers were very surprised at the strength of feeling by colleagues about their behaviour and attitudes.

The consultant produced vast quantities of data about staff responses, all supported by statistical calculations. He argued that this exhaustive methodology was needed to ensure that the evidence was accepted: the data, he argued, made it impossible for managers to dismiss any criticism as invalid. Personally, I remain unconvinced by the need for such elaborate statistical treatment and this is a view shared by those at Leyland Trucks who worked with the consultant, believing that it increased the fee considerably and unnecessarily.

Our primary overall reaction was to accept the findings and the criticism as valid and to respond to them as positively as possible. This might seem to be a statement of the obvious – of course we would accept criticism as valid and of course we should respond constructively. In fact, it is often the case in organisations that, at this stage, senior managers often react very negatively. In one case that I know the managing director of a private sector company not only sacked the consultant when the 'messenger' brought 'bad news' but also sacked the human relations director who had employed the consultant. In another case, a college that carried out a staff survey resulted in the senior managers taking the criticism made by staff personally and virtually declaring war on staff.

WHAT THE STAFF SAID

In our case, the findings fell into six key issues. These were:

- senior managers do not care about staff
- the senior management team is not a team
- the principal is to blame
- the grapevine rules
- resources are misdirected away from the classroom
- middle managers are not managers.

Although these points might seem to reduce the feedback to slogans or one-line themes, each represented a profound critique of the way that the college was being led and of the way in which we had mismanaged our response to the Education Reform Act 1990 and incorporation. The problems that we identified at Runshaw as early as 1993 were to be identified by academic researchers in the mid- to late-1990s as sector wide. These were concerns about 'managerialism'; about polarisation of values between staff and senior managers; about the special difficulties in carrying out the role of the middle manager; and about a misjudged focus on corporate matters rather than on teaching and learning. These were all revealed as significant threats to our ability to engage staff in making the commitment needed for us to succeed. It is, therefore, worth exploring what is meant by each of the slogans.

'Senior managers do not care about staff'

This first statement encompassed about 50% of the 35 key issues that staff prioritised. Staff typically felt that senior managers needed to:

- understand stress levels among staff
- be open, honest, fair and consistent in the their decisions and behaviour
- act with mutual respect
- understand the complexity and demands of the staff role
- recognise and appreciate the contribution of staff
- be more sensitive to people and their feelings
- oppose external forces and represent the needs of education
- fulfil promises made to staff.

The data presented to managers included a wealth of anecdotes and quotations by staff about real incidents that had upset people. They included, for example, several comments about the way in which certain individual senior managers walked past staff in corridors without a smile or a 'good morning'. It was often things like this that symbolised weak relationships and that were perceived as demonstrating uncaring attitudes by managers.

To put these points into context, it is worth repeating that these surveys were conducted at a time when the senior managers had been trying to persuade staff to accept new contracts. These included reduction of holidays, an increase in teaching hours and an increase in the working week – all without compensation – so many of the criticisms were hardly surprising. However, the responses were clearly not just a backlash from the contract issue; there was clearly strong resentment about the way that managers had conducted their roles, acted as 'superiors', misused their powers, treated staff as 'dependants', cared little about offending people, had not shared information, had not involved people sufficiently, and had regarded staff who had resisted change as cantankerous 'unprofessional' people who acted as a barrier to progress and who had to be made to do what was deemed necessary. There was, to the amazement of the senior management team, almost no mention of low pay, which the senior management team had predicted would be the main concern, or the other issues which senior managers had identified as those which they predicted the staff would highlight.

There were other surprises too. One was that staff experienced extreme concern about redundancy. This was strange because there had never been a redundancy at Runshaw and, with year-on-year significant growth, there was unlikely to be any. However, when follow-up focus groups explored this issue it emerged that staff really wanted to feel valued and they were not convinced that, if push came to shove, the senior management team valued them sufficiently to fight for them should a situation arise – as it had in neighbouring colleges – where mass redundancies became a real possibility.

It was clear that – without using theoretical concepts or language – staff had identified the leadership approach as 'transactional'. They perceived the senior managers as people who had no real understanding of the need to manage their feelings, emotions and relationships. They felt that senior managers were insensitive, unfeeling, detached, remote and distant. They clearly did not like or respect the apparent absence of morality in such approaches. They wanted leaders who would be caring, supportive, and who would value them as individuals as well as respecting them collectively. To use theoretical language, they wanted 'transformational' and 'moral' leadership.

'The senior management team is not a team'

Another major surprise was a strongly held perception that the senior management team did not behave like a team. This was something that the senior management team had not predicted: indeed, not only did they not know that it was an important issue for staff, but they also believed that they were a very strong team and that they were perceived as such. Staff, on the other had, perceived individual senior managers to be like 'robber barons', each fighting for his or her 'fiefdom'. Individual managers were perceived to go into 'battle' at senior management team meetings having broadcast to their respective 'camps' what they intended to say and do, and they would come out of meetings triumphant or otherwise, informing their 'followers' about who had said what to whom at the meeting. Their versions would quickly become distorted on the grapevine. Staff viewed such disclosures of confidential information as a blatant misuse of power that illustrated a lack of integrity.

Nor had the senior management team predicted that staff would criticise the personal integrity of individual senior managers. This was not just about them behaving like competing warlords, it was also about their failure to take collective responsibility for decisions. For example, it was apparently quite common for individual senior managers to leave the senior management team and inform people about a decision reached there, allocating blame to colleagues for poor decisions. One way or another, subtly or blatantly, they let others know that they were not to blame for mistaken policy or strategy. When the senior managers had been asked to identify the issues that they thought staff would view as major concerns this had not been on their list of predictions, but it was a very important issue for staff. They wanted to have confidence in their leaders. They wanted to trust them. They wanted to have a clear sense of direction and a leadership team that would collectively lead them in that direction. They wanted people at the top who had shared values and they wanted leaders who would live those shared values with integrity.

Two things were very apparent from this criticism. First of all, 'power' was seen to be at senior management level and not 'dispersed' in any meaningful way. Secondly, staff valued collaboration, collegiality and teamwork, so the fact that those at the top could not behave in such ways caused them to wonder 'why should we follow a bunch of people at the top who cannot get their act together and how dare they preach about the importance of teamwork and collaboration when they do not act like a team?'

Once again, there was an undertone of criticism about the morality of our leadership, with suggestions of hypocrisy, of double standards and of selfish individualistic behaviours at the expense of collaboration.

'The principal is to blame!'

This criticism had meanings at several levels. The most obvious was that, as a person at the very top, I was responsible for any failings in the way the college was run or in its outcomes. The college was still performing satisfactorily in 1993 but there was obvious concern about staff morale, and this indicated that all was not well in the way the college was run. Ultimately, I was literally 'to blame'.

On a more profound level, this statement revealed a critique of my entire approach to leadership. In 1984 I had arrived at Runshaw feeling that I had to take personal responsibility for 'turning it around', transforming it quickly from a poorly performing college to a good one. I had largely succeeded in that but then, from 1987 to 1993, progress reached a plateau and the college did not move on to become 'outstanding'.

I had first received an insight into how my leadership was perceived in the summer of 1990 in what was, for me, a very personal and catalytic form of feedback, as described in the following story. That is, in May 1990, a member of staff whom I liked and respected enormously applied unsuccessfully for a middle management role for a second time at Runshaw. He came to see me to ask for feedback and I explained that he was perceived as lacking interpersonal skills and might damage relationships with staff. Within three weeks he had achieved a promoted post in another college and, on the day he left, his 'farewell speech' was a long castigation of my leadership, accusing me of being Thatcherite by repeatedly promising staff that I would 'lead them to the promised land', thereby squeezing greater efforts out of them. Worse still – he received a prolonged round of applause. I was obviously upset but I also thought that he was right and that I should take on board what he had said. He nearly ruined the effect by coming to see me later that day to apologise for his speech. It was then that I came across Tom Peters's book *Thriving on Chaos*, mentioned earlier. Clearly my leadership role was too dominant and, on reflection, it is interesting to read that theorists now perceive that 'There is a groundswell towards leadership as empowerment, transformation and community-building and away from the "Great Man" theory of leadership' (Harris *et al.*, 2003). They take the view that '. . . instead of looking for saviours we should be calling for leadership that will challenge us to face problems for which there are no simple, painless solutions, problems that require us to learn new ways' (Heifetz, 1994). As Fullan (2001) argued, '. . . charismatic leaders inadvertently do more harm than good because, at best, they provide episodic improvement followed by frustrated or despondent dependency.'

I am not sure whether I was perceived in the 'great man' image or as the 'saviour', but it was certainly true that, by 1993, there was a great deal of 'frustration' and 'despondency' amongst staff at Runshaw.

Ironically, the introduction of a culture-change programme that year itself represented a fundamental change in the leadership approach. It involved movement away from an approach that relied upon a dominant leader and towards one that engaged staff in identifying the problems and solving them collectively in an atmosphere of collaboration and collegiality. This enabled Runshaw to harness the abilities, skills and knowledge acquired by all managers and staff during the process of change to facilitate subsequent changes. That is, the processes of consulting staff, listening to them and working together with them underpinned the process of culture change. Once introduced, these processes became the new 'dispersed leadership' way of doing things at Runshaw.

'The grapevine rules'

Like earlier criticisms, this highlighted the fact that, at Runshaw, we had an 'unmanaged' culture. That is, the 'grapevine' ruled the culture in the sense that rumour, gossip, hearsay, personal criticism and exaggerated or distorted versions of managers' dealings with each other were rife. Miscommunication, premature communication, leaks and so on were undermining any notion that we were managing the culture – not that there had been any really strategic, co-ordinated or coherent effort to do so.

Leaving the culture to manage itself meant that it could be managed by anybody who wanted to act destructively as well as by those who were more positively inclined. The senior management team had completely failed to see the damage that the unmanaged grapevine was causing. Once again, we had been 'transactional', failing to understand or appreciate that our most important role was to transform Runshaw by proactively managing its culture. We were bumbling along, leaving the development of staff commitment to chance.

'Resources are misdirected away from the classroom'

Staff perceived that the values of senior managers had shifted from concern about students and teaching and learning to 'corporate' roles related to competition, finance, efficiency, quality, managing staff as a 'resource' and management information. Staff had seen the central roles of senior managers change from line management of lecturers in faculties to new corporate roles. They thought that a bunch of 'grey suits' was now running the college, that senior managers were obsessed with 'businesslike' jargon and processes, and that they had become 'managerial' in a very pejorative sense. Many practical, day-to-day concerns about resources were identified in the staff surveys. These were all important in themselves but they also symbolised and illustrated leadership that no longer appeared to care about what went on the classroom; leadership that had become distracted from what was really important in a college, and leadership that did not demonstrate the values that would attract trust. Staff wanted – again without any of us knowing the existence of the theoretical term – what is now described as 'instructional' leadership. That is, leadership that assumes that the 'the critical focus by leaders is the behaviours of teachers as they engage in activities directly affecting the growth of students' (Leithwood *et al.*, 1999).

'Middle managers don't manage!'

Concerns about leadership were not confined to just senior managers. Another completely unpredicted outcome of the survey was the strongly held perception by staff that 'middle managers don't manage'! In simple terms, middle managers were perceived to be overpromoted, overpaid individuals who had many of the perks of office like reduced teaching hours, offices of their own, telephones and status, but who did not take responsibility for making difficult judgements, especially when it came to dealing with staff.

In further education, middle managers manage four primary main areas: the curriculum, students, physical resources and staff. The first three of these are relatively stress free. Managing staff, on the other hand, can be very stressful, especially in four kinds of situation:

• cases of poor performance
• dealing with non-compliance with college procedures
• casual or unnecessary absence by staff
• challenging destructive or negative behaviour by staff in, for example, meetings.

All of these situations had been relatively unmanaged at Runshaw. The one role that was most stressful to senior and middle managers, the setting of and managing standards for staff, was not being managed by most middle managers. This role had generally been left for the six senior managers to perform.

When middle managers were brought together for a two-day workshop to address the issues raised in the survey, including this one, they acknowledged that the staff perception of them was true. They accepted that part of the explanation for this was their own reluctance to do difficult and stressful tasks, but they primarily explained it by saying that senior managers had not empowered them to manage staff. For example, they argued that most college procedures for managing staff, such as procedures for managing poor performance, did not include a formal role for them. They had not been told what was expected of them, nor had they been trained in the skills and techniques required. They asserted that senior managers kept as much control and power to themselves as possible. It was this assertion that led the consultant to say to the principal and senior managers 'why try to manage the college on your own when you have 40 middle managers wanting to do it for you?'

The middle managers quickly demonstrated their commitment to this new form of 'dispersed' leadership by saying that they wanted to tackle the single most difficult problem in the college at that time – the introduction of new contracts for teachers. They pointed out that the senior managers had tried to introduce them in 1993 and had been spectacularly unsuccessful, creating immense ill feeling and achieving no positive outcome. They now said 'leave it to us and stay out of our way'.

It was a collective assertion by middle managers that they wanted to be really effective managers. They agreed with the staff that they had taken the rewards but not the responsibilities. They were quite angry and very frustrated about the situation. On a practical level they also felt that they could persuade their colleagues to sign the new contracts. They believed that their colleagues trusted them not to abuse the contracts and that, in a spirit of mutual respect and trust, they and their colleagues wanted to refocus their energies on students, teaching and learning and all the other things that had brought them into the teaching profession rather than the acrimonious battle about contracts. In the event it was agreed that middle managers should take on this task. The outcome was that, within three weeks, virtually every teacher had signed his or her new contract. 'Dispersed' leadership had worked. The challenge for us was then to embed it in the way that Runshaw would be run.

CONCLUSION

Whenever I tell the story of what happened at Runshaw, three questions are usually raised:

- Was Runshaw just unfortunate in 1993 to have a group of senior managers whose personal styles attracted such severe criticism from staff and were we, in other words, untypical of college leadership?

- Was it really necessary to go through all the traumas of a culture-change programme based on identifying staff perceptions of senior managers?

- What did we do about these findings?

The first question makes the mistaken assumption that the feedback was 'personal'. Of course, in one sense it was personal because it described the behaviours of specific individuals but, in another sense, it was almost entirely about the kind of leadership – 'transactional' leadership – which is typical of most colleges and most organisations. According to theorists, it is rare to find any other form of leadership. 'Transformational', 'moral' and 'dispersed' leadership are relatively new models of leadership and the practice of focusing on culture change is also relatively unusual. The senior managers at Runshaw were simply doing what senior managers in most organisations do. As individuals, we were hard working, value driven, student centred, inclusive, and, in my opinion, very moral people who wished to serve the needs of students in the best way possible.

But that is not how we were perceived. Our mistake was not lacking 'morality' in any way; it was our failure to focus on managing the culture in such a way that our morality was perceived. One could say that staff perceptions of us were not fair but that is not really relevant: the only thing that mattered was the reality of staff perceptions. Senior managers should have managed these perceptions but we did not do so. We should have become 'transformational', we should have offered 'moral' leadership, we should have 'dispersed' leadership to middle managers and to staff, and we should have demonstrated more clearly our commitment to students and to teaching and learning – that is, we should also have offered 'instructional' leadership. But we did not. To our credit, we at least realised that fact between 1993 and 1994 as a result of the culture-change programme and, in response, we changed. That is something that has not yet happened in most colleges. So Runshaw was not 'unfortunate' in 1993 to have the senior managers that it had: we were typical senior managers except in one respect – we underwent a transformation that moved us from what our consultant described as 'unrecognised incompetence' to 'recognised incompetence', and that was the start of becoming 'competent'.

This takes us to the second question: was it really necessary to go through such a traumatic its process to find that out?

The first thing to say is that it was traumatic. Several senior managers were very upset by the feedback they received. But it was this personal impact that created a sense of ownership that drove future individual and organisational change. The truth is that there had been a 'perception gap', we had been complacent about how we were perceived, we had not realised that staff felt the way they did or about the kind of leadership they needed, and we had not built the capacity to enable the college to deal with the challenges it faced. Ultimately, it did not really matter whether senior managers were upset; if that is what it took to change Runshaw into a college that provided outstanding service to its students and which supported staff properly, then so be it. Our consultant insisted that the process was commonplace in the private sector, that although staff surveys were rare in colleges in 1993 they were widely used elsewhere, and that real change only occurs when those at the top 'see the light', stimulated by feedback that forces them to realise that they are not 'in tune' with staff and, consequently, not in control of the 'climate' or 'culture'.

The third question often asked is 'what happened next?' The answer to this question is explained in the rest of this book. In summary, we developed new approaches to leadership and we developed what theorists call a 'professional learning community'. We introduced a multidimensional range of new approaches that later became known as 'the Runshaw way: values drive behaviours'. The heart of this was a new form of value-driven moral leadership based upon the identification of our core values and their explicit translation into behaviours. This is the subject of the next chapter.

SUMMARY

- We responded positively to the government's challenge to become more 'businesslike', to increase efficiency, effectiveness and to expand.
- Our first steps, from 1990 to 1993, were disastrous, wasting huge amounts of time, energy, money and goodwill in focusing upon systems-based approaches.
- In 1993 we changed direction, refocusing on culture change and borrowing an approach from a private sector.
- This emphasised the importance of improving staff morale, and creating a more positive and collaborative climate. Culture change became the central focus of strategic management.
- We defined the culture that we wanted to create: one based on trust and mutual respect, with a strong sense of commitment, belonging, pride and direction.
- We employed an external consultant to facilitate the process of identifying the perceptions of staff and responding to them.
- He argued that almost all senior management teams suffer from a 'perception gap', failing to identify real staff concerns and therefore failing to address the key issues for culture change. He demonstrated that such a gap existed at Runshaw.
- We took on board the issues he identified. These primarily concerned management style, workloads and facilities.
- The issues about management style focus on feelings about being valued, about the lack of teamwork at the top and about failure of middle managers to manage.
- What emerged, overall, was a picture of an 'unmanaged culture'.
- Senior managers at Runshaw had been using a very limited range of leadership styles and this adversely affected the climate, creating barriers that prevented staff from being effective in providing excellent standards of quality for all students.

3 VALUES DRIVE BEHAVIOURS

One of the most striking things about the feedback from staff in the 1993–4 culture-change process described in the previous chapter was the strong focus on values and the implied criticisms of the morality of the leadership that had previously been offered. Staff said that they wanted leaders to be caring, sensitive, to show concern for others, to behave with integrity and honesty, to work together in a collaborative and co-operative way, to make others feel valued, to show respect, to value teaching and learning and, above all else, to establish trust. These words and phrases set a moral tone to our reflections. We did not use the word 'moral' to describe our responses or to define the new kind of leadership that we developed, but a strong sense of 'right' and 'wrong' infused all of our deliberations. The lesson for us was that when you engage in meaningful in-depth dialogue with people about such things as 'leadership', as happened as part of the process of culture change at Runshaw, the outcome is that one is inevitably drawn into the formulation of what theorists would call 'moral leadership'.

In this chapter, the first section provides a review of theoretical commentaries about moral leadership and about its importance in developing the capacity to succeed. The second section provides an overview of Runshaw's six core values, showing how they are linked both to the criticisms made by staff about Runshaw's leadership and to the theoretical models of leadership associated with improvement. It also outlines the process of identifying the values and translating them into behaviours, policies and strategies. And the third section takes us through the six core values, explaining the key impacts they had on shaping behaviours, policies and strategies.

A REVIEW OF THE THEORY OF 'MORAL LEADERSHIP'

Harris *et al.* (2003) reports that 'most recent leadership studies have focused upon values and moral purpose' and she quotes others as using the term 'the moral craft of leadership'. Leithwood *et al.* (1999) envisaged moral leadership assuming 'that the critical focus of leadership ought to be on the values and ethics of leaders themselves' and went on to say that this should include a 'focus on the relationships among those within an organisation'. Harris *et al.* argued that the outcome of moral leadership is that it builds leadership capacity, meaning that it provides both the moral authority to lead and it binds the staff of the college together in a collective commitment to drive improvements forward:

> *Building leadership capacity therefore involves teachers working together and learning together to bring about effective change. It is derived from the explicit and shared values of a community. These are not necessarily 'professional values' but those which hold a community together and which, of themselves, guide actions and accountability. What people do is driven not by what is rewarded, or what works, nor by self-interest. Instead, it is led by sense of what is right and in the interests of the whole school.*

Similarly, Burns' (1978) seminal work on transformational leadership argued that moral leadership 'represents the transcendence of self-interest by both leader and led'. He argued that the effect of such leadership is generally seen to be as follows: 'Transforming leadership ultimately becomes moral in that it raises the level of human conduct and ethical aspiration of both leader and led, and subsequently has a transforming effect on both.'

Perhaps the most convincing case for values-driven moral leadership was put by Hopkins and Jackson (2003) when they outlined their model for building the capacity for a successful school. They described one of the four concepts behind their model (described in more detail in Chapter 1) as '. . . more subtle but crucially important. It is the intangible and 'higher order' domain – the territory of shared values, social cohesion, trust, well-being, moral purpose, involvement, care, valuing and being valued.'

This concept, they argued, underpins the two key components of capacity building – dispersed leadership, and the creation of a professional learning community. Their effectiveness depends upon 'the tightness around values and the moral purpose (the shared beliefs and the urgency to act and to achieve together for higher-order purposes) . . . so values making leadership tight . . .'

At the heart of all writings like this about value-driven leadership is the concept of 'trust':

> *Trust is recognised as a vital element in well functioning organisations. Trust is necessary for effective co-operation and communication, the foundation for cohesive and productive relationships in organisations. Trust functions as a 'lubricant' greasing the way for efficient operations when people have confidence in other people's words and deeds. Trust reduces the complexities of transactions and exchanges far more quickly and economically than other means of managing organisational life. (Tschannen-Moran and Hoy, 2000)*

So the challenge for Runshaw in 1994 was to respond to staff in a way that would engender trust, that would underpin the process of coming together as a community to work together collectively, that would increase the commitment, dedication and hard work of all staff and that would be open and honest in identifying and confronting our problems.

The culture-change process itself had given us a good start. It had been an open and honest search for those barriers that were impeding progress; it had provided staff with the opportunity to shape the agenda for action; it had given managers the opportunity to respond visibly in a constructive, listening way, characterised by humility; and it had clearly implied the core values that Runshaw should identify.

Overall, there seems to be a consensus that moral leadership is extremely motivating and that it inspires higher levels of commitment, hard work and productivity from staff. In summary, it increases the capacity of a college to be 'outstanding'.

AN OVERVIEW OF RUNSHAW'S CORE VALUES

Using values to manage our culture

During our reflections in the culture-change process it became obvious that managers must manage the culture, meaning that we should at least develop an understanding of the values, beliefs, attitudes, relationships, norms and behaviours that made Runshaw the kind of place it was.

We had been transactional in our leadership approach. For example, we had developed a 'personnel' function in the college but not a 'human relations' strategy. We had never considered rooting such a strategy in the value structure of the college, nor had we thought through collectively what we believed, why we believed it, how we should present our beliefs to others and how we should contest the conflicting values of others. We spent huge amounts of time discussing marketing, finance, management information and quality control, but we hardly ever discussed our values and beliefs. It just didn't seem something that senior managers should do in a college of further education during incorporation. We were wrong.

The process of developing 'value-driven leadership'

In 1994, as part of the feedback stage, we began to manage the culture by engaging in a college-wide moral debate in a formal, structured way. We created opportunities for people to say what they believed, to listen to others and to build consensus about shared values.

It is interesting to note that Hopkins (2003) argued that it is not enough for education institutions like a school or college to debate values but that they need to become explicit:

> *The important point is that each school and school system should articulate their own values position appropriate to the context within which they operate, and the broad focus on student learning and achievement. Simply discussing values in some abstract way, however, is also insufficient. Values need be translated into criteria and principles and form a way in which teachers and students behave, in the way in which school organised itself. In particular, the dialogue about values . . . provides the school with a clear sense of direction and purpose . . .*

This is exactly what we meant when, in 1995, we started to use the phrase 'ethos into action'. We felt strongly that statements about values would be justifiably perceived as 'empty rhetoric' or, to put it more crudely, 'hot air', and would create cynicism if we did nothing more than just talk about values. Hence, in 1994 and thereafter, as part of the culture-change process, we began deliberately to articulate our core values and to translate them into behaviours, policies and strategies.

The process of doing this in 1994 was initially *ad hoc* in the sense that we did not use a structured template. We simply debated the issues in senior management workshops, college management team meetings and workshops, staff conferences and on the academic board. From 1995 we began to 'stop-the-track' five times a year during term time to provide the whole college community with the opportunity to debate in depth what we believed, why we believed it and how it should shape our future vision and goals (a detailed description of this process is provided in Chapter 6). This process was very important: without it, the outcomes would have had no legitimacy and therefore no authority. During these debates the critical focus became the values and ethics that leaders and staff should practice. In developing our vision, goals, strategy and culture we became focused on defining, strengthening and articulating our values.

We eventually formalised all these approaches in 2002, when a college-wide, year-long process of consultation occurred using a template containing the six core values, requiring us to identify a set of beliefs for each core value, then a set of attitudes for each and then three sets of behaviours for each – one for the students, one for staff and one for managers. This process started with a senior management 'away-day' review. It went on to involve middle managers in a two-day workshop followed by a series of working lunches, then a staff conference (using the processes described in Chapter 6) and then students assemblies, personal tutor discussions and student feedback to senior managers. It was one of many examples of creating a whole-college sense of community that, year after year, developed a strong sense of shared values and shared direction.

As we did this, we began to manage conflict and disagreements much more effectively. The values of mutual respect, trust and treating people with dignity were an essential part of this. Difference of opinion became a legitimate basis for joint exploration and enquiry into the meaning of such differences. This was not just about win-win: it was a genuine coming together of leaders and staff in collaboration to resolve shared problems.

We constantly returned to this approach over subsequent years, always reviewing our values and exploring their implications, especially with respect to the behaviour of managers, staff and students. By 2001 this formed the basis for the manual sponsored by the Learning and Skills Council, *The Runshaw Way: Values Drive Behaviours*. It encapsulated years of debate and reflection but the essence of what it recorded was, however, formulated between 1994 and 1995 when we identified the six core values.

The emergence of six core values

During the process of surveying staff at Runshaw between 1993 and 1994, a number of specific values emerged very powerfully. Staff wanted collaboration, collegiality and a college that operated like a community. They did not want the worst aspects of what was termed 'managerialism' – managers in 'suits' aping the worst kinds of macho behaviours from the world of private-sector business. They wanted fairness, sensitivity, and consideration and they wanted all relationships to be based on the notion that everyone should treat everyone else with respect and dignity.

They wanted the college to be student centred, meaning that it valued each individual as someone who had a unique set of needs. They wanted senior managers to focus on the craftsmanship of teaching, not on the management of information systems, funding, marketing and other business approaches.

They also believed in inclusiveness, in serving all abilities and all post-16 ages. They made it clear that they were motivated by 'making a difference', by 'opening minds', by helping people to grow and to fulfil their maximum potential. This had clear implications for their belief in high standards and excellence.

They were impatient with initiatives that did not work: they wanted effective implementation of their values, not constant woolly debates that led nowhere and resulted in no action. They wanted to see practical and tangible outcomes and visible progress that confirmed their sense of purpose and their desire to ensure that what they did was worthwhile.

Hence, in summary, Runshaw's six core values were:

- teaching and learning is our first priority
- valuing the individual
- opportunities for all
- striving for excellence
- working together and with others
- putting our ethos into action.

Linking values to staff criticisms of leadership and the emergence of new forms of leadership

These six core values link very directly to the six main criticisms of Runshaw's leadership described in Chapter 2. For example, 'valuing the individual' links to 'senior managers do not care about staff'; 'teaching and learning is our first priority' links directly to the criticism that 'resources are misdirected from the classroom'; and 'the senior management team is not a team' links to 'working together and with others'. The latter also links to the criticisms of the dominance of the principal – 'the principal is to blame' – and to the assertion that 'middle managers are not managers', both subsequently addressed through the implementation of 'dispersed leadership' or, to put it more simply, the core value of 'working together and with others'.

These six core values also link to the forms of leadership identified in Chapter 1 – those that theorists believe to be the most appropriate in developing outstanding organisations. 'Valuing the individual' links to the focus in 'transformational leadership' on the management of culture and especially to the management of staff emotions, feelings and relationships. 'Teaching and learning is our first priority' links directly to 'instructional leadership'. 'Opportunities for all' articulates our moral purpose and therefore underpins 'moral leadership'. 'Working together and with others' articulates our commitment to 'dispersed leadership'. 'Striving for excellence' declares our belief in a culture of 'high performance expectations', and 'ethos into action' could correspond to the multidimensional strategies, processes and structures that implement our values and which are described in subsequent chapters of this book.

THE SIX CORE VALUES

Teaching and learning is our first priority

This value guided our new approach to 'instructional leadership'. It might seem like a statement of the obvious – so much so that it could be perceived to devalue the whole concept of core values. However, it is not obvious because in many colleges in the 1990s, with incorporation, funding, competition and intense marketing dominating the agenda, managers often forgot that their core 'business' was teaching and learning. Staff had told us in 1994 that their perception was that senior managers 'misdirected resources from the classroom'.

We took the view that, if teaching and learning is of a high quality, then everything else – success rates, student satisfaction, recruitment, funding, accommodation and so on – would all fall into place. If teaching and learning was weak, then no amount of marketing, management information system developments, funding tricks, entrepreneurial activities or anything else would make the college effective. In the last inspection in which I was involved at Runshaw, the inspector for management interestingly concluded that managers at Runshaw judged the quality of their management by the standards that were achieved for teaching and learning. I think that he was right. Ultimately, if Runshaw or any other college was to improve, it had to change what went on in the classroom.

Prioritising resources and roles for teaching and learning

This first core value was also highly 'political' in terms of the organisation's internal competition for scarce resources. There are, of course, always competing demands from a variety of sources for very worthwhile projects. In this situation, an important question is, what are the criteria for prioritisation? In our case, they were always teaching and learning and we always decided to direct resources primarily to support them. This included diverting funds to the classroom, to equipment, furniture, heating and ventilation, lighting, books, consumables and so on.

It also included prioritising the creation of management roles that supported teaching and learning and keeping to a bare minimum other support business roles. In 1995, in response to the staff surveys, we recognised that we had erred in creating new 'corporate' roles for senior managers, that this partially accounted for the distancing between senior managers and staff, that we had inadvertently sent out the signal to staff that we did not value teaching and learning or the management of teachers and students, so – as is described in the next chapter – we restructured the senior management team back to the faculty structure that existed prior to incorporation.

This core value also meant investing very heavily in professional development for teachers, in lesson observation, in research and development for teaching and learning methodologies and in information learning technologies (ILT). It meant reducing teaching hours for individual staff whenever possible to enable teachers to manage their workloads more effectively. For example, in 2002 Runshaw committed £500 000 a year to reducing the subject contact hours of A-level teachers from 25 hours a week (828 per year average) to 18 hours a week. These teachers formally remained on 828 hours per year but much of this was for subject-specific supported self-study and personal tutoring, enabling them to spend at least seven hours a week seeing individual students or small groups in workshops for coaching. Similar approaches had been taken for teachers of other students – for example, foundation students were grouped in classes of no more than 13 and had copious additional support.

Teaching and learning as our key process

Many quality gurus become extremely irritated by the focus that theorists place on vision, mission, culture, leadership and so on, arguing that the only thing that really matters is whether the key processes in an organisation are working effectively. In our case, teaching and learning was clearly a key process, probably along with assessment and monitoring, curriculum management and student support. Gurus would argue that managers, support staff and teachers should spend the majority of their time and energy on working on these key processes to improve them. They also argue that staff are more interested in whether these key processes work properly than anything else. I have a great deal of sympathy for this approach but, in this particular case, it does not conflict with our own approach because our first core value says the same as the process-focused gurus. It says that the key process of teaching and learning must be the primary focus for everyone.

This has obvious and direct implications for the behaviour of managers. They should demonstrate that they value teaching as an area of expertise. They should value teachers. Curriculum managers should present themselves primarily as 'leading professional teachers' rather than 'managers'. Collectively, they should direct resources – including their own time, energy and enthusiasm – to teaching and learning. They should talk about teaching, lead and/or attend meetings and workshops about teaching and generally behave in a way that demonstrates that teaching and learning is their first priority.

The institution should also provide a pay and career structure that enables teachers to stay in the classroom. At Runshaw one of our policies was that all curriculum managers, including senior managers, should teach – if only for three hours a week in some cases.

This first core value also implied an acknowledgement that teaching and learning happens both inside and outside the classroom. The student experience encompassed every contact that a student had with any member of staff and such contacts could help or hinder their learning experience. This implied that all staff had to be 'customer focused' at all times, courteous and helpful, ready to go 'the extra mile'. Staff also had to accept that they had a role to play in managing misbehaviour by students in public areas. No one should ever walk past a problem. Everybody has a responsibility for creating an environment for learning, and that means a safe, orderly place of work and study.

The implication of saying 'teaching and learning is our first priority' for support staff

This first core value also defined relationships between teachers and support staff. It seemed to imply that 'teachers' were more important than support staff. They were not and it was important for us to say that the role of support staff in creating effective teaching and learning was crucial, that teachers cannot do their job effectively without them and that the students' experience would not be the same without their support. Having said that, this core value did help to clarify the 'servant' role of support staff, as it did for all managers. That is, everyone who was not a teacher was employed to serve the needs of those who teach on the 'front line', doing what is most important in the college. Support roles that were not crucial should not exist in a college that prioritises teaching and learning and commits its resources to teaching and learning. So the fact that the roles did exist and did absorb scarce resources implied that those filling the roles should be enabled to do their jobs properly.

What prioritising teaching and learning meant for students

The implication of this first value for student behaviour is equally important in redefining the relationship and attitude of students to the college's staff. There is a great deal of confusion in colleges about the status of students. Some say they are 'customers', other say they are not 'customers' because they do not pay for the service or, at any rate, do not pay a full fee – so they are 'consumers' instead. Another view is that, in any case, they are 'volunteers', having chosen to enrol, and are not required by law to attend.

Does this mean that they can attend when they like, be late if they choose, leave early, and do coursework as they wish? And are the answers to these questions the same for 16–18 year olds and for the adult students? There is often a lack of clarity in response to such questions amongst college staff and consequently a lack of conviction in implementing standards of behaviour in colleges.

In a college that is driven by values there is no lack of clarity or conviction. If students expect teachers and managers to behave as though teaching and learning is their first priority then of course they must behave similarly. This means that once they make the commitment to 'volunteer' for a course then they effectively form a contract and it defines relationships thereafter. Hence they must see classroom attendance as their priority and attend on time and on all occasions; they should not take on outside commitments (like part-time jobs of more than 11 hours or tiring social activities); they should attend properly equipped; and they should meet the required standards of behaviour and work both inside and outside the classroom.

Valuing the individual

The implications for students

Our second core value was 'valuing the individual'. Behind this value are the beliefs that 'the learner comes first' and that everyone should primarily be student centred, treating each person as an individual with a unique set of needs.

These beliefs imply that each learner should fulfil his or her maximum potential, so a 'pass' for most learners would be inadequate because it would not reflect their true potential. This implies that systematic attempts should be made to achieve the 'maximum potential' for each individual in each area of study, that tangible targets should be set and monitored, that reviews of the individual's progress should be as much about raising self-esteem and creating high expectations as about monitoring progress. It also implies that one–to–one reviews, focused on maximising potential, should be used to build strong staff–student relationships, with the teachers' role being that of a coach, celebrating successes and identifying further areas for improvement in a positive way.

In the debate at Runshaw about this value, it was quickly and unsurprisingly agreed that teachers' behaviour should be characterised by sensitivity and responsiveness. However, this value did spark off a vigorous and controversial debate about whether it also implied that staff who came into contact with students should also 'enjoy' working with students. It became clear in the debate that there was a widely held perception that some staff do not enjoy working with students and that they did not like students, that they perpetually complain about them and that many of their colleagues see this as unacceptable.

It was in debates like this – and there were many of them – that people who would never articulate an opinion about colleagues in public could do so safely in a non-personal way and could thereby shape the new boundaries and disciplines of others' behaviour. Almost everybody felt very strongly about something and they had their opportunity to say what it was. Relationships, norms, 'the way we do things around here' and the culture were truly being redefined.

What 'valuing the individual' meant for management style

'Valuing the individual' implied that managers should act as role models in respecting others, praising them, being friendly, creating warm relationships, listening, being responsive, being approachable, making people feel valued, being optimistic, managing by walking about, visibly showing interest and awareness of what was important to staff and students and developing individual staff. The 'individual' in this value was, of course, assumed to include both individual students and individual staff. It was regarded as equally important that managers had to challenge behaviour that was insensitive and disrespectful. They had to ensure that staff treated students with respect at all times and they had to take action where they did not.

This had not been happening. Hence, staff had said that 'middle managers don't manage'!

Middle managers, in particular, were uncertain of their new role. They were particularly unclear about the 'morality' or 'sensitivity' of challenging staff and they were often unwilling to do anything that courted unpopularity. With the force of an explicitly articulated value system, which visibly defined roles, relationships and behaviours in unambiguous detail, it became impossible for managers to avoid their responsibilities without being perceived as lacking integrity. Peer group pressure became the new force for exercising discipline and worked to assert standards rather than to undermine them. The concept of 'leadership' was no longer defined in terms of 'transactional' arrangements; it became clear that leaders should focus on the feelings and relationships of staff to increase their commitment and capacities.

How staff were expected to 'value the individual'

These management behaviours also applied to staff with regard to their relationships with both students and managers. The new value system obliged them to treat people with respect, to treat 16–19 year olds like 'young adults', to coach students by emphasising positive feedback whilst not being afraid to give critical feedback and not being patronising.

This part of the debate raised a recurring issue that had clearly confused many staff: how to balance the need to be sensitive, positive and supportive with the need to assert high standards and to give honest feedback. Indeed, the recurring theme throughout the debate on many of the core values was how to balance the difficult and demanding art of 'tough and tender' relationships. But at least it was being debated and people had to engage with it, trying new relationships, difficult though they were, in contrast with the fudge that had existed before.

How students were expected to 'value the individual'

'Valuing the individual' meant that students should be courteous and respectful to each other and to staff at all times. One of the more subtle debates on the implementation of the concept of 'respect' was a debate about whether lateness, casual absence, missed deadlines and inadequate effort constituted a form of disrespect within the new definition of a two-way student–teacher partnership. We concluded that it did.

We also discussed how this value affected the relationships between students, especially about being supportive to new students, to those in a minority and to those with learning difficulties.

All of this involved using the value to clarify and redefine standard relationships. It was most useful in defining them in 'grey' areas – usually most behaviours can easily be recognised as 'good' or 'bad,' 'black' or 'white' but often it was unclear where some behaviours belonged on these spectrums. Often, one could feel uneasy about something without being able to say exactly what was wrong about it. We found that the value system acted as an excellent reference point: for example, 'grey' behaviour was often 'wrong' because the person was not acting with respect or was not behaving in a way that demonstrated that he or she valued other individuals.

In another example we used this core value to resolve a perennial debate about whether the rules about lateness, absence and missed deadlines applied as strictly to adults as to 16–19 year olds. We concluded that, whilst one recognises that many adult learners have special difficulties, the standards and rules should be the same. A basic skills teacher should require an adult student who is late to have the courtesy to explain and account for his or her lateness, just as a teacher of an A-level 16 year old should.

It was this kind of debate that flushed out all the areas of uncertainty and inconsistency that characterised the old culture. The new culture had explicit values and, with them, explicit rules and expectations, procedures that supported their enactment and commitment from staff to apply and implement them uniformly and consistently.

Opportunities for all

Defining our moral purpose

The third value was 'opportunities for all'. This was the only value of the six that might not apply to all colleges. For example, a sixth-form college specialising in A-level for the most able 16–19 year olds only would not share this value for the operation of its admissions policy. It could be argued that the other five values are the core values of not just Runshaw but of further education in general.

This value articulated Runshaw's commitment to respond to the needs of all abilities in both the 16–19 and post-19 age groups and its commitment to meet the needs of adults as well as 16 year olds. Again, this value might be perceived to state the obvious but it was an important public statement of philosophy and attitude and it articulated our sense of purpose. As explained earlier, Runshaw had been an elitist sixth-form college until 1984 and its staff had spoken of low achievers as 'dross' and adult education as 'Micky Mouse' courses. To achieve consensus for the value 'opportunities for all' marked a complete reversal of attitude from that which had prevailed. It was a moral statement that recognised that everyone can benefit from education, that Runshaw positively welcomed everyone who wanted to come and learn, that lifelong education should meet individuals' and society's needs for second-chance opportunities, for reskilling, for personal growth and for leisure through education. It also declared our passionate commitment to equal opportunities. It signalled that Runshaw was non-elitist, egalitarian and inclusive. It articulated our moral purpose.

Value-driven policy review

One of the most interesting debates that this value reopened was about our admissions policy. Did 'opportunities for all' mean that anybody could enrol on any course? Of course the answer was 'no'. It would have been unfair to applicants, to the college and to the taxpayer to enrol people on a course for which they were mismatched in terms of ability, aptitude or interest. But this debate gave us the opportunity to review what we meant by 'recruitment with integrity' and to be certain that our systems and structures were properly in place to ensure that we did what we said we believed was right.

It also raised the issue of how we identified the needs of our community and how we responded to them. Indeed, in the context of ministers asserting that colleges should not try to be 'all things to all people' in case they may end up 'doing nothing very well', the debate about this value presented a challenge to our mission and our strategic direction. It made us consider whether we should withdraw from certain provisions, creating partnerships instead with other agencies in our community that could share in a collaborative effort to provide 'opportunities for all'.

This core value also had specific implications for how staff operated. For example, we used the debate about this value to clarify that it meant that staff should ensure that applicants to their subjects or courses should not be refused the right to enrol, as long as those individuals met the college's entry requirements, even if staff perceived them to be 'low achievers'. There is great pressure on staff to deliver excellent retention and achievement results so the temptation for them was to be selective, enrolling only those who were highly committed and able. At A-level, for example, mathematics and modern language teachers can argue quite convincingly that a grade B at GCSE in the subject does not necessarily guarantee A-level success in that subject. However, we concluded that 'opportunities for all' meant, in this instance, that if a person has achieved a grade B then he or she should be allowed to enrol.

In another example of how this value was used to clarify policy and practice, we interpreted this value to mean that staff must not recruit in a way that aims to fill their courses; rather, the students' needs should be the only consideration in determining progression of a student and his or her recruitment to a specific course. At Runshaw this was an issue, as it is in most colleges, because staff were understandably anxious to recruit successfully to their course. An element of competitiveness was also understandable. The danger with this was that recruitment targets could take priority over the learners' needs. With a core value that was explicitly interpreted to say that the learners' needs are the priority, that we are there to provide opportunity for the student, not the staff, this was less likely to happen.

We used the debate about this value to address a third policy issue that had been contentious at Runshaw for many years. That is, in the past a small minority of staff had 'burned off' students within six weeks of enrolling them. That is, they had been required to enrol students that they would have preferred not to enrol, so they deliberately subjected those students to treatment of one sort or another that led to the student to withdraw or transfer. This may or may not have been done in a blatant manner; indeed, some argued that it was in the students' best interest. The debate about 'opportunities for all' settled this issue once and for all. It was interpreted explicitly to specify that staff should do everything in their power to support, encourage and help the students. They should go 'the extra mile' on their behalf. It spelled out that teachers must be fair to such students, that some students need a second chance and that, beyond the basic entry and admission policy, teachers should not prejudge students.

At Runshaw, this value also generated a fourth very specific debate about another live policy issue – the responsibility of staff for students whom they did not teach. This issue was 'live' because many staff identified situations in which 'their' students had not received help from other staff. This value was interpreted to specify that all staff should in future regard all Runshaw students as their responsibility, valuing all and helping all whenever they could.

So what had initially seemed a rather bland and obvious statement about providing opportunities for all turned out to be a reference point for a host of specific issues that had concerned people for many years. Staff had been divided on these issues and their meaning had not always been clear. Staff had not consistently interpreted 'recruitment with integrity' in the same way, they had been tempted to meet their recruitment targets even at the expense of students' needs, it had not been clear that 'burning off' was wrong and staff had not always realised that they had a responsibility for all students.

Many staff had quietly resented the attitudes of others with regard to these issues for a long time. The debate about 'opportunities for all' finally put them firmly on the agenda, generating an open debate about what was right and wrong and giving birth to a new set of clear and unambiguous policies, each properly explained in terms consistent with our third core value.

What 'opportunities for all' meant for students

For students, too, there were clear and explicit implications. This value required them to be tolerant and to behave without prejudice to other students. In a college of 3700 full-time students aged 16 to 19, with 50% studying A-levels, there was a possibility that some students would look down on others. Staff constantly checked on this and rarely found any evidence that this happened. Nevertheless, this value gave us the opportunity to reassert to each new cohort of students that such an attitude would be wrong.

It gave us all a platform to assert our pride in being part of a comprehensive college that took as much delight in the achievements of those with learning difficulties as in the success of its Oxbridge candidates. In many ways, 'opportunities for all' defined the political value of the student community, a community in which everyone should value and care for each other, irrespective of their level of ability, social background, race or any other difference.

In a quite different way, this value generated another important debate – a debate about the need for students to take responsibility for their own learning and the opportunities open to them. This value was explicitly interpreted in a way that required students to explain their needs, aims, ambitions and goals so that appropriate guidance could be provided. It required them to be realistic about their capability so that they could make informed choices, to accept guidance, to be open and to have the capacity to change.

This was quite demanding for the students, and that was a prevailing feature of all the debates about the way in which core values should be interpreted. Students were very rigorous in setting high standards for themselves but staff also took every opportunity to emphasise that all the core values should be used to set new standards for students' behaviour.

There was clearly a moral tone to this: they saw the core values as an excellent framework for telling students what was expected of them and explaining why it was right that it was expected. It was, for them, a form of moral education as well as a perfect opportunity to redefine staff–student relationships. But most of all, it was taken as an opportunity to assert that the student should be responsible for his or her own learning.

Striving for excellence

Redefining the concept of 'professionalism'

The fourth core value was 'striving for excellence'. This could be said to be very closely associated with the new values implicit in the concept of 'managerialism'. It articulated a powerful response to the government's challenge to low standards, to poor quality and to the demand for increased accountability that was explicit in all the government's initiatives after 1990. As mentioned in Chapter 1, the new inspection regime, benchmarking, targets, league tables, competition and accountability, all formed a government agenda that was designed to challenge the culture of individualism and professional autonomy that the government saw as the root of low standards in education.

Inside colleges, performance measurement in the form of student surveys, lesson observation, regular and frequent 'mock' inspections, team-by-team intensive scrutiny of data on student attendance, retention, achievement, added value, high grades, progression and students' satisfaction all fed a structured and systematic performance management process, a self-assessment process, a teamwork structure geared to continuous improvement and a professional development unit's rolling programme.

'Striving for excellence' acknowledged 'the new reality' of accountability and the fact that all these new approaches did promote critical judgements of colleagues' work, disturbing the comfortable, sometimes cosy and nearly always congenial culture of individualism. The real challenge was to persuade the staff that it was truly 'professional,' 'moral' and 'right' to make these changes.

Clarifying what was expected of students

To some extent, this value was driven by the strong and immediate support for a culture of high expectation for students. As mentioned earlier, staff really became engaged with the debate about core values when they saw how it clarified complex issues and helped to create a consistent approach to managing students' behaviour. They could immediately recognise how it would help for all staff to exhort students to 'strive for excellence', to take responsibility for improving their performance, for setting themselves stretching targets, for regular reviews of performance, action planning, proactively seeking support, working hard, behaving properly, meeting deadlines, attending all lessons whenever possible, accepting criticism and responding to it and striving to do their very best, whether in normal classes, enrichment activities or in personal tutor sessions. This entire debate beautifully defined what staff expected of students. When consulted, students concurred completely.

Redefining the role of staff

It was a natural next step in the process to define what was expected of staff. For students to 'strive for excellence' in the ways listed above, staff had to explain the ground rules very clearly to students, they had to enforce them uniformly and consistently, they had to work in partnership with students in setting ambitious goals, reviewing them, and so on, all in a positive manner.

More important, it was strongly asserted by all staff that everyone must follow through when faced by student misbehaviour or underachievement.

Redefining the concept of 'caring'

There was steel and sharpness in the debate on this issue, especially from staff who had felt frustrated by the way that some colleagues had defined 'caring' in the past, thereby creating a disciplinary framework that many regarded as sloppy.

At the conclusion of the debate on this issue it was agreed that we should not define 'caring' in terms that led to us accepting low standards or excusing underachievement. We agreed that being 'caring' should not lead to staff acting in a patronising way that devalued students by accepting second best. It was asserted very strongly that we should never compromise our rules, standards or expectations for the sake of comfortable relationships and at the expense of mediocre outcomes, thereby failing to prepare students for life outside college.

At the same time, it was stated equally strongly that none of the above should be implemented in a way that humiliated students. The whole debate on this issue was charged with energy and long bottled-up frustrations. Identifying our core values and defining their explicit meanings released these frustrations.

Having clarified what we meant by 'caring', we went on to spell out what we should do in a range of other situations that had irritated and confused people. For example, there were some staff who had argued that it was humiliating for students to be 'chased' for work but, after debating this in the context of 'striving for excellence', we came down firmly on the side that argued that we should 'chase' students when they failed to perform to acceptable standards but we also recognised that we had to balance this with the skills of motivating them.

Challenging inappropriate behaviour

In other contexts we also agreed that this value should be taken to mean that staff should never walk past a problem, that all staff should challenge inappropriate behaviour inside or outside the classroom, that we should monitor students' progress very carefully, raising their self-esteem whenever possible but challenging arrogance too.

The word 'challenge' emerged frequently in this debate but perhaps the most interesting articulation of the frustration that many felt with woolly standards was the requirement that staff should 'tell students what they must do to improve'. There was in this a clear implication that directiveness was a style that had been much underestimated and that it should be used much more frequently. A new tone was being set by some people who had been unable to exert their leadership in the past.

A new student culture, with new standards, new relationships, new responsibilities and new processes was created in 1995 to 1996. It was a heartfelt assertion by students and staff of a new code of conduct. Staff had taken responsibility for redefining the student culture in collaboration with students. They were using their new powers to create their own regime of accountability. Staff and students collectively insisted on the need for consistency. Staff were impatient with the notion of 'individuality' where this undermined their high standards by enabling individual members of staff to 'do their own thing'.

The idea that the government was somehow imposing a new regime of accountability or that some external body was leading a challenge to the individualism of staff now seemed absurd and irrelevant. The staff, empowered by the freedom to identify their core values and to spell out in the most explicit terms what they meant, seized the opportunity to draw a line in the sand, reinvent the culture, and set very high standards and high expectations for themselves and their students, demanded that everybody act consistently. They explicitly criticised the fact that acts of 'individualism' could undermine the whole ethos.

The changing role of managers

The role of managers in all this was to facilitate the process. Leadership could be offered by providing a clear sense of direction, a vision for the respective part of the college in which each leader operated, a set of team goals, opportunities for innovation, for continuous improvement and for staff development. It was asserted that leaders should recognise and celebrate staff successes, spread good practice, motivate and encourage staff and support them when dealing with student misbehaviour or underachievement.

Of course, it was acknowledged that not everybody would share the same level of commitment to the new standards, so there continued to be the need to manage the underperformance or non-compliance of some staff.

However, the new tone also demanded that managers stand up to be counted, that they play a leadership role by supporting or opposing the strong voices that emerged from the staff, that they act as role models in following through the implementation of the new standards, that they challenge gossip, negativity and unfairness when it threatened to lower the tone or undermine the sense of moral collective leadership that had emerged. Most of all, they were now expected to be proactive in addressing deficiencies or problems and in refusing to tolerate mediocrity.

A real sense of moral pride was created. There was no longer any question that managers would take the cosy route of courting popularity by fudging difficult decisions. The staff had said, with some contempt, that 'middle managers don't manage!' The college community had responded to this by specifying in the most explicit terms what it expected of managers: there was no option now but for managers to do what was expected. Peer-group pressure did not demand 'individualism' – it demanded consistent and highly visible management of the college community.

Working together and with others

Obtaining consensus

The fifth core value was 'working together and with others'. The first part of this, 'working together', was primarily about teamwork within the college and the second part, 'with others', was about collaboration and partnership outside the college. The whole value had its roots in the concepts of co-operation and community spirit. It was agreed explicitly that it should be taken to mean that the whole college should be unified around its shared values, thereby creating a sense of belonging and a sense of pride.

The openness of debate, the intensive and lengthy consultation process, the constant and massive attempts to involve everyone and the ongoing communication campaign meant that nobody could reasonably say that they did not have an opportunity to voice their opinion. This was the essential principle that underpinned this unity. If the 'shared values' had been in any way imposed on staff, it would have been unacceptable to expect staff to feel a sense of ownership or responsibility for them.

The strong sense of collective ownership meant that there was an explicit requirement that all staff should abide by the doctrine of collective responsibility with everyone loyally promoting the policies and decisions of the college as though they were their own. Up to the point of decision, everyone had the right to disagree and had the duty to assert their point of view, but once a decision was made, following a democratic process that produced general consensus, then every member of staff was bound by this doctrine to implement the decision and to present a united front to those outside the staff.

This approach worked rigorously for the senior and middle management team but there was always a sense of uncertainty about it amongst staff. It was one of the very few approaches at Runshaw that was never monitored rigorously but, increasingly, people asserted that it was very important that the 800 people who worked at Runshaw and who owed their living to its continued success should play their part in marketing it by positive 'word of mouth' in the local community and to existing students.

This was not quite the same thing as collective responsibility but there was a sense of impatience with those who appeared to accept the benefits of unity, like mutual support in managing students, but who then undermined others by inconsistent or half-hearted application of agreed approaches, failing to take their share of responsibility.

Teamwork

As far as teamwork was concerned, Runshaw's approach to this had been highly structured since 1984, so the debate about this fourth value did not generate as much innovation as the debates about other values.

In many ways, teamwork already formed the backbone of the organisation. In 1984 there had been no teams. Teachers had been completely autonomous and independent. When I was appointed, in 1984, I required that the teachers of each subject met regularly to spread good practice, to standardise their marking, to share their resources and to support each other in what was described as the concept of 'curriculum-led staff development'.

Most staff at that time regarded teamwork as an affront to their professionalism. Consequently, although they complied with the requirement to meet, the purposes of teamwork were not achieved initially in most teams. Within a year, however, people were saying 'we don't mind teamwork, but we do object to bad teamwork'. So by the time of the culture-change programme in 1993 there was already general support for teamwork. A number of teams had visibly been very successful and many of the staff who had been developed as leaders in the previous decade were enthusiasts of the benefits of teamwork.

Nevertheless, many still resented the concept of teamwork and there were many ineffective teams, often characterised by a strong sense of solidarity and mutual support in sharing complaints about curriculum change, students, resources and management initiatives. The identification of the core value of 'working together and with others' put these issues firmly on the agenda for staff debate.

Those who led effective teams seized the agenda, arguing that this value meant that everyone should be mutually supportive, never undermine each other and always share a consistent view of what was expected from students and from themselves. They argued that everyone should experience good communications within a team and feel involved so that they had a strong sense of ownership about decisions.

This debate also identified ways in which teamwork could be improved across the college. For example, it was recognised that it was important to support teamwork by building formal times for team meetings into the timetable; it was agreed that we should formally clarify the purposes of different kinds of teams; we should train team leaders in coaching skills and how to conduct effective meetings; and we should train team members in interpersonal skills, problem-solving skills and decision-making skills.

We also affirmed the benefits of teamwork – the advantages of sharing resources, spreading good practice, moderating standards and continuously reviewing and improving their work. Critically, ground rules were established about how the members of teams should behave towards each other. These included the importance of praising others, of challenging gossip or personalised attacks or being aggressive or being destructively negative. All of this came to define what was commonly described as 'inappropriate behaviour' in team meetings.

Learning from others

The second part of this value, 'and with others', specifically embraced the idea that everyone should systematically seek opportunities to bring best practice from outside the college into it. It eventually led to the creation of a structured process called 'best in class'. This was an opportunity for all staff to go outside the college on secondment to another organisation for two days a year. Initially we had in mind that a subject teacher could spend two days in another college where an inspection had given the respective subject grade 1. It also extended to vocational staff who could spend two days on an industrial secondment. Our support staff, too, could spend two days in a 'best practice' work placement seeing how, for example, customer care worked elsewhere or, for our catering manger, how MacDonald's organised its fast food operations. At its peak, nearly 200 staff took this kind of opportunity in one year.

Similarly, we developed policies to encourage our staff to become formally and informally involved in external learning opportunities. For example, we had a policy of encouraging at least one member of each subject team to become an external examiner or verifier. We also encouraged staff to become part-time Ofsted and Adult Learning Inspectorate (ALI) inspectors. We were delighted when our management information systems (MIS) manager became chair at the user group for the supplier from whom we had purchased our software. Our ILT manager became the project manager of an ILT network for Lancashire colleges. Managers were encouraged to speak at conferences.

We became a networking organisation, believing that external contact kept us at the leading edge of innovation, that every contact revealed at least one 'golden nugget' of a good idea and that dialogue with others helped us to think-through our own approaches. For example, in the process of disseminating *The Runshaw Way* to 350 colleges, we were convinced that we learned far more than any of them.

The implication for students

This core value was equally powerful in defining what was expected from students. We expected students to work in a constructive partnership with other students, with staff, with employers where appropriate and with their parents, again where appropriate. We expected them to take responsibility for their own learning, to contribute positively to group activities, to contribute to the community spirit within the college by taking their share of responsibility for our environment, challenging others who misbehaved wherever possible.

Like staff, we also expected them to be ambassadors for the college wherever possible, especially with their behaviour on visits or trips.

Partnerships

One of the most important ways that we developed our strategies was by working in collaboration with partners. This became so important to us that we developed a structured approach towards the management of partnerships. The first element of this was to distinguish between ordinary external relationships and substantial partnerships which required formal management by using a set of criteria as follows:

1 Is there a working relationship?
   * Has the college and partner committed resources?
   * Is there a mutual sharing of risk and reward?
   * Does the college and partner exchange information?
   * Does the college and partner regularly meet to review performance and progress?

2 Is added value created?
   * That is, is the student experience enhanced?
   * Would a loss of the partner lead to reduced quality of service?
   * Does the partnership attract new students?
   * Are costs per student reduced?
   * Is risk reduced for the college?

On the basis of these criteria we had identified 25 key partnerships and we subdivided these into three subcategories: 'primary' for funding bodies; 'secondary' for those partners who worked with us to produce or develop core products or processes; and 'organisational' for those that focused on our support services.

We also supported the development of partnership relationships, firstly by allocating responsibility for partnerships to a senior manager, secondly by allocating response for liaising with specific partners to other senior managers, and thirdly by arranging regular meetings to assess and review performance of the respective partnership and to plan new developments. Reports of these meetings went to the senior management team for review at its regular meetings where actions would be agreed. Each partnership relationship was also recorded in a written agreement, often linked to bids for external funds and subject to audit.

Although these agreements were formal, we were aware that a strong personal relationship between ourselves and each partner was a key to success. Hence, we worked hard to develop close relationships. For example we systematically surveyed the satisfaction of staff who served us but who were not employed by us, as in the case of the drivers of the 30 special buses that transported our students. When we surveyed their level of satisfaction, we found that they were very dissatisfied with the behaviour of our students. When, in turn, we surveyed the satisfaction of our students, we found that they were very dissatisfied with the 'rude' behaviour of these drivers. Serving both enabled us to identify problems and then to solve them. The outcome was the deployment of student monitors to each bus with the role of trying to negotiate better relationships.

The most successful partnerships were based on the principle of win-win in which all parties achieved clear and significant benefits. One example was an ILT partnership involving 13 colleges in a consortium. Runshaw obtained £200 000 of government funds in 1999 to support the creation of 18 subject groups to develop their ILT approaches in their respective subjects. It also created networks of ILT managers, IT managers, and staff development managers. In another case, we worked with three other training partners to bid successfully for European Social Funds. We also formed mutually beneficial franchise agreements with a variety of private and public sector organisations such as Age Concern. We formed a partnership with a housing association with which we made a successful joint bid for funds for a mobile IT classroom to visit housing estates. We formed an alliance with the Countryside Agency to bid successfully for funds to enable people in local villages to borrow college mopeds and bicycles to improve their access to adult education classes. In the case of our MIS, we developed software that filled the gaps in the commercial system that we had bought. We sold the software that we developed to the commercial supplier. So partnerships were a very important way for us to identify needs and to respond to those in a collaborative way to everyone's benefit.

Putting our ethos into action

Doing what you say

Of all the six core values, the one that created most enthusiasm was 'putting our ethos into action'. In summary, it could be interpreted to mean 'just do it!'

In our case, many people at Runshaw were simply fed up with ineffectual, tortuous debates about various aspects of theory related to, for example, the difference between a 'customer', 'consumer', 'stakeholder', 'student' and 'learner'. They were equally fed up with the jargon of management initiatives. There was almost an institutional aversion to 'paralysis through overanalysis'.

To some extent, this explains why there was such enthusiasm for turning the core values into practical, hands-on, meaningful statements about behaviours that addressed the real, everyday issues of college life. The whole tone of the culture-change process was down-to-earth. Its power was in the anecdotes and language that made the debate so recognisably 'Runshaw', relevant, 'owned' and not in any way pious or bland.

It is interesting to note that a study by Ian Taylor into Beacon Colleges (unpublished report by the Evaluation Unit at the University of Liverpool on behalf of LSDA, 1999) concluded that they are not particularly innovative, that what they do can generally be found in commonplace textbooks on educational management, but that what makes them special is that they all systematically implement their approaches. They simply 'do what they say' in a consistent, rigorous way.

Implementing the 'hard Ss'

This last value brings us back to the model of the seven Ss with its subdivision of the four 'soft' Ss relating to management style, shared values, skills, and staff morale. It is argued that these 'soft' Ss must be addressed first to create a climate in which the 'hard' Ss can be implemented effectively. But the equally important part of the seven S model is that the 'soft Ss' are worthless unless they are implemented through the 'hard Ss', the strategies, structures and systems of an organisation. In Runshaw's case we interpreted this to mean that value statements and other elements of culture are, on their own, virtually ineffective without the processes and structures that make them real and that implement them.

An example of what was meant by this can be drawn from the story of how the phrase 'ethos in action' was first used at Runshaw in 1995 to describe a new process called minimum target grades (MTG). This was a process used at Greenhead College and we decided to adopt it for Runshaw. It involved determining target grades for such student in each subject, based on an added-value calculation of what it would mean for each student to achieve his or her 'maximum potential'. We developed procedures and structured times for our staff to set these targets, to review them on a one-to-one basis with students, to develop action plans with students, to monitor these and to take corrective action when needed. Nothing was left to chance: a complex system was developed, staff were intensely trained in it and managers monitored it.

As part of the debate on this, one person remarked that the MTG system was our 'ethos in action'. By that he meant that this process empowered staff to implement the ideal that 'each individual student should fulfil his or her maximum potential'. It also enacted concepts like coaching, reviewing, action planning, rigour, standards and high expectations. Without a process that underpins systematic implementation, there was a danger that all these words might simply be meaningless platitudes and empty rhetoric.

A compliant culture?

By the same token, anybody who failed to implement the process properly would be undermining the values and behaviours that the college community had agreed as the way we would turn our ideals and values into action. It may sound odd, but it could be suggested that Runshaw thereby became a 'compliant culture', meaning that non-compliance with agreed processes that implemented our values was not an option for an individual member of staff. Non-compliance would undermine the values that the process implements and it would undermine the efforts of others who were complying.

The phrase 'compliance culture' does sound pejorative, conjuring up images of systems being centrally imposed on reluctant staff, who are then 'commanded and controlled' into compliance. In Runshaw's case, the identification of core values, their translation into explicit beliefs and behaviours and the debate about how to implement these was conducted in a democratic way, with general consensus and staff ownership of outcomes. Rules about behaviour, processes about supporting students, roles and structures, were all agreed by consensus. If it was a 'compliance culture' then it is important to qualify this by emphasising that we also accepted the notions of challenge and debate.

In practice, however, there are always people who, for one reason or another, do not do what they are supposed to do. Hence, the need to require and 'manage' consistent compliance. What was relatively unusual was for a college to be explicit in its rationalisation behind the 'morality' of the demand that staff comply with agreed processes.

At the same time, the teamwork structure and the process management model provided ample opportunity for staff to challenge compliance in a structured way, to review processes, to evaluate them, to have their say about whether they were effective and to generate changes in them in the search for continuous improvement.

Incidentally, most staff regarded MTG as the single most powerful curriculum innovation that Runshaw had ever introduced, judging it in terms of the fact that it appeared to result in the single greatest step-change improvement in student achievement and overall performance. Nevertheless, there was always a minority of staff who did not believe in it and who paid lip service to its implementation. Constant reviews, intensive workshop-style training and the management of compliance were very important in making it generally very effective.

What made the management of compliance acceptable in this instance is, firstly, the fact that those managing the process, in this case MTG, passionately believed that it did help to 'fulfil the maximum potential' of students. Secondly, it was acceptable because the general approach to process management ensured that reviews were bottom-up and consequently included a great deal of listening by managers to those who operated individual processes.

Challenging individual autonomy

Virtually all of these six core values challenged the concept of individual autonomy in one way or another. All explicitly demanded consistency by staff in meeting high expectations, but none was as powerful as 'ethos into action' in this respect. It was this value above all others that required that the three 'hard Ss' – systems, structures and strategies – were used to convert the 'soft' Ss into tangible, concrete, visible tools, techniques and methodologies.

The presence of this value also raised an often-heard objection to the whole approach taken in 'the Runshaw way' – that it is 'all about systems'. Ten staff left Runshaw to move sideways to a neighbouring sixth-form college that achieved comparatively mediocre results. Most of them said that they wanted to move to a college that was 'not so driven by systems' – they wanted more individual autonomy. With its traditional 'professional' approach to individual autonomy, we felt, at the time, that it could never be a real threat. Ironically, the governors there recruited a senior manager in 2003 from Runshaw as its new principal and he, in turn, recruited other managers from Runshaw. All of them were fully committed to the idea that standards would only improve significantly and quickly if a culture of high expectation were implemented in a systematic, structured way. They believed passionately in the value of 'ethos into action' and they understand how it works. That college will now quickly become a real threat to Runshaw and, ironically, the new managers from Runshaw will disturb the cosy, comfortable life of those who left for a quieter life. Indeed, they may well find that they have moved 'out of the frying pan and into the fire'.

Their voices, however, were representative of a minority of others within Runshaw's staff. It was also a constant challenge to explain 'the Runshaw way' to new staff and it was always necessary to demonstrate to existing staff that processes and systems were justifiable, that they did clearly add value and that they were not 'unnecessary bureaucracy'.

This meant that new staff had to be trained and coached in how processes work. They also needed to understand why they were justified. In particular, new staff had to be inducted properly into process management because, if they were not strongly committed and skilled in the processes, their non-compliance would quickly undermine the efforts of others and create inconsistencies and lower standards.

CONCLUSION

So what contribution did Runshaw's approach to identifying its core values and then translating them into explicit behaviours, policies and strategies make to its transformation to becoming an excellent college? It contributed in at least four critically important ways.

The first was that every value emphasised student centredness. Every value had clear and important implications for real issues and problems rooted in the classroom experiences of students and teachers. The values acted as the basis for a fundamental review and redefinition of staff–student relationships, emphasising the aspects of teacher responsibility for treating students with care and respect and the students' responsibility for their own development and their relationships with others. It was not just a debate for the sake of it – it was about problem solving, about practical, hands-on solutions to issues like whether a teacher should 'like' or 'enjoy' teaching students, about the meaning of 'caring' and about many other everyday concerns for both staff and students.

The second way in which Runshaw's approach to identifying its core values made a contribution was by creating a culture of high performance expectations. It repeatedly defined, clarified and reinforced norms of excellence, for the work of both staff and students. It clarified complex issues and helped to create a consistent approach. It gave staff and students a powerful platform from which to assert high standards and to cast inconsistency as 'unfair', 'lacking in integrity', a 'fudge', 'patronising', and 'cosy and comfortable mediocrity' – phrases that were all charged with moral condemnation.

The third contribution was the 'constancy of purpose' that values gave to the direction of the college. This phrase comes from the eight fundamental concepts behind the European Foundation for Quality Management's Business Excellence Model (Runshaw was awarded a European special prize in 2003 for 'leadership and constancy of purpose'). Apart from being quite a mouthful, it is a very important concept in building a clear and long-term sense of direction based on shared values and shared vision. The core values were not short term or temporary: they articulated Runshaw's moral purpose, what it stood for and how it conducted itself over the long term. They acted as reference points – as beacons – for all decision making.

Perhaps the most important contribution that our approach made to building capacity for long-term improvement was in the way that the process of debating the values defined our approach to 'dispersed leadership'. This chapter has given many examples of the way in which the processes for debating those values enabled staff at all levels to participate in decision making about fundamental policies and strategies. It suggests a democratic process and a form of dispersed leadership in which the role of managers was transformed from directing staff to one of facilitating decision making by them. It could no longer be said that decisions were made at Runshaw by leaders who were not 'in tune' with staff. Dispersed leadership meant that decisions were made by the staff who 'played the tune'. It meant that better decisions were made, it meant that there was strong commitment to the morality of the decisions and strong ownership of the values that shaped them, and it meant that Runshaw had established the foundations for social cohesion.

As Hopkins and Jackson (2003) said:

> *[Dispersed] leadership occupies the space between the pebbles in the jar. It is the cohesion that surrounds the management structures, the coherence, and grows within and across schools. It requires spaces. Leaders . . . will orchestrate and nurture the spaces – create the 'shelter conditions' for collaborative learning . . . the lubricant for community and social cohesion.*

SUMMARY

- Moral leadership is a form of transformational leadership. It implies that a college should articulate its core values and translate these into explicit behaviours, strategies and policies.
- If done successfully it can be motivational, inspiring staff to work harder and more productively and thereby improve standards.
- It can also give the leadership of a college a strong sense of conviction, determination and moral authority in managing the culture.
- The first core value focused Runshaw on teaching and learning, prioritising resources and management time to it, clarifying the centrality of the importance of the teacher and defining the focus for students as that of learning.
- The second core value, 'valuing the individual', reinforced the concept of student-centred, democratic, affiliative and coaching management styles and asserted that students should show that they value staff and other students in all of their actions and behaviours.
- The third core value, 'opportunities for all', articulated our mission to serve all post-16 age groups and all abilities. This also clarified numerous complex issues regarding admissions policies and practices.
- The fourth core value, 'striving for excellence', articulated a new culture of 'high-performance expectations'. It clarified the high standards expected of students and staff. It provided a new framework for redefining concepts like 'caring' and provided the rationale for challenging inappropriate behaviours.
- The fifth, 'working together and with others', spelled out our commitment to collaboration, teamwork, learning from others and partnerships.
- 'Putting our ethos into action' was about implementation, doing what we said we would do, and using structures, systems and strategies to implement our culture.
- This sixth value raised concerns about 'a compliant culture' and about 'the place of individualism'.

4 FROM 'UNRECOGNISED INCOMPETENCE' TO 'COMPETENCE'

One of the key conclusions from the analysis of what happened at Runshaw in the culture-change process was that senior managers moved from a position of complacent 'unrecognised incompetence' about managing the culture to a position of 'recognised incompetence'. In this latter position they at least understood that they were not 'in tune' with staff and had little control over managing a culture in which commitment by staff to high performance expectations was absolutely necessary. A study of leadership in further education by the Hay Group in 2002 titled *Further Lessons of Leadership* (Franks *et al.*, 2002) said:

> *In every organisation, leadership has an enduring impact on performance. It's not just about the chief executive setting strategy, or making the right decisions, but about motivating and engaging staff, about developing their willingness and ability to take decisions. Ultimately, in any enterprise driven by the knowledge and ability of people – which seems to describe education well – it is the discretion and productivity of all people who work there that makes the difference.*

The next step, therefore, was to become 'competent'. But competent in what?

Two dimensions shape the answer to that question. The first is the obvious one: what staff complained about was the management style of both senior and middle managers, criticising the former for being too directive and lacking sensitivity and criticising the latter for failing to manage staff performance to consistently high standards. So management style was the first dimension.

The second was much less obvious. The introduction of a culture-change process changed the role of leaders and created an entirely new set of relationships for both managers and staff. It was not just a matter of management style – it was a profound role change that demanded new competencies. That is, the culture-change process both identified the key concerns of staff – things like their perception that 'senior managers do not care about staff' and that 'middle managers do not manage' – and suggested core values that had profound implications for the concept of leadership and the roles of managers. Using theoretical language, implementation of these new values demanded new forms of 'transformational', 'moral', 'dispersed' and 'instructional' leadership. This implied that all staff should in future participate in decision making in the same way that they had shaped the culture-change agenda through staff surveys and staff focus groups. It also implied that they play a full and active part in shaping a shared sense of purpose, that they continue to work in collaboration with managers and with each other, and that they accept joint responsibility for the outcomes.

The new role of leaders was to empower staff to play their new roles. It meant that managers had to recognise the central importance that managing and developing people rather than systems should play in their roles. As Patterson *et al.* (1997) said:

> *Managers know that people make the critical difference between success and failure. The effectiveness with which organisations manage, develop, motivate, involve and engaged the willing contribution of the people who work in them is a key determinant of how well those organisations perform . . . employee commitment and a positive 'psychological contact' between employer and employee are fundamental to improving performance.*

The staff surveys of 1993 and 1994 had clearly demonstrated that we had signally failed to make that 'positive psychological contact'. We had to rectify this by first recognising that leadership was separate from the role of leader, that leadership henceforth lay in the hands of the many staff who had asserted their values and who vented their frustration when setting new standards and specifying new relationships – including staff–student relationships – in the debate about values and their explicit translation into behaviours, policies and strategies. In this debate, staff had taken responsibility, they had welcomed collaboration, and they had created a culture of high standards for themselves and their students. They had behaved as a community in taking ownership of decisions, and in doing so they had learned from each other and translated that learning into the capacity to succeed together. The role of leaders was, henceforth, to build that capacity further by investing in people, by focusing on teaching and learning, and by developing connections and relationships between staff. How they did that is described in Chapter 6.

Becoming 'competent', for managers at Runshaw, meant developing the ability to fulfil a reconceptualised role of 'leader' as well as the ability to deploy the full range of management styles on a spectrum that we called 'tough and tender'.

This chapter, therefore, addresses these questions:

- How did we conceptualise the new role?
- How did we develop a 'tough' approach based on moral leadership?
- What were our core competencies and where did they come from?
- How did we develop them in leaders?
- What were the implications of all these changes in the roles of senior managers: the changing role of the principal as an illustration of becoming 'competent'?

How did we reconceptualise the role of leader?

The 'great' teacher and 'great' manager

To help us understand the role that we wanted managers to play in these new forms of leadership we used the concept of the 'great teacher' to act as a role model for all other roles in the college. That is, we repeatedly referred to the teacher who had completely mastered the skills of teaching as the kind of person to whom we should all aspire. We described the 'great teacher' as someone who stimulates, enthuses, inspires, creates a warm, friendly, positive atmosphere and who engenders a love of the subject. We argued that 95% of the 'great teacher's' focus was on these positive behaviours but, at the same time, he or she would demand high standards, would not accept late or poor work and would have the energy and integrity to follow up and confront poor performance, thereby revealing a passion for high standards. He or she would have mastered the very difficult skill of balancing 'tough and tender' approaches.

A similar description could then equally be applied to the concept of the 'great' manager and, below that level, to the role of the 'great' team leader – one who enthusiastically leads other staff by creating the 'right spirit' but who would never shirk from managing poor performance. It was always clear at Runshaw that such role model descriptions stemmed from the concept of the 'great teacher'. We consciously and deliberately replaced a culture based on the concept of 'professionalism' as defined simply by 'expertise in one's subject discipline' with one based on admiration for those who, additionally, could effectively manage both the learning process of students and the efforts of the staff. 'Professionalism' became defined by people skills rather than simply by academic knowledge.

In the same way, 'great' managers would focus primarily on managing people rather than their specialist subject knowledge or expertise. They would take responsibility for creating a 'professional learning community' within their team and within the college. They would do that through inspiration, enthusiasm, support, care, communication, involvement, coaching and a passion for quality as defined by the 'customer' who received the services of the respective team. Most of their efforts would be focused on creating positive relationships, warmth and a spirit of camaraderie but 5% of their effort might be devoted to challenging poor performance and demanding high standards from everyone on all occasions. If there was any doubt about how to do this in a college environment without, in any way, creating a culture of fear or oppression, the manager had simply to turn to the many role models of 'great teachers'.

This new approach implied that the manager needed to be particularly competent in motivating and engaging staff.

A framework of management styles

The Hay Group uses a framework of six management styles: they are, 'democratic', 'affiliative', 'coaching', 'coercive', 'authoritative' and 'pacesetting'. Using this framework, we had clearly not deployed the types of leadership described as 'democratic' ('what are your views on the matter?') or 'affiliative' ('its important that we all get on') or 'coaching' ('how can I support your learning?'). We had probably excessively deployed the types of leadership described as 'coercive' ('you must do this now!'), 'authoritative' ('this is where we are going and why') and 'pacesetting' ('this is the way to do it'). The key message of the Hay Group's work is that effective leaders possess a repertoire of styles and use whichever of the six styles is appropriate to the situations in which leaders find themselves.

It was clear that at Runshaw we had to develop the capability to use all six styles appropriately. To do this we had to develop a model of 'transformational leadership' that would engage the hearts and minds of all staff. We had to adopt the full repertoire of leadership styles, which meant, in particular, acquiring new competencies in being democratic, affiliated and coaching. In short we had to change the emphasis on our use of management styles and, thereby, change the climate in the college.

Developing a caring and supportive management style

It had become clear from the feedback from the 1994 staff surveys that their key concern was with the management style of senior managers. During the process of receiving feedback from staff, the strength of the levels of staff dissatisfaction and the personalisation of the anecdotes about senior managers made us recognise the level of our incompetence and how badly we were perceived. Naturally most senior managers were upset by this feedback. There was a sense of anger and frustration at what some felt was the unfairness of the feedback but they were intelligent people so they recognised that, fair or unfair, the perceptions of staff were a reality that had to be addressed. They also recognised that they were not skilled in certain leadership styles and it was self-evident that the climate was not one that fostered high levels of commitment or outstanding performances by staff or students. So it was clear that we had to change.

If one uses the Hay Group's framework of six leadership styles, then it was evident that senior managers had to develop three particular new leadership styles: they were democratic, affiliative and coaching, in addition to the established and predominant styles that the Hay Group would term authoritative, coercive and pacesetting. Hence, on the basis of the feedback from staff about what they needed from managers, we concluded that the management style at Runshaw should include being sensitive, caring, encouraging, praising, appreciative. Managers should show that they valued staff, provide positive feedback, act as coaches, train and develop staff capabilities, communicate, facilitate and organise staff to help them identify and solve their problems, provide frameworks for reflection and analysis and provide guidance as to the use of these frameworks, and establish trust and respect.

It was one thing to say what we should do; it was an entirely different thing to enact it. Changing behaviour is very difficult and it requires a great deal of support, development and time. The danger was that, with all the other problems of running a college, we might have easily slipped back into the style we found most natural, irrespective of whether it was appropriate. We had to find ways to ensure that we were disciplined and rigorous about monitoring our behaviours and styles to ensure that this did not happen.

We had become aware of the need to develop what Tom Peters calls the four 'soft Ss' – style, staff morale, skills and shared values. We now needed to find ways in which to enact these through the three 'hard Ss' – strategy, structure and systems. Hence, we radically changed the college's management structure (see the next chapter), in so doing creating the concept of 'one united management team' with a set of ground rules that rigorously implemented our new management style. One example was the requirement that all managers be 'mutually supportive'. We developed new formal and informal approaches to communicating with and listening to staff. We developed new recognition strategies, new consultation strategies aimed at creating a strong and shared sense of direction and new approaches to staff development. And we developed a new process-management model to support the continuous improvement of all these approaches.

So we said that we believed that managers at Runshaw should be caring, supportive, sensitive communicators, and that they should listen, encourage and develop others. We enacted these aspects of management style in our strategies, structures and systems. We provided managers with the means and mechanisms to behave in a way that was consistent with these styles. It was not left to chance. Managers were required to carry out certain processes – like briefing and performance management – which required them to be coaches, communicators and trainers. This whole approach is described as 'putting our ethos into action'.

How did we develop a 'tough' approach based on moral leadership?

'Tough and tender'

The first difficulty of implementing a new approach to management style was the tension between, on the one hand, the obvious need to respond constructively to the needs of staff for a more caring, supportive style of management and, on the other hand, our determination to confront poor performance, including attitudes that produced low standards. Out of the debate on this came the phrase 'tough and tender', describing what we perceived to be one of the highest levels skills of the 'great' teacher and 'great' manager: the ability to balance a range of management styles and to choose the appropriate one in a particular situation.

Managers at senior and middle levels seemed to have been polarised at these two extreme ends of the range of management styles. Some were authoritarian, grim, almost always directive and completely undemocratic whereas others seemed to be desperate to be popular with staff, fearing to make any decision that left them open to appearing to be anything other than 'nice'. In our reflections on this, one of the most interesting and telling comments was that this latter group erroneously took responsibility for making their staff 'happy'. We concluded that this was not the job of the manager.

What happened to those who couldn't or wouldn't change?

One of the questions that I am frequently asked when I talk about what happened at Runshaw is 'what happened in 1995 to the existing managers and staff whose roles changed – did they buy into the changes required of them?'

To answer that it is worth recalling that, in Chapter 1, I explained how, in the period after my appointment in 1984, I challenged the prevailing culture at Runshaw, introducing compulsory teamwork, mandatory staff development and requiring completion of various forms of documentation like schemes of work and assignment plans. At the same time, a number of senior managers took early retirement, partly because I introduced new standards and challenged their performance. It was not a new thing, therefore, in 1993–5 for poor performance to be challenged at the senior management level, but it had never really occurred below that level and managers did not think it was their role. It was somehow perceived as 'unprofessional' and 'ruthless'.

In the culture-change process of 1993 to 1994 it was assumed that there would be no dismissals or redundancies and that we would take the feedback of staff 'on board' and respond constructively to it. If individuals had to change their management styles then they would do so and they would receive every available support.

By 1997, two years after the end of the culture-change process, only two of the original six senior managers remained, myself and the 'champion' who subsequently helped to lead the implementation of many of the changes that followed thereafter. Nobody was sacked from the senior management team and it would have been difficult to sack them, even if one had wished to do so, because they were hard working, dedicated, technically competent and had contributed to the development of a good college. But, at the same time, it was patently clear by 1995 that some individuals had to change because they significantly lacked the range of skills and leadership styles that were expected of the new role of a senior manager at Runshaw.

In the final analysis, it would have been unacceptable and inconceivable for some managers to remain as they were. Had the situation not changed, the college would not have moved forward, staff would have remained demoralised and, ultimately, excellent education for students could not have been provided. Students would have missed out on life chances as senior managers remained out-of-touch, cosseted and relatively unaccountable. We therefore took the view that it would have been immoral for us to fail to confront the performance issues identified by the staff surveys.

Redundancy versus dismissal on grounds of poor performance

So what would have happened if a senior manager or anybody else had refused to change or could not change sufficiently and refused to leave?

In our case it was all done on a voluntary basis. Had it not been voluntary, it would have been possible for any individual to have been dismissed or to have been made redundant. For example, it would have been possible to restructure the management team, requiring managers to apply for the new posts and making redundant those who were not appointed. Roles of all managers are constantly changing as new strategies, new financial situations and new responsibilities develop in a college so this was an obvious option. However, it is not one that we pursued at that time at Runshaw.

For one thing, we were trying to create a culture based on trust, mutual respect, honesty and integrity, and restructuring may have been perceived as a disingenuous way of removing people and therefore contrary to these values. Secondly, it would almost certainly have had a destabilising impact on others who were highly competent, hard working and committed because restructuring usually means that all those affected by the disappearance of existing posts potentially face the threat of redundancy. At Runshaw, we later came to believe that the first of these arguments is particularly compelling – that it was preferable for an 'incompetent' person to be dealt with on the grounds of poor performance rather than on grounds of redundancy through reorganisation.

The moral power of self-realisation

It never came to that. The four senior managers who departed did so voluntarily and it is important to understand why it was voluntary. To explain this it should be repeated and emphasised that the culture-change programme occupied two years – a long time – and that, even when it finished as such, in 1995, there was an ongoing intensive process of reflection, training and development (this is partly described later in this chapter). Managers were saturated in management education about the meaning and development of management styles. They were also part of a team that took responsibility for changing the college's culture, partly by redefining management styles. They understood what was required and agreed with it. They were also intensely aware of how they had been perceived as individuals by staff and what their weaknesses were perceived to be.

In the context of all this, they were gradually able to come to terms with the judgements of their performance that were made by others. In a sense, they could empathise and sympathise with their colleagues who suffered as a result of their management styles and they knew that this was 'wrong' for the organisation. There was, in fact, a strong moral feeling about what was 'right' and 'wrong' and there was a view that if a person would not change or could not change then it would be 'wrong' for us to fail to confront the situation.

The morality of such a situation itself created an irresistible level of accountability. Hence, it was recognised that, if we had tried everything possible to improve the situation – including the intensive development and support of the individual – and if the standard of performance still fell short of acceptable standards, then the individual would have to leave the management team. In the event, this was not necessary because individuals felt a strong sense of responsibility for their own performance and believed that it would have been wrong for them to stay. In short, they acquired a profound understanding of the importance of management style and an acute level of self-realisation.

Providing the opportunity for 'a dignified exit'

In a culture like the one we were trying to create at Runshaw – that is, one based on trust and mutual respect – it was important that an individual would be able to leave a particular job in a dignified way. One way was early retirement. Another was for a person to announce that he or she was to stand down to a less senior post, citing personal or domestic reasons or simply that, on reflection, the person preferred to be a teacher. This kind of situation really did happen and it happened on a number of occasions at middle management level too. Some people simply found that, having tried the role of senior or middle manager they really did not like it for one reason or other and preferred their old job.

In such situations, we would usually allow individuals to retain their salary at its existing position and freeze it until the salary point of the new role caught up with it. There was never any adverse staff reaction to such changes of status, possibly because those staff nearest to the situation would probably have contributed in some way, perhaps through the feedback that informed upward appraisal, to identifying the individual's weaknesses and therefore welcomed the change. Possibly they also agreed with the notion that mediocrity should not be tolerated, especially at management level.

Challenging those staff who opposed 'the management'

Throughout this whole period of culture change, a number of staff opposed 'the management' whatever we did. This was primarily the outcome of the inadequate way that we had led the college before 1993, using 'transactional' leadership approaches based on notions of 'leaders' and 'followers'. The new 'transformational' leadership approach used a different paradigm: it was one based on the democratic principle of staff participation in decision-making. Runshaw did not become a 'democracy' with majority rule for all decisions, but it did empower staff to participate in a meaningful way in decision-making and this did 'disperse' leadership, changing the role of staff and giving them a full opportunity to have their say about new policies, processes and strategies.

This meant that they also shared responsibility, so 'opposing the management' became an outdated concept. The role of managers became one of facilitation of staff participation in decision making and 'opposition' could be expressed legitimately as disagreement rather than conflict in new forums designed to reach consensus. Hence, one of the unintended outcomes of the culture-change process was that the militant trade union branch of NATFHE that existed at Runshaw between 1993 and 1995 simply disappeared by 1997: members stopped attending meetings and officers left unfilled vacancies so the branch effectively ceased to function (this, incidentally, presented real difficulties whenever we sought trade union agreement to changes in personnel procedures).

One view is that it would not have made much difference if we had not engaged our 'opponents' in decision making because their real motivation focused on a power struggle, with a small minority of staff taking the ideological view that all managers were 'capitalist lackeys' – 'Thatcher's children' – implementing 'managerial' policies, and that the workplace was a place for the 'proletarian struggle'. They were, to a large extent, supported in this view prior to 1993 by everyday examples of unnecessarily hierarchical, autocratic management behaviour that relied on status rather than the merit of an argument for authority or moral judgement – some would suggest that this was the natural outcome of transactional leadership. In many ways, the whole culture-change programme in 1993 and 1994 provided ample ammunition for those who ideologically opposed the concept of management by identifying strong levels of staff dissatisfaction with the leadership of the college. However, it also changed our concept of leadership, resulting in the new 'transformational' and 'dispersed' leadership that simply did away with the concept of a 'power struggle'. Conflict simply disappeared as disagreement and difference of opinion became increasingly recognised as genuine opportunities for exploration of meaning.

So, in the medium term and long term, 'opposition' became a notion that was out of tune with collaborative work structures and processes. In the short term, between 1993 and 1995, it was a really big issue. Hence, we developed an approach for it that integrated 'moral' leadership with a clear understanding of the need to deploy the full range of management styles, including those that addressed aspects of poor performance.

As we reflected on what we had heard from staff in the culture-change process, we could not forget one voice that, from our point of view, articulated unacceptable values that were linked to a narrow and selfish form of individualism. A minority of staff heatedly argued that they should be allowed to act as 'autonomous individuals', developing their craft, knowledge and skills on their own through personal and individual reflection and not as part of either a team or as part of an ongoing staff development programme. They opposed the concepts of compulsory teamwork and compulsory staff development. Indeed, they opposed the notion of 'compulsion' about virtually everything. There were also expressions of resentment about the concept of 'value for money'; for example, some argued that the range of courses should meet all the needs of the community, even if this meant having class sizes of three or four. At its most extreme, this resentment and opposition expressed itself as contempt for management, seeing it as a 'necessary evil' rather than as a positive activity.

Moreover, all of these views were expressed with moral indignation and those who expressed them occupied what they thought was the 'moral high ground', claiming that they were dedicated to their students and implying that managers were not. Some managers resisted these views on an individual basis for years, using their authority to combat them through coercion. What managers at Runshaw had never done collectively at a college level was to explore the morality of these assertions, to engage in a debate that argued that they were not fair, correct or moral and that those who held such views were not necessarily acting in the best interests of the student.

As we explained in Chapter 3, in the theoretical literature on schools there has long been a debate about the importance of what is termed 'moral leadership' (see, for example, Hodgkinson, 1991 and Bates, 1993). It has been asserted, for example, that values are a central part of leadership practice. Indeed, Hodgkinson claims that 'values constitute the essential problem of leadership . . . if there are no value conflicts then there is no need for leadership.' As we grappled with our conflicts with our 'opponents', we increasingly developed our own sense of shared values.

We acknowledged that many of the arguments of our 'opponents' had considerable merit. They had been right to castigate senior managers for concentrating on 'corporate' roles rather than on teaching and learning. They were right to criticise insensitive behaviour because it demonstrated that senior managers did not value staff sufficiently. But they were profoundly wrong when they argued against quality assurance and quality control policies and practices that aimed to improve standards. And they were 'wrong' to oppose the confrontation of poor performance. What was interesting here was the way that our debate began increasingly to focus on 'right' and 'wrong'. It is interesting that this focus was not unique to Runshaw: for example, Leithwood *et al.* (1999) argue that, in the schools sector, 'moral leadership assumes that the critical focus of leadership ought to be on the values and ethics of leaders themselves. So authority and influence are to be derived from defensible conceptions of what is right or good.'

Challenging the 'opponents'

Our consultant's view was that such opponents exist in all organisations that practise 'transactional' leadership. He argued that, in most organisations, 20% of staff enthusiastically supported the senior management, 60% were indifferent and 20% almost always actively opposed the management as a point of principle or out of habit. In times of difficulty – like the introduction of new contracts – the latter group could often take control of the culture, strongly influencing the 60% to join them.

In our case, we reflected that we had probably been guilty of focusing too much on those who expressed such dissent. We might have distorted our overall approach by overreacting to their agenda. We may have been overly coercive, authoritative and pacesetting partly because the climate created by transactional relationships generated hostility and aggression. If that was the case, it was our fault. First of all, we had adopted the wrong leadership approach. Secondly, even within that approach, we had not really collectively thought through what they were saying, whether it was justified or not, what we really believed was 'right' or 'moral', what our responses should be and how we should best present our view.

Our consultant constantly told us that we had two options: to have a 'managed culture' or an 'unmanaged one'. We had clearly had an 'unmanaged one', partly as an inevitable result of our transactional leadership approach but also by permitting those who opposed the whole concept of management to seize and retain the 'moral high ground'.

One of the other things that our consultant urged us to do was to address the behaviours and, if possible, the motivations of the individuals in this group. We began to do this and, in the event, discovered that some of them were motivated by long-held and long-ignored grievances that could be resolved. Others just needed to be challenged on an intellectual level and persuaded to work with us in developing a new leadership approach. There was also a minority who could not be persuaded. This made it even more important that we addressed their behaviours. We could not do much about what they thought but we were responsible for managing their behaviours, actions and performance.

In addition to this group, there were a few people who simply did not work hard enough or who did not do their job properly for one reason or other. Senior managers had been 'brought up' in the culture of colleges in the 1970s and 1980s (as illustrated by my experiences, which were described in Chapter 1), when local authorities were responsible for staff discipline and, consequently, often created a culture of lax standards in which performance appraisal played little part. Managers had been virtually powerless to require staff to perform to high standards. Sickness levels throughout the public sector, including colleges, were much higher than the private sector. There was also a general culture of non-compliance, with 'professionalism' elevating the primacy of subject expertise over the importance of teaching of students and generating a general contempt for registers, documentation and procedures, described pejoratively as 'unnecessary bureaucracy'.

All this seemed to us to be, in a moral sense, 'wrong'. The more we became engaged in the process of listening to staff and in an intensive process of reflection, dialogue and debate, the more we began to realise that staff expected us to 'demand' and 'require' high standards from everybody – ourselves included – in the service of students. This was one of the most striking features of the debate on values described in the last chapter. Staff had articulated an intense feeling of conviction and determination. They believed that that it was 'wrong' to be insensitive and uncaring to staff, but it became equally clear that they believed that it was just as 'wrong' to accept mediocrity and poor performance when it damaged the life chances of students.

Clearly there is a strong link here between the development of a form of moral leadership at Runshaw and the creation of a high performance expectation on behalf of students. This became the dominant ethic that shaped the way that management styles were deployed. We developed a strong sense of moral purpose and this gave us the power to drive forward and to implement all the approaches described in the remaining chapters of this book. In this context, it is interesting to note the following:

> *it is the underpinning values and beliefs that give leadership its power. It is these values and beliefs that also inform the moral purpose of education and leadership style . . . it is clear that effective leadership is infused by a commitment to clearly articulated values and beliefs. In all of these settings this also has profound implications for style of leadership and the predispositions of leaders. It implies a personal style that is congruent, intuitive and unafraid to selectively show weakness; and a leadership style that provides focus, engenders trust and is unafraid to practice 'tough empathy'. Above all school leadership should be infused with a moral purpose. (Hopkins, 2003)*

The moral purpose that drove the entire culture-change programme forward at Runshaw was the desire to provide excellent standards of education for its existing students and to develop the capacity to widen participation for low-achieving school leavers and adult returners, providing them too with first-class education. It was not about making managers 'popular' or about making staff 'happy' – it was about improving staff's performance and thereby raising standards. The challenge was to find a way to do this by creating a climate in which staff could willingly give their best. To create this climate we needed leaders who had certain qualities and competencies. The report by the Hay Group, quoted earlier, goes on to identify the key qualities of leadership and concludes that:

> *what really makes a difference in leadership is behaviour rather skills, knowledge or even IQ. In terms of motivating staff, personal traits like integrity, persuasiveness, humour, courage and conviction outweigh your ability to write a perfect business plan or interpret a balance sheet.*

The role of 'champions'

One of the most important lessons that we learnt from the culture-change process was that effective leaders are, as Sergiovanni (1992) argued, likely to be 'reflective, caring and highly principled people who emphasise the human and emotional dimensions in preference to managerial requirements. They place a high premium upon personal values and are more concerned with culture than rather than structural change.'

Runshaw was very fortunate to have a significant number of people like this who came to the fore in 1994 and 1995 and thereafter to 'champion' the new culture. One was a senior manager; another was somebody promoted in the summer of 1995 to the senior management team. Both had outstanding levels of emotional intelligence. They were sensitive, aware, empathetic and considerate but both were also driven to an almost obsessive degree by an unflinching loyalty to their values. I frequently described the second one as 'the most moral man I had ever met'. He was not at all religious but he oozed a spirituality born by his single-minded focus on the welfare and progress of students and on the view that were all individuals, to be respected and valued for their differences.

Both of these senior managers were completely 'in tune' with the staff. They were both also strongly 'achievement orientated', wanting to get things done and to make rapid and significant progress. There was almost a military tone about their approach – clarity of direction, strong discipline, conviction, determination, rigour, structure. And they were not alone. There were many 'zealots' who delighted in the articulation of a clear vision and mission, infused by values that were used to define explicit behaviours and criteria for policies and practices.

Hence, in redefining our management style at Runshaw, we took the view that, although it was all very well to develop democratic, affiliative and coaching leadership styles, we also needed to reassert our firm belief in being directive where necessary. We therefore redefined our leadership style to include the caring and supportive language used earlier in this chapter – words like 'encouraging', 'communicating' and 'praising' – and the explicit assertion that it is equally important for us to set and maintain high standards for staff behaviour and performance. Specifically, we included in our definition the need to 'challenge negative, destructive behaviour in others that flouts our values and undermines our spirit'. We also made specific reference in the new definition of management style to 'actively managing poor performance, non-compliance and absence'. We already had a procedure for dealing with poor performance and, in 1995, we introduced a return-to-work procedure for absence so it became clear why and how managers should manage both. In the case of non-compliance, our debate on this and the strength of our feeling about the need for compliance are explained in the section on 'ethos into action', in Chapter 3.

It is interesting now to reflect that this 'tough' approach to managing poor performance appears to be regarded by current management theorists as crucially important in managing the culture of a high performance organisation. For example, the Hay Group identifies six dimensions to the concept of 'climate' and these include one called 'reward'. This is composed of two related concepts, 'performance' (that is, a strong link between individual performance and the way someone is rewarded) and 'recognition'. The Hay Group points out the danger that, whilst leadership style can help to create congeniality and co-operation, it can also lower the sense of 'reward' by not confronting poor performance.

Furthermore, in a study of Beacon colleges, another of non-Beacon colleges, and a third of private sector companies, the Hay Group found that in all three cases the weakest dimension in creating an effective climate was the failure to confront poor performance rigorously. They argued that the toleration of mediocrity was probably the most harmful influence on an otherwise very strong climate. Even Beacon colleges were relatively weak in tackling poor performance and the non-Beacon ones were substantially worse, scoring only 38.8%, the lowest score of all six dimensions. Scores on this dimension, incidentally, were the weakest in both further education colleges and sixth-form colleges. The Hay report concludes that '. . . action here – which was to focus on both cultural preconceptions and processes such as performance management – could help make the average good, and the good excellent.'

WHAT WERE OUR CORE COMPETENCIES AND WHERE DID THEY COME FROM?

The origins of our core competencies

We believed that the new role of leader at Runshaw required eight new core competencies and these are outlined in this section. They did not originate at Runshaw. We used a variety of frameworks drawn from elsewhere, which, over the years, contributed to the formulation of our core competencies. This section outlines the key developments in identifying them.

In 1991 we had adopted another Hay framework which identified eight characteristics expected in a leader and we thereafter used this framework in appraising managers. These characteristics are as follows:

- achievement motivation – constantly striving to improve by seeking out and comparing one's work with standards of excellence, efficiency, effectiveness or innovation
- complex thinking and problem solving – intellectual initiative, looking deeply into critical problems, analytical thinking
- interpersonal understanding – sensitivity and understanding of unspoken thoughts, feelings and concerns of others

- relationship building – building and maintaining friendly, warm relationships of networks of contact with people with whom you work, ideally at all levels
- team orientation – to hold a genuine desire to work co-operatively with others, to be part of a team, to work together as opposed to working separately or competitively, to empower and encourage others
- initiative – to have the bias for taking action, proactively doing things and not simply thinking about future directions
- directiveness – to understand when it is appropriate and necessary to obtain compliance from others, with a long-term good of the college in mind, and to do so effectively by demanding and monitoring high performance against goals
- customer service orientation – to desire to help or serve the needs of others, whether internal colleagues or external clients, and to take personal responsibility for correcting customer service problems.

Because we used this framework for appraisal, the words in it were studied very carefully by managers and reflected upon over a number of years. They became part of the language for management development at Runshaw. Hence, concepts like 'directiveness', 'a bias for taking action' and 'achievement motivation' gained widespread recognition as the sort of qualities that earned promotion at Runshaw. Clearly, we had not been very good at 'interpersonal understanding', 'relationship building' or 'team orientation'. But given that Runshaw was, nevertheless, a good college, we must have been better at the other five characteristics. In particular, I believe that most senior managers were excellent in 'achievement motivation'. Indeed, the introduction of the culture-change programme itself was an excellent example of 'constantly striving to improve by seeking out . . .' The way that we followed up the staff feedback with reflection and the development of values was an example of 'complex thinking and problem solving'. The way that multiple and innovative approaches to enacting the new culture were devised was an example of 'initiative'. The way that we developed our position on the 'tough' aspects of the new 'tough and tender' approach was an example of 'directiveness'. And, with regard to 'customer service orientation', it should be remembered that Runshaw was a 'good' college: it was popular and attractive to students, it achieved a grade 1 in the 1996 inspection for 'student support' and a grade 1 for 'responsiveness'. One of the most commonly reported comments from staff feedback in 1994 was that 'Runshaw was a great place to be a student but not a good place for staff to work.'

Over subsequent years we developed this framework further. For example, in 1994, as the first wave of feedback from the culture-change staff surveys began to have an impact, we collectively reviewed a study of 'blue ribbon' principals in the US. It reported that staff who worked under such principals identified five outstanding qualities. We reflected on these in one of our management development workshops and decided that they should apply not only to myself as principal but to all managers at Runshaw. We therefore adopted them as additional criteria for measuring the performance of managers through the appraisal process. We also added to these five qualities our interpretation (listed in brackets behind each of the five) of what, in practice, they meant. They were:

- being caring (for example, being considerate, sympathetic, tolerant, empathetic)
- optimism (for example, 'can do', 'no problem', 'we will succeed', 'things are getting better', visionary and setting ambitious goals)
- honesty (for example, displaying integrity, trustworthy, standing up to be counted, challenging negativity or unfairness)

- enthusiasm (for example, being positive, dynamic, enjoying work, being cheerful, taking the initiative, tackling difficult issues, never walking past a problem)
- friendliness (for example, liking people, smiling, saying 'hello', having warm relationships, praising others, not being aggressive).

It can be seen that these five qualities represented a change of direction from the original eight characteristics listed above. Being 'friendly' and 'caring', in particular, had not figured prominently before the culture-change programme. However, the Runshaw managers would not entirely let go of their original approach. Hence, they insisted on adding a sixth. This was:

- being conscientious (for example, hard working, dedicated, rigorous, following through, being consistent, structured and disciplined).

Echoes of the core value 'ethos into action' were evident in adding this.

Throughout the process of reflection and development in 1994 and 1995, we also constantly reviewed the meaning of 'leadership' and contrasted it with the concept of 'management'. We interpreted 'leadership' to be about vision, values and morality, about setting a direction and goals, about creating an ethos, and about listening and motivating others in a way that made them feel valued. We interpreted 'management' as akin to administration, to reinforcing the status quo, to implementing legislation, to operating routine processes, to handling difficulties and to running meetings. We did not see 'management' as a pejorative term – just one that was a worthy, necessary but uninspiring activity.

These processes of reflecting and developing the range of management competencies continued after 1995. For example, as we began to engage with the business excellence model in 1995, we added to the list of competencies the need for managers to understand strategic planning and process management. We constantly introduced and developed specific processes. As managers were responsible for them they therefore had to understand them.

Our core competencies

In 2002, we reviewed all of our previous attempts to define the competencies of a Runshaw manager and concluded that we should focus on eight core competencies. These were defined and lists of 'positive behavioural indicators' and 'negative behavioural indicators' were added to each. They were as follows.

Strategic perspective

We defined this competency as: 'Demonstrates a sound awareness, broad knowledge and comprehension of the values, vision and mission at Runshaw in the wider environment in which the college operates.'

The positive behaviours attached to this definition included 'one sees the "big picture" rather than becoming embroiled in the detail' 'understands the college's culture and its importance', 'builds a shared vision with others' and 'seeks to obtain value for money where possible'. The negative behaviours include 'not aware of or ignores factors which impact on the college', 'approaches problems with a limited perspective', 'little understanding of Runshaw's values, vision, mission and culture' and 'appears parochial – has too narrow a focus'.

Customer focus

This was defined as: 'Anticipating the needs of both internal and external customers, providing a superior quality service and constantly delighting them by exceeding their expectations. Understanding that students are customers as are colleagues in providing internal services.'

The positive behaviours included 'builds relationships and partnerships with customers', 'takes personal responsibility for meeting – and exceeding – customers' needs' and 'constantly looks for ways of adding value or otherwise making a difference for students'. The negative behaviours included 'does not accurately assess customers' needs and wants', 'quality of service delivery fluctuates and lacks consistency', 'takes no personal responsibility for meeting customers' needs' and 'where conflicting demands arise, chooses to tackle other tasks before resolving customers' problems.'

Analytical thinking

We defined analytical thinking as: 'Effectively and thoroughly assimilates, analyses and evaluates all available information. Develops effective solutions that are in the best interest of the college.'

The positive behaviours include 'checks data and information for errors or omissions and anomalies', 'makes links to all other data or information', 'looks beyond symptoms to identify key issues and root causes', 'develops workable solutions', 'identifies knock-on effects' and 'identifies the key issues in ambiguous or inconsistent data'. The negative behaviours include 'jumps to conclusions', 'becomes overwhelmed or daunted by complex issues or problems' and 'fails to go beyond the superficial'.

Planning and organising/prioritising

We defined this competency as: 'Thinks ahead in order to effectively organise workload. Prioritises activities, efficiently establishes appropriate causes of action and monitors progress, accomplishing goals on time.'

The positive behaviours included 'prioritises tasks logically and efficiently', 'prepares in advance and sets realistic timescales', 'builds in contingencies', 'plans time effectively to meet deadlines' and 'concentrates efforts on activities that have the most significant impact on effectiveness'. The negative behaviours included 'haphazard approach: disorganised and unstructured', 'no clear priorities', 'tasks are handled on the hoof' and 'allows tasks or the project to continue without monitoring.'

Working in a team

Working in a team was defined as 'Willingly works with others and supports them in order to achieve the best results as a team, over and above individual success. Creates an environment where people are positively motivated.'

The positive behaviours included 'helps to promote and sustained team spirit, pride and trust', 'co-operative working relationships', 'actively participates in team situations' and 'explores possible ways forward by working with others'. The negative behaviours included 'works in conflict with others: is outspoken and domineers and oppresses others in the team', 'participates infrequently', 'seems unwilling to engage with ideas, thought or views', 'unwilling to share information', 'approach is dominating and overbearing towards others' and 'fails to persuade others'.

Leading and managing a team

This was 'The will and ability to actively manage performance in ways that deliver high standards and ensure delivery of results. Guides and coaches individuals or groups towards the accomplishment of tasks.'

The positive behaviours were, in this case, subdivided into 'tender' approaches like 'leads by example and shows personal enthusiasm', 'gives a clear direction', 'delegates effectively' and 'communicates regularly'; and 'tough' approaches like 'knows when to use authority and will use it to ensure results are delivered', 'brings difficult issues into the open and helps to resolve them', 'tackles problems firmly, addressing process and procedural issues', 'takes difficult or unpopular decisions when addressing performance and is prepared to stand by them', 'prepared to take ultimate responsibility when things go wrong', 'has the courage to confront issues or people were necessary' and 'can inspire a team to deliver the vision'. The negative behaviours included 'lets poor performance go unchecked', 'makes excuses for poor performance rather addressing the real issues', 'sets or applies standards inconsistently', 'is unnecessarily directive when working with others', 'fails to delegate appropriate tasks', 'fails to communicate targets or set expectations', 'does not accept responsibility for delivery of results or tackling performance', 'unprepared to take ultimate responsibility when things go wrong' and 'perpetuates a blame culture'.

Interpersonal style

Interpersonal style was defined as: 'Considers and responds appropriately to the needs, feelings and capabilities of different people in different situations whether internal to Runshaw or external to the college.'

The positive behaviours included 'body language indicates an interest in others in the subject being discussed', 'intuitively reads situations accurately', 'acknowledges and supports others' contributions', 'remains courteous and polite at all times', 'develops and uses a range of behaviours which are appropriate for particular situations', 'questions and challenges without being offensive', 'shows empathy and patience with others: handles difficult staff and students and situations without becoming emotional', 'shows respect for and interest in the views and opinions of others at all levels', 'handles objections convincingly' and 'facilitates win-win solutions'. The negative behaviours included 'misreads or ignores others' body language', 'is rude or discourteous when dealing with people', 'shows insensitivity and impatience towards people from different backgrounds', 'argues in a non-constructive manner', 'adopts a confrontational attitude and antagonises others', 'becomes angry or withdrawn or upset or shows other negative emotions', 'comes across as self-opinionated and uses posturing to boost ego', 'wins at all costs' and 'shies away from conflict and disagreements and is unable to manage and successfully resolve them'.

Quality focus

This meant that: 'Actions are guided by a high need for integrity in all aspects of work and for reaching exceptional standards of performance.'

The positive behaviours included 'maintains integrity by being honest, responsible and ethical', 'adheres to the proper procedures, processes, standards and regulations required', 'sets exceptional personal standards: takes pride in their work', 'works to get things right first time every time', 'ensures work is completed to the highest possible standards: only satisfied with the best', 'finds the best and aims to beat it' and 'challenges processes and seeks to continually improve them – asks "why am I doing this, how can it be done better?"' The negative behaviours included 'lacks integrity, shows dishonesty, irresponsibility or unethical behaviours', 'deviates from procedures, processes, standards and regulations or disregards them altogether', 'personal standards are lax: little evidence of pride taken in work and is satisfied with mediocre work and results', 'approach indicates a lack of attention to detail: mistakes are made, errors occur and are not corrected', 'rarely checks on work for errors or omissions', 'maintains the status quo rather than looking for opportunities to make improvements' and 'satisfied with good enough'.

In a sense, these eight sets of core competencies, definitions and behaviours represent what became known as the 'Runshaw way'. They were at the heart of our drive for excellence.

HOW DID WE DEVELOP THESE COMPETENCIES IN MANAGERS?

There were four key approaches. The first was the concept of individual critiquing, including a variety of feedback mechanisms. The second was one of these that was so important that is worth describing as an approach in its own right – the establishment of an assessment centre. The third was the creation of a modular training programme for our managers. And the fourth consisted of biannual two-day management workshops.

The power of feedback

One of the most powerful lessons that we learned from the culture-change programme was about the extraordinary impact of individual feedback. That is, we had all attended countless lectures and conferences on 'culture', 'team-building skills', 'management styles' and 'interpersonal skills' but we had all absorbed what we heard with a sense of complacency, believing that we already fulfilled the criteria for excellent practice. It was only when we received the feedback about our individual actions and behaviours, the actual offensive and insensitive things that we had said and done, that it began to really register with us that we were not as good as we had thought we were. It forced us to listen and, when we did, we realised that we had misunderstood and misinterpreted what people had thought. It was individual critiquing that penetrated the complacency of individuals, that caused individuals to have sleepless nights and to feel embarrassed, and that made individuals determined to take individual responsibility for and ownership of the changes that we had to make.

Hence we resolved that we should develop and implement a series of new approaches that provided managers with feedback in a systematic and structured way. It includes processes related to staff focus groups, annual surveys on the management style of individual managers and a college-wide annual staff conference to identify the strengths and weaknesses of 'leadership and management'. In addition we operated a performance management process for individual managers and staff and this included appraisal, based on the evidence gathered by the respective line manager over the year on an individual's performance. In 2002 we introduced 360-degree appraisal for senior managers and in 2003 we began to pilot it for a group of middle managers.

Establishing an assessment centre

In 2002, we also introduced an assessment centre for managers. Its purpose was to put all of the middle managers through a two-day process at an external venue in which they were assessed against each of the eight core competencies listed above. During the two days they would undergo a series of activities, each designed to assess a specific competency. These activities included a structured in-depth interview, a role play, a presentation, a group exercise, a written exercise, psychometric tests and verbal and data rational tests.

The assessment centre was primarily operated by two external consultants. They first trained the senior managers by putting them through the exercises. Then they prepared for the events by working with senior managers to develop relevant case studies, questions for interviews, and briefs for the roles in the role-play exercise. It was then arranged that each activity and assessment would be led by one of the two consultants but that one or two senior managers would assist them. Many of the activities simulated the kinds of task that managers carried out in their jobs. For example, the role play exercise involved each manager being observed playing a role interviewing an actress who played the role of a poorly performing member of staff. The actress's role had a brief that allowed her to explain her poor performance in a very plausible way, if she was given the opportunity to do so.

In the event, the performance of managers varied significantly. At one extreme, one manager was very stressed by the need to hold the actress responsible at all and behaved in a very timid way, apologising constantly for being so 'uncaring' as to ask her to explain her outrageous behaviour to colleagues and students. It is difficult to see how he could have been doing his real job properly in challenging poor performance given his lack of assertiveness skills. At the other extreme, several managers were brusque, intimidating and they had clearly already made up their minds that firm directness and discipline was the only appropriate action. They did not give the actress the opportunity to explain herself. All of our middle managers had been through countless interpersonal training sessions: they all knew what they should do but very few actually did it.

Immediately after the event, the senior managers and consultants met to agree strengths and weaknesses of each individual manager against each competency. The consultants then produced an in-depth written report on each middle manager. Once this was agreed with the senior managers, they arranged an in-depth feedback session with each middle manager.

Observing and assessing the behaviours of middle managers and providing each with individual confidential feedback by trained external coaches was an extraordinarily effective way of developing them. With hindsight, it seemed obvious that this it would be the case: we routinely observed teachers in the classroom and provided them with feedback about their teaching competence, so we knew that this format was extremely powerful. We had also routinely used student feedback to inform our assessments of teachers' performance, so we had experienced the power of such feedback.

All this was conducted in a context in which the senior management team held regular 'away days' with the consultants, exploring the concept of leadership, particularly the framework used by Hay. We also went through assessments and received 360-degree feedback from the consultant, with individual senior managers receiving individual and confidential coaching from the consultant on an ongoing basis. After the 1993–5 culture-change programme, we took the view that it was imperative that every senior manager should be very effective and competent in deploying the full range of leadership styles if we were to create the climate that would sustain and develop the standards of excellence to which we aspired.

A modular management training programme

The outcome of the assessment centre was that there was a clear need and demand by the managers for refresher training sessions on the eight competencies. When we provided these, managers attended them with a new insight and a new sense of urgency. In the same way that senior managers had been made to recognise their failings in the culture-change programme in 1993–5, thereby generating in them an intense level of commitment to improving their management style, many of the middle managers similarly became determined to acquire greater competence in the skills required, especially in interpersonal skills.

In truth, we also probably felt guilty that we had not done enough to enable existing managers to develop their competencies prior to the assessment centre. A significant number of them had clearly not understood what was expected of them as managers and some acted out of character on the assumption that senior managers expected something other than their normal behaviour. Several of those who were too brusque in the role play, for example, thought that senior managers were assessing their ability to be 'tough'. The whole process, therefore, provided an opportunity to explore what behaviours would have been appropriate in each activity, what was expected by senior managers and what exactly each competency meant in practice.

One of the unintended side effects of this process was that we became keenly aware of the need to train future managers in each of the eight competencies that we expected our managers to demonstrate. We therefore introduced a rolling management-development programme for team leaders. This was open to all, but individual senior and middle managers strongly encouraged about 30 individuals to participate in it. We wanted to create an upward flow of potential managers. We then introduced a similar college-wide programme in team leadership, developing a range of competencies that were drawn from the college's eight core management competencies.

Annual management workshops

Our fourth key approach to management development was the provision of two annual two-day management development workshops for our managers. We had introduced these prior to the culture-change programme that started in 1993. The first was in February 1991 when all middle and senior managers went to a hotel in the Lake District for a two-day management development workshop. The entire party travelled together by coach from the college and, *en route,* watched a Tom Peters management video. On arrival at the hotel, several middle managers (including the two who later became the 'champions' of culture change) pretended to vomit, showing their contempt for management gurus and management development and their apprehension about what was to come. But somebody else said that it was an important achievement to get all middle and senior managers together on the coach in the first place. My memory of that first management development event was that, in terms of the content of what was achieved, it was far from notable, but in terms of beginning to create a team spirit amongst all the managers it was a breakthrough.

We began to hold three such two-day events each year, in the February half term, in July after the teaching staff started their summer holiday and in the October half term. We were sufficiently sensitive to staff views, even in 1991, to be concerned that such conferences might be seen as 'junkets', so it was important to us that they were held in times when staff were on holiday. For the first three years, the February workshop was residential but increasingly the attraction of the bar on the first night made the second day almost useless. Consequently, the management team was asked to vote on whether we should continue with the concept of a residential and, by a very narrow majority, it voted that we should not do so. Around about 1994 we also stopped the October workshop, simply to ease the workload burden for managers in a very tiring term. Since then, however, we continued with two two-day workshops each year, in February and in July.

These workshops were always arranged in such a way that each produced a tangible, concrete new policy or process or an action plan. We were always conscious that middle managers would be tired and that these events were held in 'holiday' periods when other staff were relaxing, so it was imperative that these workshops should not be seen as 'a waste of time'.

Two of the earlier workshops, in 1993 and 1994, were hosted and run by local employers. In one case, the training unit at Matthew Brown Brewery provided the entire team with a two-day programme on briefing, a process that we introduced immediately after the workshop. On another occasion, a similar team at Leyland Trucks provided a two-day event on how they managed culture change, and on the basis of this we introduced a number of new processes, like 'stop-the-track' staff conferences and recognition processes like 'team of the month'.

On both occasions the hidden advantage was that we were able to assess practitioners of what was regarded as 'best practice' in the private sector and compare ourselves with them, and this helped to develop our sense of confidence. We also felt like a team, going out of college together as colleagues, to learn together, thereby developing a strong sense of collaboration.

The sense of collegiality that this kind of experience generated became stronger over the years. In every evaluation of every conference, most middle managers said how much they valued and enjoyed mixing with colleagues in both the middle and senior management team levels, meeting and working with people whom they would never normally encounter during the day-to-day running of the college.

Every workshop was very interactive. Buzz groups gave everybody an opportunity to reflect on everything and to feed back their views. The tone of presentation was 'conversational', laying out the background to issues, the alternative ways forward, the advantages and disadvantages and, sometimes, making recommendations, followed always by key questions for colleagues to consider in the buzz groups. The atmosphere was friendly, there was always a great deal of laughter, lunch was lavish and much appreciated as a symbol of care, and the management style was democratic, affiliative and coaching.

The content and tone of the workshops improved significantly over the years as we became better at arranging them. The secret was to begin to plan for each event three or four months ahead, identifying a really important topic that would be self-evidently relevant and that would mean that the workshop was, in effect, providing the management team with the time, space and focus to develop an important policy or strategy or action plans that would create a real breakthrough for the college in some particular way. An obvious example was 'preparing for inspection'. Another would be to review and develop human relations approaches related to, for example, either staff development or communications or consultations or the management of poor performance, or managing quality assurance and processes like the self-assessment review process or the process management model. It was always a concern and constraint that, of the 60 managers present, about 15 were managers of support services, so it was not normally possible to focus on teaching and learning at these events.

Finally, one of the attractions of these workshops for many managers was that it gave them easy access to 'leading-edge' thinking by external agents or bodies. They appreciated, for example, the opportunity to catch up with and fully understand recent publications from Ofsted, the DfES, the Learning and Skills Council, the Learning and Development Skills Agency, the Further Education National Training Organisation (FENTO) and other bodies, and to share in the formulation of Runshaw's responses to such publications and in the development of our plans to implement the significant changes that many of them required. Managers also valued having access to recent theoretical and academic research on, for example, leadership and management, strategic planning and on the business excellence model. Such access made them feel more confident and capable – so much so that, from 2001, about 20 middle managers urged us to seek accreditation for the management development that they were already receiving. In the event, we were amongst the first colleges to link up with the accreditation offered by the Centre for Excellence in Leadership (CEL).

Overall, these workshops were the most important structural part of our approach to management development and they were strongly supported over the period 1991 to 2004 by a second structure, the monthly meetings of the college management team and by what we described as 'one united management team', itself a developmental concept that underpinned the whole concept of management style, core competencies and management development. Both of these latter approaches are described in the next chapter.

THE CHANGING ROLE OF THE PRINCIPAL AS AN ILLUSTRATION OF BECOMING 'COMPETENT'

During the culture change programme of 1994, the role of the principal emerged as one of the most significant symbols. The actions, behaviours, speeches, decisions about such things as staff promotions, all seemed to highlight the importance of this role in the running of the college. Sometimes these contributed to the lowering of staff morale. For example, at staff meetings I had always tried to explain external environmental factors that were affecting the college during incorporation, especially funding changes, and consequently these meetings became known on the grapevine as 'doom-and-gloom' meetings. I also tried to present government policy and initiatives in a positive way, thereby often communicating inadvertently a lack of empathy with staff who were struggling to fight against some of these policies.

In response to the feedback received, it was decided that a guiding principle should be that the principal should, if possible, always be perceived as someone to whom every member of staff could relate positively. Irrespective of who was in the role, it was agreed that, ideally, the image of the principal that should be presented should be that of a moral person, as somebody who was competent, driven by educational vision, somebody who is hard working, committed and conscientious, somebody who cares about students, who is genuinely interested in teaching and learning, who embodies a collaborative approach to creating a community spirit and who is passionate about quality – in short, someone who lives the core values that emerged as the central focus of the new culture.

To achieve this, we collectively had to decide how I should change the way I presented myself. It was agreed, for example, that my speeches had to become more focused on vision, values, students, teaching and learning, celebration about success and less about the 'doom and gloom' of government initiatives. I had to be very visible, meeting students and staff on a regular basis. I had to return to being 'the leading professional teacher', not a chief executive with the image of being a 'grey suit'.

As this was really important – something that we were going to take seriously – then it had to have a clearly defined and carefully structured approach to communicate the appropriate image in a systematic way. It was decided, therefore, that another guiding principle should be that the principal should be 'presidential', symbolising all the good things that Runshaw stood for. I should not, for example, be perceived to be too involved in the day-to-day operational management and I should rarely communicate 'bad news', leaving it to other managers, especially middle managers, to do this. Earlier it has been described how, in one of the culture-change workshops with the middle managers, the principal and senior managers had been challenged with the question, 'Why try to run the college on your own when you have 40 managers who want to do it for you?' Being 'presidential' was part of the response.

This required changes for all managers, partly to take on the roles and responsibilities previously exercised by the principal but also to communicate that the principal was the kind of person with whom staff could relate positively.

As a matter of policy, the management team agreed that it would have been impossible to create the new culture if the person at the top was perceived negatively. Nor could this be left to chance. Processes, structures and approaches had to be carefully 'stage managed' to ensure that the principal was seen in this way. Opportunities had to be created in which he could offer visible leadership. This new role was perceived to be highly 'political' within the environment of the college's community; it was vital to get it right.

One of the opportunities created, for example, was linked to the introduction of five one-day staff conferences during each year. They were to be introduced by the principal with a 30-minute presentation that was intended to introduce the agenda for the day, thereby providing very visible opportunities for leadership to be displayed by him. In order to ensure that the speeches hit the right note, the content for them was identified by the senior management team as a group and the draft of the speech, including the format, style and language, was checked ('spin-doctored'?) by the deputy principal beforehand.

The speeches provided a classic opportunity for 'boss watching' so every precaution was taken to ensure that staff could relate to them and to the speaker. Another example of creating an opportunity for visible leadership was the weekly 'principal's diary' page written by the principal for the staff update, described in Chapter 7.

CONCLUSION

By February 1996, when Runshaw achieved the best set of grades for any further education college in that inspection cycle, including a grade 1 for governance and management, the inspectors reported: 'In a relatively short time, staff perceptions have become more favourable. Morale is generally high. Staff feel the senior management team is open, flexible and accessible. Internal communications are much improved.'

That year we repeated the staff survey that in 1993 had produced the appallingly low score of 35% satisfaction levels and achieved about 90%. We repeated the survey every year thereafter and achieved similar scores. After 2002 we were able to benchmark these with the sector and we could then see that Runshaw had much higher levels of staff satisfaction than most other colleges.

So what were the responses by management that produced such a turnaround in staff morale in such a short time?

First of all, the overall response was one of resilience and resolution to take the criticisms on board and to respond in a strategic and constructive way. This was important because it was so tempting, with all the emotional turmoil of the time, to simply bury one's head or to respond angrily. A previous section of this chapter described our most important approaches to management development. The first built on the power of the concept of 'individual critiquing' that had had such an extraordinary impact in the culture-change programme between 1993 and 1995. It was the force and impact of feedback from staff that had shaken our complacency and galvanised us into transforming Runshaw. If we were to avoid slipping back into bad habits we needed to repeat this process over and over again in systematic and structured ways. Hence, the concept of staff feedback became a central feature of our approaches to management development.

We had not known then that Hay describes this approach as 'best practice leadership training': we simply recognised that the impact of the staff survey of 1993 was that it had led to the introduction of the entire culture-change programme and that the subsequent multiple staff surveys of management style in 1994 had a transformational impact on the attitudes of senior managers. Runshaw continued to build on this experience in subsequent years, introducing, for example, 360-degree appraisal and the assessment centre concept. One of the key reasons for this was the commitment shown to change, the determination to take on board the criticisms that staff had made and to act on them in a strategic way, investing huge amounts of time, energy and emotion in developing and implementing approaches that were very innovative in colleges at that time. It is interesting to note that one of the conclusions of the Hay report on college leadership (Franks *et al.*, 2002) said:

> *This leads us to the conclusion that successful leadership is as much about personal conviction and self-determination as it is about resources, policy constraints or cultural*

factors. If you have the courage to examine your own behaviours and seek feedback from others, you can make changes to factors within your control (i.e. your own actions) that will ultimately make their way down to the bottom-line. Perhaps the most important resource that one can bring to the table is the combination of self-awareness and empathy that drives these changes. Outstanding leaders . . . were in tune with their employees' opinions and able to reflect on whether their own behaviour was appropriate. It is worth noting that these are the techniques . . . that are used in best practice leadership development training.

The second important response was that there was no significant debate about what the 'tender' aspects of the new management style should be: senior managers already knew about interpersonal skills, emotional intelligence and the need to provide support for staff; they simply did not recognise that they had not been 'doing' this and that they had, in fact, been doing the opposite. The impact of feedback brought about the realisation by managers that they were not 'living' their values.

The third key response was the further development of the 'tough' approach. This was critically important to the improvement of Runshaw's performance as a college and its transformation from 'good' to 'outstanding'. The question was how to present it in such a way that it did not make staff morale worse? The answer was that it grew quite naturally from a moral debate about what was right and wrong. Values were identified and these were interpreted into explicit behaviours, and the staff engaged with them positively and then embraced them.

A fourth key feature of the overall response was the role of 'champions' who were equipped with very high levels of emotional intelligence and a passionate conviction in the morality of what we were doing. Their leadership was critical to the success of this process. Their example became the role model for what became known as the 'Runshaw person', and we used this model to redevelop all of our staffing policies and practices.

The fifth key feature of Runshaw's approach was the long, reflective development of the eight core competencies and their development into criteria for positive and negative behaviours. The words used in these descriptions of behaviour can be traced to earlier attempts to capture the critical balance between 'tough' and 'tender'. The constant repetition of the focus on the need for managers to 'challenge', 'confront' and 'direct' staff says much about the reason for Runshaw's culture of high expectations.

This sixth key feature was the biannual two-day management development workshops for the college management team. These provided time, focus and energy for reflection and development. Their link to tangible outcomes is another illustration of Runshaw's 'bias for action' and 'achievement orientation'. But the most important aspect of these was the consistency of the approach, constantly building the team spirit of the management team and helping to make it into an effective team. It constantly reinforced the notions of collaboration and 'dispersed' leadership, it built capacity, it provided intellectual stimulation and it developed self-esteem and self-confidence. It also provided the time for managers to meet at leisure to reflect, digest and internalise theory, to review current policies and strategies and to learn from each other in a collaborative way.

The seventh key feature was that Runshaw's management development approaches owed much to the way in which they were informed by external inputs of academic theory and best practice from the private sector users of the business excellence model. Throughout this time, Runshaw demonstrated a spirit of intellectual openness and willingness to learn, which characterised the whole organisational approach

The final response was that words would not be enough, that actions were needed and that to deliver these we needed the systematic and structured approaches to the implementation of core competencies that are described in the forthcoming chapters.

Summary

- Half of the issues that emerged from the culture-change staff surveys in 1994 involved concerns about the management style of senior managers.
- There was a clear need for senior managers to develop democratic, affiliative and coaching styles and to be less coercive, pacesetting and authoritative.
- Four of the six senior managers employed during the culture-change programme left within two years, so there was an opportunity to recruit senior managers with a wider range of styles.
- It was recognised that senior managers had to either change or leave and that it would have been unacceptable to continue as we were. With such limited management styles, the college's climate did not create the conditions that encouraged the improvement of standards.
- The new management style at Runshaw included a requirement to challenge poor performance.
- This tied in with external research that argued that even Beacon colleges are relatively weak in doing this and that they should focus on developing this area.
- We defined the eight competencies and related behaviours that we expected from managers at Runshaw.
- In 2002 we introduced the concept of an assessment centre to observe and assess our managers' performance with regard to our eight core competencies, and then to act as the basis for individual coaching and further training. This approach was based on the premise that feedback and individual critiquing was the most powerful form of management development.
- We arranged two two-day management development workshops twice a year to help managers develop their competencies and these provided a consistent approach over many years towards building a team spirit and providing time and focus for reflection.
- It was agreed that all staff should be able to relate to the person holding the office of principal. This implied significant changes in the way that the role was performed, moving to more deliberately visionary, value-driven activities that focus on successes by students and staff, teaching and learning and mission.

5 'ONE UNITED MANAGEMENT TEAM'

Experience and educational theory show that colleges can become outstanding by using transformational leadership and by creating a 'professional learning community'. The assumption here is that, broadly speaking, the model of capacity building used for schools is transferable to colleges. I believe this is true, but there is at least one significant difference between schools and colleges that implies that such a model for colleges must include the additional concept of 'one united management team'. This difference is that colleges are significantly larger than schools, with hundreds of staff – over 800 in Runshaw's case – or even over a thousand, compared to between 50 and 100 in a typical school. This difference in size creates additional and complex problems related to coherence, co-ordination, connectivity and relationships for colleges. A college, therefore, needs to create a dynamic unifying force that can create coherence and, at the same time, co-ordinate the dispersal of leadership to staff, whilst avoiding fragmentation.

The senior management team in any organisation also needs to model collaboration, co-operation and mutual respect if it is to be credible in asking staff to demonstrate such behaviours to managers, to each other and to its 'customers', in our case, to students. One of the strongest staff complaints in Runshaw's culture-change process between 1993 and 1994 was that 'the senior management team is not a team'. Another was that middle managers 'were not managers'. The perception of staff at Runshaw was that the college was run from the top, that there was no sense of 'dispersed' leadership and therefore no obligation for staff to accept joint responsibility for the success of the college.

All of these issues had to be addressed vigorously. Runshaw may have defined its core values and may have developed core competencies in individual leaders, but it also needed to create a collective leadership that would work together in facilitating the involvement of staff in direction setting, goal setting and continuous improvement in a sustained pursuit of excellence.

Runshaw did this by creating the concept of 'one united management team'. This chapter explains how this happened. The first section describes how, in 1994, we created 'one united *senior* management team'. To do this we created six ground rules that defined the nature of the 'unity'. The second section describes how, when we explained these to middle managers, they immediately said they felt very strongly that there should be 'one united *college* management team' which included them. Hence, the concept of a 'united team' was extended to middle managers, thereby creating 'one' united management team. The third section explains that the process was fraught with difficulties, particularly regarding acceptance by middle managers of the ground rule of 'collective responsibility'. It was simply unrealistic and unfair to expect middle managers to accept this without first addressing their role conflicts, their position of being 'caught in the middle' between staff and senior managers, and particularly their need to participate fully in decision making and policy formulation. So this section describes how we resolved these role conflicts.

DEVELOPING ONE UNITED SENIOR MANAGEMENT TEAM

The reasons for staff suggesting that 'the senior managers were not a team' were based on criticisms of managers' behaviour. For example, they said that some senior managers lacked integrity by blaming others for poor decisions, that some were disloyal and courted ego-seeking popularity by leaking information about decisions or discussions in the senior management team, and that they behaved like 'warring fiefdoms' in 'empire building'. Quite clearly this had to change if we were to create a sense of community with a moral purpose. It was also simply inept and incompetent behaviour to act in a way that some senior managers had behaved. It gave credence to those staff who would justifiably say, 'why should we follow leaders like these when they cannot even get their own act together?'

Most importantly, we needed to develop a mechanism to drive a coherent, co-ordinated, highly structured and long-term strategy for improvement. It was clear that leaders at Runshaw had to focus primarily on managing the culture if we were to become outstanding and if we were to develop the capacity to cope with the constant flow of external initiatives. We had to create a sense of unity, shared purpose and shared direction for all staff, and we had to create a culture of 'high-performance expectations'. One of the key problems in doing this was to change the norm of 'individual autonomy' where this impeded consensus building or created isolation rather than collaboration. Leithwood argues that 'the culture among professionals in schools is typically characterised as weak (little consensus) and isolated, whereas strong, collaborative school cultures contribute more substantially to school improvement initiatives'.

The culture at Runshaw was clearly weak. If we were to survive, let alone become 'outstanding', then we simply had to find a way to marshal the talents, energies and commitments of the senior and middle managers and then, hopefully, those of the staff into becoming a 'professional learning community'.

A crucial part of our approach to strengthening Runshaw's culture was clarifying our core values and translating them into explicit behaviours. Another was defining our management style and competencies. Another was the way we set about developing a shared sense of direction, described in the next chapter. In all these, we built our vision in a collaborative way and, crucially, re-focused on student-centredness, reinforcing norms of excellence for both students and staff.

In all these approaches, we developed what Leithwood *et al.* (1999) described as very clear 'content' for our new culture – explicitly spelling out, for example, what behaviours were expected – and we thereby 'strengthened' our culture significantly. But we were also concerned with the 'form' of our culture; from the moment in 1993 when we introduced the culture-change programme based on bottom-up feedback, we were determined that it should be collaborative in form. That whole approach was premised on beliefs about listening, about sharing power and responsibility with others and about the notion of 'dispersed' leadership.

During the culture-change programme I had been confronted by middle managers who had said 'Why try to run Runshaw on your own when you have 50 managers who want to do it for you?' That was a defining moment, along with other moments like those when the senior management team was told that it was not perceived as a team and when middle managers were told that they were not perceived as managers. When we put all these things together, it became self-evident that all 50 managers – and then perhaps others like team leaders and, eventually, all other staff – should unite in managing Runshaw collectively. In making that decision, we apparently aligned ourselves with best practice elsewhere. Harris *et al.* (2003) argued:

> *There is a growing recognition in the increasingly complex contexts of educational change and accountability that deep and sustained improvement will depend upon the leadership of the many rather than the few. There is a groundswell towards leadership as empowerment, transformation and community building and away from the 'Great Man' theory of leadership.*

So part of our response in 1994 was to become a real team, united in our new approaches to communication and consultation and determined to offer collective leadership in the creation of a strong sense of direction that could inspire all staff. We believed that creating a sense of belonging and of pride in this community was contingent upon managers' role-modelling behaviours that demonstrated loyalty, unity, camaraderie, liking and respect for each other.

THE GROUND RULES

To develop the concept of a 'united' senior management team we realised that we needed to identify ground rules that would govern our behaviour. We also then needed to monitor these ground rules as rigorously as we monitored hard targets like data on student achievement or financial performance. We therefore created six ground rules. They were as follows.

Collective responsibility

We agreed that we should debate issues fully in private, disagreeing as much as we wanted, but that once we had made a decision we should then present a united front to staff. That meant that, once we had made a decision, every member of the senior management team must then actively promote the decision of the team as though it was their own, even if the individual had privately disagreed with the decision. Staff should never be able to perceive a difference between senior managers on policy or strategy.

The alternative was what we had been doing – sometimes individual senior managers had let it be known that they disagreed with a policy, thereby undermining the credibility and authority of the team's decision. This legitimised staff paying lip service to new policies and approaches rather than being wholeheartedly committed to their implementation. It also gave the impression that there was no clear sense of direction from the top.

One of the most interesting examples of the way we monitored ourselves was to introduce what we called 'leak watch'. This was obviously to monitor leaks. We made it the first item on the agendas of our weekly senior management team meetings and used it to review leaks that had occurred in the previous week. Often leaks had occurred inadvertently rather than, as in the past, as a result of deliberate misuse of information or as a basis of power but, nevertheless, they were just as destructive. Constant reviews eventually eliminated them, partly by increasing our awareness of how they happened and the damage they caused and partly by being clear about our collective determination to change – it showed that we were really serious about getting our behaviour right.

Disciplined communications

The second ground rule was that there should be disciplined communications. We had become notorious for leaks and for premature communication. This meant that we communicated a decision before it was properly thought through. The truth was that we had rarely had a communications strategy for any decision. Hence, we seemed – we were – incompetent.

In future, we decided to record on the minutes of each senior management team meeting both the decisions that we made, the actions agreed and a communication strategy for each decision, spelling out who would tell whom, when announcements would be made and whether we would use one form of communication or multiple forms.

We also recognised that ill-disciplined communication presented most difficulties in informal settings. We acknowledged the truth in the saying that 'everyone tells what they know to someone' – that is, everyone has a 'trusted' friend but they too have a 'trusted' friend and, before long, the grapevine has taken over the communication system, allowing the destructive spin of gossip to shape the culture. So no senior manager was to tell anyone anything unless it was agreed as part of our communication strategy. In this context, we had an interesting debate about whether one of us could tell his wife – who was a middle manager – and we decided that he could not.

Mutually supportive behaviour

The third ground rule was that we should act in a mutually supportive way. There were, within the senior management team, rivalries and personality clashes as in any group and it was certainly true that individuals fought for their faculty or function, behaving sometimes like warring fiefdoms in verbal battle.

We decided that this had to stop. We wanted the team to work towards college goals collectively and collaboratively in the common interest of the student. We could hardly expect staff to behave like that if we did not do so.

So we began to address specific issues that revealed to others that we had not been mutually supportive. One of the most obvious ways was the way in which curriculum senior managers publicly criticised the work of support services, saying, for example, that 'MIS is hopeless' or something similar about estates or cleaning or about the refectory. These support services were managed by other senior managers, so there was a suggestion here that one senior manager thought or implied that another was incompetent or did not share his or her moral commitment to students.

Another specific issue that undermined mutual support was the way in which senior managers dealt with disagreements within the team. It was commonplace, for example, for one manager to e-mail another severely criticising the other's approach and copying the e-mail to a host of other people, including his or her staff to show that their leader was 'fighting on their behalf'. We banned this practice and agreed that e-mails or any form of written communication generally represented an inadequate and inappropriate way of dealing with disagreements between colleagues. In future, disagreements should be handled frankly, face-to-face, in confidence and with mutual respect.

These kinds of issues addressed the more blatantly obvious incidents of unsupportive behaviour. Less obvious was the issue of how to handle gossip or negative comments made by others about a colleague. We decided that part of being mutually supportive was never to accept negativity about a colleague. Even silence would be an inadequate response, whether the criticism was made in a formal or informal situation, because silence implied that the comment was acceptable.

A related issue was whether we should pass on 'intelligence' about such negativity to a colleague. Should we tell each other what people say about each other on the grapevine? Our response was that we should, that one could choose to manage the grapevine or not to manage it – no choice really – but, if people do not know what people are saying about them then they cannot manage it. If they do know, they have the choice of either acknowledging the criticism as 'fair comment' and responding constructively or they could challenge it as 'unfair'. Telling someone what other people are saying about him or her is difficult and the precondition for this is trust. The senior managers had to trust each other so they had to be truly mutually supportive in their behaviour with each other to earn that is trust.

Conduct at meetings

The fourth ground rule covered conduct at meetings, the battleground for most conflict. In fact, we created a long list of rules governing the way that we should behave in meetings and, whenever we reviewed these, we always seem to add another two or three rules, constantly identifying new behaviours that threatened to undermine the team ethos.

These often represented specific behaviours that irritated others, which flouted the ideas of 'collegiality' and 'colleagues' and which did not demonstrate 'mutual support'. They included, for example, a ban on 'empire building', on assuming the 'high moral ground' to win an argument or disparaging another's opinion. For example, one senior manager would sometimes say that another senior manager held a particular opinion because 'he was only interested in money' – that kind of comment was no longer tolerated.

It was also agreed that there should be no aggression or hostility; that people should come to meetings on time; that they should listen respectfully to each other; that they should come prepared with a detailed understanding of the papers produced by others; and that they should accept the views of the majority. Coming late, being unprepared, behaving aggressively or in a domineering way were all examples of behaviours that, we decided, demonstrated lack of respect.

How decisions should be made

The fifth ground rule covered the way that decisions were reached. This ground rule addressed the criticism that decisions had already been made before consultation, that there was a pretence at consultation, that such pretence was disingenuous, and that false consultation would create cynicism.

Hence, it was agreed that we should agree to use three words that communicated the status of a decision-making process. They were 'inform', 'involve' and 'consult'. All three described decision-making processes that could be regarded as legitimate, as long as they were used appropriately and as long as it was made clear before a discussion which status was to operate.

The first, 'inform', meant that the principal (perhaps in liaison with, for example, the director of finance and resources) could tell the rest of the team about a decision that he had made. This was very rarely used as a decision-making process and, whenever it was it threatened to impede the concept of collective responsibility, but at least it recognised that the principal had the right to do this where a team decision was inappropriate. An example might be that the principal wanted to change the composition of the team in some way and it would have been very difficult for the senior management team to agree, as a team, to changes which affected other senior managers.

The second term was 'involve'. This was where a member of the team thought that he or she understood a problem and what the solution should be, but wanted the view of the team and would accept the team decision. Most agenda items for management team meetings were like this.

The third term used was 'consult'. This was where the person who was initiating the debate said that there was a problem but that he or she did not really understand what the problem was or what had caused it and did not know the solution – so help was needed.

Monitoring the ground rules

The sixth and final ground rule was that we should monitor these ground rules as rigorously as we would monitor hard data like student achievement. These ground rules represented 'soft' standards and targets but they were at least as important as many 'hard' targets that we would automatically measure. Our whole approach to this is described in the previous chapter but it is worth, in this context, summarising some of our most important approaches to it.

The first was that we should make available the time, space, energy and commitment to review our performance properly and to undergo management development to support the implementation of these ground rules. We recognised that changing behaviour is very difficult but that it was essential. To achieve such change people needed a great deal of support and development. For some it almost required a change of personality.

The second was that we agreed to adopt a range of methodologies that involved individual feedback about one's behaviour. This included 360-degree appraisal conducted by an external coach who used the outcome of the feedback to provide confidential coaching to individuals. In some cases this was extensive and consequently expensive – but we judged it to be worthwhile. If one senior manager 'misbehaved' and was seen to get away with it, this would undermine the credibility of our entire approach to culture change.

The third was that if a person could not change sufficiently, could not stop empire building in an aggressive manner or miscommunicating or using information as a base for personal power and ego building, that person would have to leave the team. In practice this happened at both senior and middle management levels but, at both levels, the individuals understood and agreed with the need for 'one united team' and recognised that, despite support, they could not change their behaviour sufficiently or consistently.

The fourth was that at the heart of this approach to monitoring ourselves was the concept of individual critiquing. On the basis of the experience of the staff surveys in 1994 and feedback to individuals as well as groups we had come to believe that many people lacked the emotional intelligence to recognise that criticisms of group behaviour applied to them. They recognised the misbehaviour in others but did not think that, on balance, their own behaviour was significantly wrong or that it significantly impacted on others. Feedback therefore had to be specific to the individual. It was necessary to feedback precisely what the person had said or had done that had offended others and to explain why it had offended them and with what impact. The senior managers at Runshaw agreed that we should do this to each other informally as well as in formal situations like appraisal, 360-degree feedback and coaching. It demanded a very high order of skills from both the person doing the feedback and the person receiving it and it required a very high level of trust. Nevertheless, it did happen and it happened to me. It was part of a culture that recognised that feedback and evaluation should be a natural way of going about our business and that it was unintelligent to receive feedback as though the person giving it was motivated by personal animosity.

EXTENDING THE CONCEPT TO THE MIDDLE MANAGERS

Everything about 'one united team' was openly discussed at Runshaw. We acknowledged that the staff were right to criticise us for not being a team and we wanted to take their criticisms on board. Making positive efforts to create a united team was our open response. There was nothing devious or secretive about it.

When we explained to the middle managers that we were trying to create a united senior management team, they responded that they should be included, thereby creating one united college management team. They felt very strongly that this should be part of our overall response to the valid criticism by staff that 'middle managers don't manage'! They wanted to share in decision-making processes about policy and strategy and they accepted that it would be impossible to have meaningful debates if what was said in meetings was publicly leaked or miscommunicated.

They also accepted that being part of such a team would change their role and relationships with lecturer colleagues fundamentally. They would no longer be simply higher paid staff with increased responsibilities. They would have stepped over a line that divided staff and those who managed staff in situations related to performance issues. These included managing incidents of poor performance, non-compliance, casual staff absence and the need to challenge negative behaviour. The whole culture-change programme had been designed to reduce such divisions but it could never eliminate them. There was an important and difficult staff management job to be done and middle managers accepted that it was their job.

For some, particularly those who placed a very high value on being popular with staff, this was very difficult. Some had seen their middle management role as that of being the 'representative' of staff, upwardly communicating staff needs as their primary function, avoiding any perception that they were responsible for the decisions made by 'the management', happy to 'pass the buck' to those above them. They did not want joint responsibility because it changed their preferred image but, in the context of peer group pressure, they were now obliged to accept it.

Others had become quite adept at manipulating the situation. For example, one would frequently bring staff with him to see a senior manager, arguing for his or her promotion or some other cause, take the credit for a favourable decision and openly expressing disappointment if the senior manager rejected the individual's case. This had been seen as quite acceptable, the norm, but this now became unacceptable; thenceforth, it was the job of middle managers to deal with staff on their own, to take responsibility for 'bad news' and to present the 'management' case in the most positive way possible. Middle managers had to combine with senior managers to become the college management team, bound by collective responsibility and all the other ground rules that helped to create one united management team.

Senior managers welcomed this development. We believed that it was essential for middle managers to act as effective mediators of policy and strategy, implementing these in a positive and sensitive way. We believed that middle managers 'had the ear of staff', were trusted, were 'in tune' with staff feelings and could implement decisions in a way that we could not. We wanted to 'disperse' leadership to them. We would have agreed with Briggs (2005) when she said 'middle managers occupy a pivotal role within a complex setting, translating the purpose and vision of the college into practical activity and outcomes.' So the stage was set for the creation of 'one united management team'.

Middle management role conflict

But it was not as simple as that. Middle managers were not prepared to participate in the ground rule of collective responsibility without first sharing in decision making. This ground rule said that all managers should 'sell' every management decision as though it were their own, even if they disagreed with it on an individual basis. But they were not prepared to do this unless they were first properly involved and consulted in making the decisions.

The two areas of decision making that most concerned them were resource allocation and the introduction of new processes, which they were then required to implement with their staff. With regard to the first, they complained that the process of allocating resources had been clothed in secrecy, that they never knew what other managers had bid for, what was allocated to them or on what basis. They wanted the decisions about resource allocation to be open, honest and based on behaviour that involved them in trusting each other and listening to each other empathetically, thereby coming to appreciate the 'fairness' of allocations.

As it was, they felt that senior managers did not trust them to participate as reasonable people and they confessed that the current arrangements did not foster trust between them. Some admitted that they 'played games' when it came to bidding, deliberately exaggerating the merit of their case and 'overbidding'. They expressed frustration with the role of being a 'bidder' – they wanted to be strategists, seeing things from a college perspective and acting accordingly. They felt that their relationship with the senior management team had been a classic 'transactional' one, not a 'transformational leadership' relationship based on trust, which they now wanted.

With regard to implementing new processes on behalf of senior managers, they felt quite angry and frustrated about the way that decisions about such matters were 'passed down from up high'. Many new processes, they argued, were often deeply flawed, often irrelevant to the operational needs of the college, would simply not work and would add to a sense of initiative overload to the workload problem. They argued that things were not properly thought-through and that it was, therefore, 'embarrassing' to ask staff to do something that was often 'nonsensical and ludicrous'.

A related issue was that 'representation' on the senior management team for those who managed large cohorts of students and/or large areas of the curriculum was weak. They felt that they interfaced on a daily basis with the 'customers', that they were very aware of what the customer needed, and that the senior management team was not prioritising resource allocation properly to meet those needs. They felt that senior managers were insufficiently focused on customers, that their new corporate roles had caused them to 'take their eye off the ball', and that, therefore, senior managers would not support them properly when it came to being responsive to student needs. The lines of communication and accountability between themselves and senior managers were, at best, tenuous because the senior managers saw their roles in terms of corporate activities rather than line management. In short, they felt that they lacked access to decision making about key matters concerning the way that students were served and that the decision-making process was unbalanced and flawed.

They also felt that there was a lack of opportunity for demonstrating the ground rule of mutual support and that, when it came to the ground rule of disciplined communications, the norm was for them to learn about decisions 'by default', finding out about, for example, the allocation of a scarce resource – like a key room – only when it became obvious that other middle managers had acquired it. With such miscommunication at management level, it would have been impossible to expect them to practise a set of ground rules that required them to communicate in a 'disciplined way'.

Middle managers felt that they were caught 'in the middle', unsure about whether they were teachers or managers, unclear about what was expected of them, and they were unable to explain policies, strategies and decisions made by senior managers because they had not sufficiently shared in the decision-making process and consequently did not fully understand or agree with the decisions.

Reviewing our management structure

So there was clearly a set of preconditions to put in place before middle managers could realistically be expected to sign up for the ground rules that shaped and governed the concept of 'one united management team'. There first had to be new approaches to shared decision making, there had to be proper 'representation' or linkage between them and the decision-making process at senior level, and there had to be new structures that enabled middle managers to communicate with and be consulted by senior managers. We had to review our management roles and structures, to look back at what had worked before ERA and incorporation, to review what had happened since and why it had created such confusion for middle managers, and to decide how we should restructure in such a way that middle managers were enabled to participate fully in 'one united management team', accepting the ground rules as fair and reasonable.

In 1984 I had introduced a simple faculty structure to manage the day-to-day operational life of the college, with a second tier of schools below them and then curriculum or continuous improvement teams at the level of the subject or course teams and support service teams. I tried to avoid the traditional problem of competing 'fiefdoms' by creating a neutral faculty for student support. It did not have any students of its own but it co-ordinated the pastoral systems across college for all students. The presence of this neutral department meant that the funding units earned for students were shared out between various faculties, with the consequence that the salaries of senior managers were not dependent upon the size of their individual faculty, so there was no financial incentive for any individual senior manager to compete with others in recruiting students. Our focus as a college could be to serve the needs of the student rather than any particular faculty.

Generally, the faculty system had worked well up to 1990, but the impact of the Education Reform Act and incorporation created new corporate roles and responsibilities. I did not want to spend scarce resources on expanding the senior management team so these roles were allocated to existing senior managers. This happened in most colleges. In a study of college management structures, Harper (2000) reported that 93.5% of colleges in her study had restructured over the previous 10 years in much the same way that Runshaw had, replacing faculty structures with corporate functions. She reported that:

> *the common features are that the senior management team most typically consists of a chief executive and 2, 3 or four senior managers, each accountable for one or more broad areas of operational management. Academic and support functions are centralised and middle managers coordinate varying aspects of support for teaching and learning within flatter organisational structures.*

She found that it was usual for one senior manager to be responsible for the curriculum and to line manage the curriculum leaders at middle management level, whilst other senior managers managed combinations of resources, finance, human resources, quality, business development, marketing, student services and management information systems. The latter generally had fewer line management responsibilities.

Developments at Runshaw were similar. Our senior managers developed new corporate roles between 1990 and 1993 but, unlike the typical situation described by Harper, we did not create a single senior management role to line manage all curriculum managers. We left such line management as a secondary role for each of our new corporate managers. I do not think that this difference was particularly significant: in both our case and that of the 'typical college' described by Harper, the focus shifted in the senior management team from students and the curriculum to the new corporate roles.

We had inadvertently created a staff perception that the values of senior managers had changed and that we were no longer interested in students, teaching and learning or staff. The externally imposed imperative to reduce costs had not helped but neither did our naive and insensitive voluntary adoption of business terms and job titles, which were perceived by some staff as a manifestation of 'managerialism'. Nor did our equally naive assumption, introduced by the consultant whom we employed between 1991 and 1993, that the wholesale adoption of a private sector package of process-management roles and structures would solve our problems.

The culture-change programme stopped us in our tracks. It challenged virtually every assumption that had led to the emergence of the new management structure. It forced us to think again about the importance of managing staff morale, about strengthening the lines of communication, about refocusing on the development of the teaching skills of our staff and, most importantly, on the importance of creating a shared vision based on shared values.

The acid test for us became the answer to the question, 'Would our new management structure support the management of culture or would it hinder it?' On reflection, I believe that the answer to that is that one of our biggest mistakes in trying to respond to the challenges of ERA and incorporation in the early 1990s was to create a senior management team composed predominately of corporate roles. There were three main reasons for this. Firstly, it led to a breakdown in lines of communications with teaching staff; secondly, it sent out a signal to all staff that teaching and learning and the leadership of teachers was not our priority; and thirdly, it under-resourced the key structure – the faculty – that could have supported the integration of our approaches to the management of staffing, finances, and quality into a coherent, student-centred service that was focused on the student experience. In short, I agreed with the perceptions of middle managers that, in losing strong faculty voices in the senior management team, the decision-making process had become fundamentally flawed and that the creation of corporate roles fragmented our focus on the students' experience.

In addition, one of the consequences of this shift was that curriculum and line management roles had largely been passed down to middle managers. This was a very big mistake. No matter how well disposed or how hard working those middle managers were, they were not part of the senior decision-making team, so they could not communicate new policies and strategies to staff with the same level of understanding or conviction as senior managers. This was a major reason for the breakdown in communications that was detected in 1993 and articulated strongly in the culture-change programme.

Reintroducing faculty management

Consequently, in 1995, we restored faculties, initially by expanding the size of the senior management team although it was reduced back to its original small size by shedding corporate roles. There were eventually seven senior managers, including myself. The restoration of effective line management by the recreation of heads of faculty posts in 1995 was, in my view, a significant contributor to the rapid improvement in staff morale thereafter. Since then, the implementation of our corporate matters has been deployed largely through this faculty management structure.

What was different at Runshaw was that we operated a second, cross-college process-management structure. In summary, it consisted of a series of process improvement teams (PITs) for each of our key processes, each led by a senior manager. In practice, one process improvement team managed the core processes for teaching and learning and I chaired it. There was a separate PIT for student support and another one for equal opportunities, both chaired by the senior manager responsible for these. The director of finance and resources chaired two separate PITs for financial management and facilities management. The senior manager responsible for MIS chaired the PIT for knowledge management (she was also a head of faculty). The senior manager for Runshaw Business Centre chaired the PIT for partnerships. The whole senior management team reviewed strategic planning as a process and it was reviewed during an annual away-day senior management team conference. Quality assurance was reviewed by the quality council, a body chaired by the principal and consisting of the senior managers and several middle managers such as the quality manager. The principal chaired the PITs for human resource management and for marketing.

We did, of course, also have central support service specialists in a range of areas but their role was generally to support developments in the faculties, not to manage them directly. For example, there was a central information learning technology (ILT) team, with an ILT team manager, and ILT staff trainer and ILT technicians to help teachers develop online self-study materials. Initially, responsibility for our ILT strategy was delegated to them. This did not work, partly because they lacked the detailed understanding of conditions and priorities within different faculties, schools and curriculum improvement teams but also because they lacked the authority to make things happen in the faculties. Once we agreed that heads of faculty and their respective managers and staff would be responsible for ILT developments, the role of the central ILT team changed to that of support, facilitator, 'critical friend', mentor and trainer, there to serve the faculty staff. Put simply, this worked and the college then made significant and rapid improvements.

Exactly the same model operated for personnel: the central unit performed some central tasks but, in terms of managing staff, its role was to act as a 'consultant' to those who needed help in matters like managing poor staff performance or staff absence. The onus was ultimately on the shoulders of the managers and staff in the faculty. The same operated for finance: the faculty designed and operated business plans and these were their responsibility, but the finance team performed specialist tasks and acted as advisors to those in the faculties who were responsible for business planning.

In some ways I am tempted to agree with those who say that principals of colleges focus too much on management structures. Certainly I would agree that managing the culture is the most important thing for a principal or senior management team to do and that developing senior managers' leadership styles and thereby creating an effective climate is fundamental to a college's success, but I do believe that management structures contribute significantly to the implementation and support of effective leadership. In our case, the changes made in 1995 to our senior management structure supported the transformation of culture by successfully addressing the key frustrations of middle managers with respect to participation in decision making.

THE CHANGING ROLES OF MIDDLE MANAGERS

These changes in the roles and structures of the management team had a significant impact on the role of middle managers. Runshaw probably involved middle managers in decision making more than the typical college because, since 1991, it had operated the monthly college management team meetings and the biannual management development workshops. There was, therefore, a track record of attempting to share and work together, though it would be wrong to overstate their importance in terms of shared decision making. Clearly, notwithstanding these regular meetings, senior managers had been perceived as the decision makers by middle managers.

After 1995, the majority of middle managers at Runshaw in 1995 were intellectually stimulated, personally challenged and very excited about the potential to develop both themselves as individuals and their professional role as managers. The changes to structures helped enormously and there was no longer the same sense of role conflict. For example, they were no longer in any doubt that they should be managers, not teachers; they accepted their role within the ground rule of collective responsibility; they greatly appreciated the new opportunities to participate in decision making; and they welcomed their role in leading staff in building a shared vision.

In a recent study of the role of middle managers, Briggs (2005) has developed a typology of five distinctive roles that middle managers perform – 'corporate', 'implementer', 'staff manager', 'liaison', and 'leader'. Each is problematic within the college sector in terms of the kind of role conflict that middle managers at Runshaw had experienced between 1990 and 1995. In Runshaw's case, we addressed these in general through the management restructuring and, additionally, through a variety of developments described below. It was these that thereafter enabled middle managers to participate fully in the concept of 'one united management team'.

The corporate role of middle managers

In the case of the 'corporate' role, we believed that middle managers had a very significant role in contributing to and carry out the corporate work of the college. Being members of 'one united management team' meant that they shared collective responsibility for all corporate decisions. We recognised, of course, that it was not as simple as that. We had to create the opportunity for them to 'own' corporate policies and strategies and to feel a real sense of responsibility for them before they could reconcile the sometimes competing interests of corporate decisions with those of their special areas of responsibility. When it was necessary to explain corporate decisions to their staff, especially when these were unpopular, we wanted them to do so with personal conviction and understanding. Hence, we had to create structures in which they could meaningfully participate in corporate decision making. These included the two annual management conferences. Two others that were just as important were the faculty management team and the college management team, described below.

Faculty management team

In Runshaw's case, the creation of a new faculty structure in 1995 was accompanied by the development of faculty management teams with a strong linkage between senior managers and middle management teams. These ensured that all managers benefited from flows of information and shared in decision making processes. That is, at the top level the senior management team met weekly to consider the views of senior and middle managers. Its minutes – which included actions agreed, who would implement them and by when – were then circulated to all middle managers within 24 hours. Each senior manager met his or her faculty management team each week to review these minutes and to ensure that middle managers understood them and their own role in implementing them where appropriate, and that they shared in developing future decisions, especially where – as in most cases – the recorded senior management team decision was to 'explore' or 'consider' a particular way forward.

These weekly faculty management team meetings also enabled middle managers to propose agenda items for the senior managers' meetings and, as they received the agendas for senior management meetings as well as the minutes, they had the opportunity to contribute to developing the views that their line managers would present. In some ways the senior management team was like a creature with six tentacles, with constant flows to and from the six middle management teams, each led by a senior manager, each facilitating a constant flow of information and contributions to decision making.

Below the faculty management team was a tier of continuous improvement teams and curriculum improvement teams (CITs). The former were composed of support staff and the latter of teaching staff. All staff were members of at least one team and these met weekly. In addition, all members of staff met their respective line manager, a middle manager, at least once a month at a briefing and CIT leaders met their respective middle manager on a monthly basis to discuss operational matters that were being considered at the faculty management meetings.

College management team

This met monthly on Wednesday afternoons between 3 p.m. and 5 p.m. It was chaired by myself as principal, partly because it was perceived as symbolically important that the principal should attend to listen to the views of middle managers. All senior and middle managers attended the meeting. Attendance was seen to be important in creating a sense of community so it was monitored carefully by senior managers. The seating arrangements were cabaret style, with groups of six to eight managers sitting around each round table in such a way that they could participate in discussions on agenda issues. Senior managers were dispersed to join different groups.

The meeting was preceded by a social gathering – a team-bonding activity – of 15 to 20 minutes for tea. The agenda consisted of a number of key items. The first was a report back and follow-up (we called this 'closing the loop') to the decisions made at the previous meeting. The second, third and possibly fourth items consisted of short presentations by senior managers and occasionally by middle managers about recent developments in policy and strategy, usually followed by 'buzz groups' and then feedback on what managers thought about the proposed issues. The next item was a briefing for middle managers by the deputy principal on the proposed content of the next monthly college briefing (described in Chapter 6).

The final items on every agenda were 'hot-spots', 'just-in-time' and 'what's on the grapevine?' The first of these provided an opportunity for buzz groups to identify things that needed to be addressed urgently in the college. These could be, for example, about student behaviour, or poor cleaning, or operational worries about forthcoming events, or anything at all. This item provided a safety net for managers to identify any day-to-day crises that were not being addressed appropriately through normal procedures. The issues would be addressed the next day by the senior management operations team that met every Thursday morning and its minutes, including the actions agreed in response to each hot-spot, would-be circulated within 24 hours. Apart from anything else, it generated an extraordinary feeling of empowerment and enabled middle managers to 'set the agenda'.

The second item, 'just-in-time', was related to training needs that had just been identified by any particular manager and that needed to be addressed urgently but that were not included in the planned training schedule. The third item, 'what's on the grapevine?' provided middle managers with the opportunity to discuss any rumours that were in circulation about either the college or about its competitors. It was part of our attempt to ensure that we operated a 'managed culture'.

At the end of each meeting of the college management team, the principal would make a farewell speech for any manager who was leaving the college before the next meeting. By 2004 there were over 60 managers and each of them could leave at any time of the year, once they had served 2 months' notice, so there was often one manager leaving each month. This provided a pleasant opportunity for recognition and appreciation, not just of the individual concerned but, by implications of many of the remarks made, of his or her immediate colleagues and their achievements. It also provided an opportunity for humour, laughter and a focus on feelings and relationships. The individual would reply, thanking colleagues and wishing them well. It was a small ceremony, which helped to create a sense that the management team was a team in which it was pleasant and mutually supportive to work.

Overall, these monthly meetings reinforced a sense of collaboration and they provided an opportunity for managers to demonstrate mutual support. But its greatest value was in sustaining the momentum of the concept of 'one united management team' between the two annual management development workshops, developing in middle managers a feeling of self-worth and self-confidence – they perceived themselves, and were perceived by others, as 'key players' in the running of the college. It enabled them to share and contribute to the shaping of the direction of the college and its goals on an ongoing basis and, as such, it helped to create a sense of clarity in the climate of the college.

Hence, on balance, middle managers at Runshaw very successfully exercised their corporate role. They did have a strong sense of ownership about policy and strategy, they were very aware about the college's values, they knew how Runshaw 'worked' and they were acutely aware of the college's environment and competitive strategies. They also had a very strong understanding about the need for accountability and the framework for implementing it. In particular, there was no real difficulty – given the existence of our six core values – in reconciling potential conflicts between 'professionalism' and 'managerialism' which, as explained in Chapter 1, have featured so strongly in the literature since 1990. Middle managers were saturated in regular and repeated debates and reflections on our core values and there was never any real doubt or dispute about what behaviours and attitudes were expected from them after 1995.

The implementer role of middle managers

Using Briggs's (2005) typology of the roles of the middle manager, that of 'implementer' is that of 'carrying out college policy through the purposeful and effective organisation of departmental activities'. Briggs notes that this role is associated with a feeling of 'pressure on managers, a feeling that there is simply too much to do and thus of inadequacy'.

At Runshaw, there was never any doubt about the value we placed on implementation. One of our core values was 'putting our ethos into action' and it was all about translating concepts, beliefs and ideas into hands-on, practical action. It was about making sure that we were never guilty of 'empty rhetoric' and it articulated a widespread dislike for words without action. It also expressed our ethos of 'achievement orientation'.

It was supported by the identification of our core management competencies. These included 'planning and organising/prioritising', defined as 'thinks ahead in order to effectively organise workload; prioritises activities, efficiently establishes appropriate courses of action and monitors progress, accomplishing goals on time.' The required behaviours include 'prioritises tasks logically and efficiently', 'prepares in advance and sets realistic timescales', 'plans time effectively to meet deadlines', 'concentrates efforts on activities that have the most significant impact' and is 'proactive'. Another management competency was 'analytical thinking', defined as 'effectively and thoroughly assimilates, analyses and evaluates all available information: develops effective solutions that are in the best interest the college.' Its behaviours included 'checks data and information for errors, omissions, anomalies', 'makes links to other data', 'looks beyond the symptoms to identify key issues and root causes', 'develops workable solutions based on correct analysis', 'identifies knock-on effects' and 'identifies the key issues in ambiguous, inconsistent data'.

It is clear from this that we asserted very clearly that implementation was very important and we were explicit in defining what it meant. But that was not enough. We also had to provide middle managers with access to information and to other staff across the college with whom they needed to interact; understanding about the way that the college worked, including who did what in other parts of the college; and the professional expertise to make effective decisions. This is why it was so important for Runshaw to introduce a cross-college process-management structure, which cut across the faculty structure, enabling managers to come together from different faculties and from services to develop integrated and coherent approaches to such processes as student-tracking, staff development, health and safety, equal opportunities, marketing, quality assurance, student support and, of course, teaching and learning. This structure gave clarity to what the cross-college processes were, how they could be reviewed, the role of the manager and others in reviewing them, and how they could gain easy access to each other. It gave 'easy navigation of the college systems and structures' (Briggs, 2005).

The new management structure also helped because, unlike corporate structures elsewhere in which most lecturers are line managed through a single 'curriculum' senior manager, our structure shared line management of curriculum managers between four of the six senior managers. This meant that a great deal of time and energy was spent by senior managers on coaching and mentoring curriculum middle managers and that the latter had very easy access to decision making at senior management level. This ensured that resources were allocated in the way that was responsive to the needs of curriculum managers and that new policies and processes were fully 'tested out' at the formulation stage with middle managers before the latter were obliged to implement them. They, in turn, 'tested these out' with the team (CIT) leaders whom they line managed. The same flows of information, negotiation and 'testing out' went on at that level with face-to-face interactions between managers and their teams before any decision was finalised. Consequently, on the whole, implementation was well done at Runshaw.

The staff management role for middle managers

The third role in Briggs's typology is the role of 'staff manager', complementary to that of 'implementer', together enabling middle managers to carry out their 'corporate' function. Briggs argues that 'middle managers are the focus of the staff management'. That was certainly true at Runshaw. Overall, it was regarded as a critically important role for middle managers. They had demonstrated, in negotiating new contracts successfully with their respective staff in 1994, that they were trusted by staff and that, consequently, they had the credibility to get things done quickly and effectively, but it was still a very challenging role for them, especially when it came to balancing 'tough and tender' appropriately. Some desperately sought constant popularity. Others were quite the opposite – autocratic, distant, a personification of 'them' against 'us', coercive and almost always directive. All were now required to balance those styles with those of coaching, being affiliative and being democratic. In the event, as explained in Chapter 4, some could not change sufficiently. The constant repetition of feedback and reflection through performance management processes and management development meant that they fully understood and generally agreed with what was required and that, through a process of self-realisation, they came to the conclusion that they could not manage staff effectively and would never be able to do so. In such circumstances, they found 'dignified exits', again as explained in Chapter 4. What was not acceptable was that they would not do their job properly.

There was no doubt that the most difficult issue for middle managers in their 'staff management' role was that of managing poor performance. What was crucial here was the 'mutual support' amongst managers at Runshaw. It was the feeling of solidarity, of camaraderie and of trust that kept managers feeling well supported professionally and personally. It is very difficult and very stressful for an individual to conduct poor performance procedures and it would have been impossible to do so effectively if they had worked in isolation. But, in the new culture of 'high performance expectations', it had to be done and sometimes that meant that middle managers had to be made to do it. In one instance, where a middle manager continuously avoided dealing with a weak member of staff through poor performance, the senior manager not only required him to put the member of staff on poor performance but then put the middle manager on poor performance too for not having done his job properly in the first place.

In Runshaw's case, this was not just about managing the extreme few cases. In 1995 we relocated middle managers back into staff workrooms so that they could manage the culture there, and this included challenging staff who were negative and destructive . We had chosen to have a 'managed' as opposed to an 'unmanaged' culture, and this meant that middle managers had to play a key role in managing 'informal communications'. It was very difficult for them to retain the necessary sense of distance from their colleagues, enabling them to make objective and detached judgements while sharing in the banter of the workrooms. This is why we went to such pains to develop interpersonal skills in managers in the ways described in Chapter 4. Their skills and the constant support they received in both training and 'mutually supportive' management teams were crucial in making them effective staff managers. Equally crucial to this aspect of their role were their roles in the communication processes.

On the whole, staff management was by far the most difficult role for middle managers at Runshaw as, I suspect, it is in most colleges and other organisations. I cannot claim that the difficulties managers experienced in managing poor performance were ever overcome but Runshaw did have a very clear, robust and value-driven approach to managing staff – described as 'tough and tender' in the previous chapter – and there was an enormous amount of management development in it. Overall, I do believe that it was a role that was performed relatively well at Runshaw and this made a significant difference to the creation of a culture of 'high performance expectations' for staff as well as for students.

The liaison role for middle managers

The fourth dimension of the middle managers' role in Briggs's typology was that of 'liaison' – that is, managers liaising with others laterally and vertically and with external agents to ensure that the student received a coherent and successful educational experience.

As Briggs (2005) says:

> liaising is underpinned by the college's collective ability to work as a coherent whole. Managers are supported in their liaising by easy access to, and co-operation from, teams and managers across the college structure . . . liaising is mainly facilitated by systems and potentially impeded by people . . . and by locally focused systems and purposes devised by other managers.

Given that Runshaw reintroduced a faculty structure, there was a real danger that, in doing so, it would create a major barrier to liaison across faculties and between middle managers. As Briggs said:

> If the faculty-based management structures are valued as a framework for the college – and given its educational purpose, this is a reasonable framework to choose – the college needs to address the deficiency in whole-college understanding and the differential values placed upon managers' roles. In other words, the college needs to address how it is to work as a coherent whole . . . there has to be a unity of college design and a mutual valuing of roles if the different aspects of college function which the various managers represent are to be enabled to work together as a coherent whole.

Many of the structures that enabled middle managers to liaise at Runshaw have already been mentioned – vertically through faculty management teams and laterally through the college management team, management development conferences, the 'faculty' of student support and process improvement teams, all enabling the college to work together as a whole. There were three additional approaches that were particularly important to the way that we supported this role. The first related to centres of excellence, the second to portfolio development groups and the third to a particular way in which we developed relationships between business support managers and curriculum managers.

Centres of excellence

Centres of excellence were a structure that was introduced after we subdivided Runshaw into three federal units, one for the sixth-form centre, one for the adult college and the third for Runshaw Business Centre. One of the effects was that we created separate curriculum delivery teams for each sub-college so, for example, there was a separate IT curriculum team in each of the three sub-colleges. We wanted these curriculum teams to be separate so that they could focus upon the respective needs of the student cohort they served, whether these were 16–19 year olds, post-19 students, or those sponsored by employers. This suited one set of our needs but a disadvantage with it was that subject experts from across the college did not then have the opportunity to work together naturally to share resources, spread good practice and standardise their work. Centres of excellence provided the forum do this, thereby overcoming the disadvantages of our federal structure.

Portfolio development groups

Similarly, managers of subject specialists across the college came together in portfolio development groups to analyse information about the environment, local needs, competition from other colleges and agencies, and their own strengths and weaknesses so that they could collectively plan the introduction of new courses, irrespective of which particular faculty introduced them.

Partnership agreements

The final distinctive way that we supported liaison was with respect to linkages between business support managers and curriculum managers. That is, in most colleges, there is often a destructive, negative tension between support staff and lecturing staff. Briggs (2005) found that 'Curriculum managers in powerful faculties are accorded respect and status within their role . . . other managers are impeded by having little status in the eyes of curriculum managers and received conflicting, competitive demands from them, resulting in ineffectiveness which reinforces a lack of respect.'

Typically, support staff feel undervalued and often resent the better conditions of service – especially the holidays – of the lecturers. The lecturers, on the other hand, often feel that support staff have a relatively 'easy' life, not having to manage student discipline or motivate unwilling students and not having to spend hours at home on marking. Relationships between the two groups are not usually good and this sometimes spills over into 'territorialism' with, for example, curriculum managers openly criticising business support managers and attempting to take over their roles.

During the culture-change process at Runshaw between 1993 and 1994, we explored the other root causes of this feeling and found that they were, firstly, that lecturers or curriculum managers routinely failed to comply with business procedures, making it difficult for support staff to do their jobs properly, wasting their time and energy and creating low morale as support staff felt devalued. Secondly, lecturers and their managers often made last-minute and unrealistic demands on support staff, frequently assuming that they had direct authority over and access to support staff and the right to determine their priorities. In both situations, the concept of 'service' and 'servant' was misinterpreted by lecturers, possibly because the language used – 'service' and 'servant' – gave the impression of a one-way relationship.

At Runshaw we tackled this by developing 'partnership agreements' for all support services – about 20 in all – which defined the mutual, two-way responsibilities and behaviours of support staff and lecturers, each providing the information and support to the other so that all the students received the service to which they were entitled. These behaviours required quite specifically that lecturers should communicate with support staff in a positive manner to get the best positive response from them.

The 'leader' role for middle managers

The fifth and final role of middle managers in Briggs's typology is that of 'leader', described as 'potentially the most contentious, not least because the term "leader" is little used in further education colleges.' At Runshaw we had used this term since 1993 when we used one of the twice-a-year management development workshops to distinguish between the concept of 'leader' and 'manager' in the way described in Chapter 4. Our entire approach to culture change in 1993 led to intensive development of dispersed leadership and every chapter of this book is about how we developed the concept of leadership at Runshaw. So it was not at all contentious for us as far as the role of middle managers was concerned.

What was slightly contentious, but only in a 'conversational' sense, was the way in which we began to explore how far the concept of leadership extended down the organisation. That is, in 2003 we were interested to find out whether 'CIT leaders' and other staff perceived themselves as 'leaders'. Hence, in a staff conference that year which evaluated 'leadership and management', staff were asked to identify who they thought were the 'leaders' in the college. The majority of responses identified 'leaders' as staff, and everybody included course team leaders, subject leaders and support function leaders (all of these were called 'CIT leaders'), almost all of whom were on basic grade posts.

The latter did have access to training in the same kind of management development modules as middle managers, using the same eight core competencies described in the previous chapter but there had never been any formal acknowledgement that they held a formal leadership role. Nor was there a formal agreement that they would be subject to the ground rule of collective responsibility but there was a growing assumption that they should be and there was a growing identification by them with the roles of managers.

Similarly, as all staff became increasingly involved in collective planning and collective decision making about college policy and strategy in the ways described in the next chapter, the concept of collective responsibility became integrated with the notion of staff rights and responsibilities. By 2004, when I left Runshaw, this notion had progressed to the stage where it was frequently asserted that everyone who worked at Runshaw had a responsibility to promote its policies, strategies and achievements to the external world. It was an implicit assumption that, with all the opportunities to feedback their views and to participate in all the consultative debates, there was also an obligation to be loyal to the organisation. Increasingly, the concept of collective responsibility was being extended to all staff and embedded within our culture.

CONCLUSION

In terms of deciding on the first steps towards becoming an 'outstanding' college, I would put the creation of 'one united management team' as second from the top of my list of priorities, only after the definition of core values and the related management competencies, styles and behaviours. It is such an obvious thing to do and yet, in my experience, it rarely exists in colleges or other organisations in the disciplined and structured way that Runshaw developed. It is also easy to do because middle managers generally welcome the opportunity to contribute and share in decision making and they would certainly welcome the flow of information. In terms of leadership styles, it lends itself naturally to the democratic, affiliative and coaching styles, whilst providing the opportunity to explore collectively the ways in which other management styles – coercive, authoritative and pace setting – should be interpreted and applied.

In terms of creating an appropriate climate that encourages better quality, it provides a forum in which all managers can participate in the creation of a clear and shared vision and a strong sense of direction. It enables all managers to collaborate in raising standards and in identifying ways for future improvement. It creates a sense of empowerment, fostering in each manager a sense of control and responsibility for decision-making. Most of all, it creates an intense feeling of team commitment, based not only on creating a congenial and co-operative atmosphere within the management team but also on developing a strong sense of pride and dedication.

The ground rules supported this approach by articulating positive leadership behaviours. Collective responsibility demanded that managers act democratically by requiring them to accept the majority view and behave with integrity in presenting that majority view to others, even when it was difficult to do so. It also required that middle managers truly accept the role of 'management' and step over an invisible line in accepting the responsibilities that go with the status of manager. All six ground rules recognised that behaviour was crucially important and that it should be regulated with the same level of discipline as other more tangible and measurable standards.

It quickly became clear that ground rules were not enough. We needed to change the management roles and structures too. This did not just mean the reintroduction of the strong horizontal lines of control, authority and communication that enabled middle managers to understand and take part in decision making and policy formulation. It also meant that we had to create lateral structures that complemented the faculty structure. These structures supported collaboration and liaison and helped managers to manage staff, to liaise with each other and to implement decisions.

Within the structures was the micropolitics of the status of different middle managers and the danger that 'territorial' barriers might impede effectiveness. Whenever we formed a role or structure to meet one particular need, it seemed to create an imbalance in power relationships that threatened to reduce the effectiveness of other roles and structures. Such issues – like the tension between business support managers and curriculum managers – had to be identified and confronted as a 'system failure', depersonalised from the negative force of the issue and resolved by creating collaborative structures in which face-to-face contact eased tensions. 'Partnership agreements' and 'process improvement teams' are examples of such approaches.

Many of these tensions occurred in the operational cross-college systems, creating feelings of excessive bureaucracy and frustration with the difficulties of accessing accurate data. Managers wanted clarity and consistency and easy access to 'user-friendly' information and support. The difficulty of providing such is commonplace in colleges and it was ever present at Runshaw but it was partly for this reason that we invested heavily in creating first-class management information systems and a cross-college process management system.

This may all sound very technical and scientific: the focus on structures and systems sounds rather like the focus on which we mistakenly concentrated between 1990 and 1993 when things went wrong for us. But it was not a mistake this time because we were using structures and systems to implement the new form of this 'dispersed' leadership that emerged from culture change. Middle managers were encouraged to question, to challenge, to use their initiative and to be autonomous, but all this was contingent upon them understanding the boundaries to their authority and the way that the college worked. It was also contingent upon excellent communications between managers at both senior and middle management level and across the college. We could not afford role conflict or role ambiguity if middle managers were to act effectively as leaders, thereby creating a level of coherence and collective dynamism which would transform the college successfully.

But above all, in simple terms of creating a dynamic force for change inside an organisation, the power of 60 managers operating together at senior and middle management to effect change seemed to be almost irresistible. It could almost be said to be dangerously powerful in the sense that, if it decided to take a college down the wrong path, there was little that could stop it. Hence, it is important that the creation of 'one united management team' is balanced by strong consultative processes involving staff in a college, that the purpose of a strong united management team is seen as the mechanism to develop a strong 'united staff team', and that it should operate within a framework of agreed and shared values, which implicitly limit its power through the exercise of democratic principles. The way that Runshaw tried to create one united staff team and a shared sense of direction, both within a framework of core values, is described in the next chapter.

SUMMARY

- The concept of a united team was the central mechanism for managing the culture and driving forward a coherent strategy for improvement.
- Staff perceptions between 1993 and 1995 were that the senior management team was not a 'team' as such and that middle managers were not 'managers'.
- Runshaw decided that one of the central strategies to progress from 'good' to 'outstanding' was the creation of one united management team composed of both senior and middle managers.
- To create this team it was decided that there should be explicit ground rules governing managers' behaviours. These covered collective responsibility, disciplined communications, mutually supportive behaviour, conduct at meetings, the decision-making process and monitoring the ground rules.
- When we came to extend this concept to middle managers we found that the way their roles were structured made their wholehearted participation in ground rules requiring collective responsibility impossible.
- The management structure was changed to strengthen lines of communication between the senior management team and middle managers and to enable middle managers to share in decision making more effectively.
- We supported the creation of the united management team by arranging a monthly schedule of meetings for all senior and middle managers at which policy and strategy were shaped and a team spirit was carefully nurtured.

- This was supported by management development activities like the biannual management conferences.
- We also introduced a wide range of approaches to support five key middle management roles – that is, 'corporate', 'implementer', 'staff manager', 'liaison' and 'leader'.
- The creation of this team enabled Runshaw to model new leadership styles, it supported the creation of a climate that encouraged improvement and it created a dynamic force for change.

6 CREATING A SHARED SENSE OF DIRECTION

In a review of the educational literature about leadership, Leithwood *et al.* (1999) concluded that direction setting is one of only two basic attributes that are common to definitions of leadership. Moreover, he found that direction-setting practices explained about 50% of the effects of leadership. These included strong commitment to change by teachers and the extensive individual and collective learning by teachers. Leithwood *et al.* argued that, in practice, direction setting was enacted through building a shared vision and developing consensus about goals. These, he argues, lead to the creation of high performance expectations.

This view was supported by Harris *et al.* (2003) when they argued that efficient leaders will be those '. . . who are able to build collaborative cultures through generating positive relationships . . . who build a capacity for improvement through working collaboratively and through building professional learning communities'.

Sergiovanni (2001) similarly argues that '. . . developing a community of practice may be the single most important way to improve.'

Since 1990, with the implementation of the Education Reform Act, the key process in colleges for delivering vision and goals has been that of strategic planning. This chapter therefore explains how Runshaw developed its approach to strategic planning so that the latter underpinned the development of a sense of community within the staff, working together within a framework of shared values to develop a joint vision and a consensus about goals, all of which made a very significant contribution to the development of a culture of high expectations at Runshaw.

The first section of the chapter argues that the decision in 1993 to introduce the culture-change programme itself represented a direction setting 'strategic' choice of the utmost significance. The entire process of engaging staff in a college-wide collaborative exercise to determine our way forward established a set of consultative practices, which developed into a massive consultative infrastructure. It also changed relationships, roles and expectations and began to establish a new culture based on shared problem solving, collaboration and co-operation.

The second section of the chapter illustrates all of this by describing the way in which Runshaw grappled with the real 'strategic' issues that emerged from the culture-change programme. This led to the reorganisation of the college's management structures with the introduction of a new federal structure. It also led to a new marketing strategy that was built on a collective identification of how Runshaw should develop a strategic competitive advantage by being different from other colleges in both the way it presented itself and the way it established new, rigorous standards of behaviour and performance for students.

The third section explains the consultation processes and the enormous investment of time and effort that went into creating the conditions to support unhurried, collaborative and shared direction setting. This was highly structured and it quickly became integrated into the strategic planning process, providing the time for staff to share in developing the college's values, vision, mission and goals. This whole process not only demanded a very high level of commitment of time and energy, but it was also innovative in borrowing approaches from the private sector and in radically revamping the existing staff representative body, the academic board, which is often perceived in colleges as boring, bureaucratic and a waste of time.

The fourth section explains how the role of staff changed Runshaw. The concept of a 'Runshaw person' was created and human relations processes were aligned with this. This approach raised concerns about whether Runshaw was creating an overly conformist culture so the concept of individualism is explored in this context.

The fifth and last section of this chapter explains the strategic planning process that was developed at Runshaw by 1995. This acted as a vehicle for vision building, developing consensus about goals, translating these into tangible, ambitious but feasible objectives, targets and strategies, and that enabled college-level aspirations to be cascaded into aligned team and individual goals.

'CULTURE CHANGE' AS A FORM OF STRATEGIC PLANNING

A bureaucratic incumbrance

The introduction of the culture-change programme in 1993 was our first conscious attempt at strategic management. Before then, there was almost a sense of 'muddling' along, doing whatever seemed to be the most urgent priority. Under the Education Reform Act in 1990 all colleges were given explicit responsibility for strategic planning. This was to be one of the new elements of being 'businesslike'. We initially regarded strategic planning as a bureaucratic incumbrance, something we had to do because it was 'required' and not something that added any real value to the running of the college. Our attitude to this formal process remained like that until we began the culture-change programme in the summer of 1993. Then we began to develop new informal practices to what became, by 1995, an entirely new approach to strategic planning and, with it, a systematic and structured approach to vision building, goal setting and creating a shared sense of direction. The key to this approach was the fact that, in introducing an expensive and time-consuming culture-change programme in 1993, we were tacitly acknowledging that managing the culture was the most important job for senior managers and that we should prioritise it in terms of our time and energy.

The context for all this was as described in Chapter 1. In summary, Simkins and Lumby (2002) described it in the following terms:

> *Colleges in England have not been a comfortable place to work since 1993 . . . The double burden of being asked to take the responsibilities which were previously those of the Local Education Authorities and the unremitting pressure to recruit more students, make efficiency gains and improve achievement have exacted a heavy price from staff of all kinds.*

Our strategic choices

Notwithstanding all the external pressures, Runshaw still had choices about both the way it conducted itself and its strategic direction. With regard to the latter, we could have allowed, for example, its four neighbouring sixth-form colleges to capture the A-level 'market', or it could have become more elitist, reducing its provision for the less able, or it could have cut out those post-19 areas of provision that did not 'pay their way'. In fact, we chose not to do any of those things.

With regard to the way that colleges conducted themselves, as explained in Chapter 1, colleges responded quite differently to incorporation – some by interpreting 'best practice businesslike' to imply 'macho-management' styles, with some senior managers appearing to relish the opportunity to settle old scores through mass redundancies of staff. At Runshaw, we chose to take the opposite direction. We interpreted 'best practice businesslike' approaches to mean culture change and to imply the kind of listening management style that had made Leyland Trucks so successful. Our central strategy was to listen and to respond constructively, to work collaboratively with staff and to identify what the whole community of staff saw as the right direction for the college. The effect of this was to make us rethink our sense of purpose, our vision for the future, and to determine the goals that would move us forward in the right direction. Without necessarily formalising the process, we had begun to engage in the essence of strategic planning. We began to realise what 'strategy' really meant and what it looked like.

The key issues that were identified by staff in the 1994 surveys and focus groups required us to rethink fundamental aspects of the college's work, like the standards of behaviour expected of students in public areas, how these should be managed, what should be expected of students in terms of, for example, attendance and completion of assignments, the way that the accommodation should be developed to support teaching and learning, the provision of facilities for staff, and whether 16–19-year-old students should or should not be integrated with post-19 students. Other key issues, especially those about the 'misdirection of resources away from the classroom' and staff concerns about workloads, made it increasingly clear that our whole approach to resource allocation would also have to change.

The intensity of staff dissatisfaction that emerged from the culture-change programme also made us understand that our ability as a college to engage staff in 'marketing' the college to existing students and potential students whom they met at 'open evenings' was contingent upon satisfying staff that the college would properly support the teaching and learning processes, that it would focus its attention and resources on the student experience, and that it would really fulfil our core values, particularly that of maximising the potential of every student. It became imperative for our future that we re-focused on the students' experience and on the key process of teaching and learning. It was absolutely clear that staff believed that these should be our priorities.

Becoming strategic naturally

We did not consciously marry up what we thought of as the bureaucratic and mechanistic strategic planning process that already existed with this new perception of the main 'strategic' issues at Runshaw, but we did begin to borrow key concepts – like the concepts of 'vision', 'mission' and 'goals' – from it to clarify the meaning of these issues and to provide structure to the way we developed coherence in addressing them.

So, in 1994, strategic planning began to become for us a meaningful, relevant and positive tool in helping us to address the issues that emerged from the bottom-up culture-change consultation exercises that occurred in 1993 and 1994. Strategic planning as a concept and as a process grew out of the college's need to plan and manage its responses to culture change. It was rooted in the real issues, the real problems and the real perceptions of staff. The formal process increasingly became a vehicle or framework that enabled us to build solutions in a collaborative way and to sustain the sense of collective engagement that had been created in the culture-change programme.

HOW TACKLING THE REAL ISSUES DEVELOPED A SENSE OF STRATEGY

By the end of 1994, we had really begun to understand what strategic planning was all about. We could see its potential for determining our sense of direction and how we should conduct our 'business'. We could see that it could help us to develop a coherent and integrated approach to responding to the external pressures and local needs, to developing competitiveness by being distinctively better than other providers. We could also see how we could use measures of our own performance to inform the way that we should build on our strengths and address our weaknesses.

Those 'real issues' included all the new human resource approaches described elsewhere in this book, like the redefinition of our management style, the creation of 'one united management team', and the new communications and staff development approaches – but four others stand out as extremely significant in shaping our new sense of direction. These are outlined below to illustrate the meaning and relevance of strategic planning and management at Runshaw.

'Three colleges in one'

An immediate outcome of the culture-change strategy was the subdivision of the college into three separate parts – a kind of a federal structure – a strategy that was called 'three colleges in one'. This meant that we created a sixth-form centre for the 16–19 year olds, an adult college for the post-19 students and Runshaw Business Centre for employers and their employees. This ultimately led to the separation of students onto different sites, the attachment of staff to one of the three colleges, separate budgets and separate management teams. Where bottlenecks had existed in obtaining central services, the adult college and Runshaw Business Centre were now empowered to find their own ways around the bottlenecks. The only thing that really mattered for them was that their students should not suffer from the bureaucratic barriers created by the size and complexity of the college.

There were three key reasons for developing this new strategy and all had been identified by staff in the culture-change process as 'barriers' to our becoming fully effective.

The first emerged from concerns about staff workloads. When we explored the root of the problem with staff, it became clear that one of its principal causes was the way in which the college was organised and the way that staff were deployed. That is, it became clear that individual staff were struggling with the workload demands of focusing on serving the needs of a wide range of students on a range of different courses. The background to this was that, in 1984, I had been determined that the comprehensive ethos that was being introduced would require that staff who taught A-level students exclusively should share in the difficult task of introducing new courses for the less able and for the post-19 age group. By 1993–4, these new students included vast numbers of 'second-chance' adult students and low-achieving school leavers, including over 600 on foundation courses. The culture-change process identified the fact that those staff who had resisted change to the ethos of the college had by then left or had adapted, so the reason for my original approach had virtually disappeared. Hence, the balance of concern in 1994 shifted to that of staff workloads. It was far easier for staff to specialise on specific areas of provision and, for many, this also increased their motivation and commitment.

The second key reason was that the college was becoming very big and very complex. Not only had the 16–19 provision expanded to include a wide range of vocational courses at all levels, but adult education had similarly expanded and the college had introduced a thriving business centre, which provided short courses for employers. Students and parents had begun to provide negative feedback about the size of the college and about the fact that school leavers and the post-19 students were mixing in social areas and in classes, so we began to consider separating these.

The third reason arose from a different concern for many staff. Whenever a management 'queue' formed for the demand of any service like MIS developments, the 16–19 year old provision always took priority. The college had originally been a sixth-form college. The sixth forms of all the local schools had closed down so, when a youngster became 16, he or she had little option but to progress to Runshaw college if he or she wanted to stay in full-time education, so it was understandable that the 16–19 age group should take priority. However, this meant that adult education and the business centre always took a lower priority, creating frustration and concern about their quality.

This was a major change of policy and strategy for the college. Hence there was a major debate about it involving all stakeholders. Some staff strongly disagreed with it, believing that it was beneficial for school leavers and adult students to mix. However, the vast majority of staff, parents and students supported the proposal because they were impressed by the arguments about reducing workload and about creating a more simple college structure that appeared to reduce the size of the environment in which learning took place. They were also impressed by the argument that this strategy would improve the marketing position of the college by offering parents and school leavers a 'sixth-form centre' experience and offering adults an 'adult' environment.

This whole debate occurred at the end of the culture-change programme in the autumn of 1994 and it was conducted in a very constructive and positive way at a staff conference. Staff appreciated the opportunity to have their say and they saw that the debate was conducted in a truly consultative manner. The process of using one simple theme – 'three colleges in one' – for a meaningful debate about an important new strategy had been very successful, so we decided to build on this practice and replicate it annually thereafter.

'Attract the top 5% . . . and the rest will follow'

In 1995 circumstances provided the opportunity for a similar in-depth review of a major strategy. We faced a real strategic dilemma. That was, there were four local sixth-form colleges near Runshaw as well as four further education colleges and two of the former began to succeed in 'creaming off' the most able local school leavers in our area, promoting themselves as selective institutions. Runshaw prided itself on offering 'opportunities for all' and we were proud of our comprehensive ethos but we did not want to become a 'sink' college and we were worried that we could do so. Our dilemma was how to compete effectively with what were perceived to be elitist institutions whilst not becoming elitist ourselves.

A local headteacher who was sympathetic to our dilemma said that, in the playground at his school, children of all abilities judged colleges on the basis of where the top 5% of the ability range in their school was going to enrol. His advice, therefore, was that, in order to attract the mass of his pupils, Runshaw should first attract the top 5% and the rest would follow them. In 1995, therefore, the staff conference in March considered the proposal that the theme for that year should be that we should 'attract the top 5% . . . and the rest will follow.'

It seemed the perfect strategy to enable us to compete effectively with sixth-form colleges and, at the same time, remain true to our values. The staff overwhelmingly supported this strategy, as they had the previous year the idea of 'three colleges in one'.

This was the second time in two years that we had focused on what both staff and managers perceived to be an urgent and very relevant 'strategic' issue. It was also the second time that, in implementing our new communication strategy to keep things simple, we had used a slogan as a form of shorthand to focus debate. The idea of a major annual theme had been born.

'The New Beginning'

The following year came the development of the most important strategy and slogan of all, 'The New Beginning'. This was a college-wide commitment to a consistent approach to a new approach to staff-student relationships and to a collective determination to create a new student culture.

In the review of relationships, roles and responsibilities during our culture-change process in the period of 1993 to 1995 it had become glaringly obvious that staff wanted to take ownership of the way that they and the college management collectively managed students. They had immediately taken the opportunity to express their frustrations about the student culture. On reflection, Runshaw was probably no better or worse than the average college but staff complained about poor behaviour by students in the public areas. Their main complaints concerned litter, spitting and sitting in doorways and corridors. As far as the classroom was concerned, their key concerns were about inadequate effort by students in coursework, lateness for class, lack of effort in class, missed deadlines for assignments and casual student absence. They were also fed up with the fact that, by being inconsistent, they undermined each other's standards and made it difficult for themselves to maintain high standards.

So we started with these issues. These were perceived by staff to be the most pressing problems in the college and that they needed to be tackled collectively. Hence, during 1995 and into 1996 there was a major review of student–staff relationships. By March, 1996 we had developed an entirely new approach, called 'The New Beginning'. Collectively we decided that we would draw a line between what had gone on before and what would happen in the future. There would be a new student ethos with a new set of standards and rules and these would be implemented in a consistent way by all staff.

The students fully participated in the whole process. The majority of them were as keen as staff to establish higher standards and high expectations. They also complained about inconsistency, seeing other students 'get away' with breaking the rules. They wanted to belong to a college that was rigorous, which demanded high standards from them and which acted consistently.

Overall, this process of redefining the student culture was predominantly a bottom-up initiative driven by the staff in a collective effort to redefine standards and to ensure that everyone would enact them consistently. It was a spectacular example of empowerment because it went to the heart of the college's 'business' and gained a very high level of commitment by being completely 'owned' by both the staff and the students.

The emergence of a systematic and structured approach towards strategic planning

Until 1993, the process of developing strategy had been relatively unplanned, even anarchic and ad hoc. Even the strategic decision to adopt a culture-change programme in 1993 was rather like a plunge into the deep end without really knowing what would happen next. But by 1995 and 1996 strategic planning and management had become well supported by managers. They created opportunities for staff to have their say, for groups to meet to solve problems, for effective communication and consultation and for intensive training in the new policies and practices. They also played a leading part in implementing these. So the process became structured and systematic.

Looking back at the whole process of creating these three strategies and comparing them with the pre-1993 approach to strategic planning, our approach had become relatively structured and disciplined. It was also a very responsive approach – following strong staff criticisms of management in the culture-change programme, the traditional leadership style had given way to a much more listening approach. Staff had really appreciated the fact that the management had taken on board their criticisms. For managers, it became rather like 'pushing on an open door' as staff seized the opportunity to create a new agenda comprised of the real problems that beset them every day. Both managers and staff welcomed the opportunity to redefine college policies and practices.

The benefits of staff involvement were numerous. The whole process fostered shared decision making and problem solving, producing not only better solutions but also a strong sense of commitment by staff. It also created new college-wide norms of excellence, creating a culture of high expectations. It clarified the shared beliefs and values held by most staff so that staff could thereafter act in greater accord. It built confidence and self-esteem. It energised and focused staff. It changed relationships in a way that built trust and mutual respect.

Not surprisingly, in the light of all this, we formed the belief that the new role of college managers was to provide the framework and support that would sustain and develop this sense of ownership. We believed that we had to formalise the college-wide consultation process that had been developing since 1994 and had been seen by all to have supported the emergence of 'The New Beginning' – a tangible and incredibly popular articulation of the way that management had refocused 'strategy' back on to the students' experience and on to teaching and learning.

THE CONSULTATION PROCESS

'Stop-the-track' staff conferences

One of the key practical difficulties that obstructed the development of a systematic and structured long-term approach to the continuance of staff engagement was finding the time for all staff to meet and work together. In the summer of 1994 the senior and middle managers together attended a two-day training course on 'culture change' that was provided for us by managers at Leyland Trucks. During this we became increasingly aware of the importance that their managers placed on creating a shared sense of direction but we were puzzled as to how they overcame the practical difficulties of bringing the whole workforce together. They told us that periodically they would 'stop the track' for a day, literally stopping the conveyor belt on which trucks were assembled so that the whole workforce could come together. There was a clear cost to this in terms of the number of trucks that did not get assembled when the track was stopped, but they were convinced that it was worthwhile because it did so much to create a sense of community, a sense of purpose and a sense of direction in the company. They argued that this, in turn, created the commitment, motivation, pride and trust that produced higher quality, higher productivity, secure employment and, ultimately, higher profits.

We were absolutely convinced of the merit of this view so, in 1994–5, we introduced five term-time 'stop-the-track' days at Runshaw. We explained the origin of the term to staff and it stuck as part of our language. Staff welcomed it as an opportunity to build on the consultation processes that had been so popular in the culture-change programme and were reassured when it was agreed that we would start the teaching year five days earlier than usual to ensure that no teaching time would be lost.

The five conferences were held in November, December, January, March and May. At each conference all staff came together to consider college-wide issues. Over time, this generated an intense understanding about and commitment by staff to our values, vision, mission, policies and strategies. Staff felt knowledgeable about 'what was going on around here', about the direction of the college and about its problems. Collectively, they decided what needed to be done for the college to succeed and they felt able to contribute effectively to the shaping of successful policy and strategy.

Preparations and arrangements for 'stop-the-track' days

The mechanics of how each 'stop-the-track' staff conference worked were important. These were similar for each conference. Each included:

- intensive preparation involving three levels of 'leadership' – first senior managers, then middle managers, then team leaders – in shaping the content for the conference
- formal communications through a special staff update and presentations at the conference by senior managers
- the opportunity for all staff to participate in decision making during the staff conference
- the use of staff representatives from the academic board to provide feedback
- the rigour of the follow-up by managers to ensure that action plans were agreed, enacted, monitored and evaluated.

An illustration of how one of these 'stop-the-track' days worked – the first of each annual cycle – is described below. The November event provided the opportunity for a bottom-up self assessment of the strengths and weaknesses of each subject, course and business support team against a checklist based on the Ofsted inspection handbook. The sequence of stages in the consultation process was as follows:

1 *Senior managers' away day.* The first stage occurred when the senior managers spent a day in early October going through the Ofsted-based checklist, trying to identify generic issues that were recurring across the whole curriculum range.
2 *Involving middle managers.* We then cascaded this process to the middle management team in mid-October. This had three main purposes: firstly, raising their awareness about the inspection criteria; secondly, doing the same about the self-assessment process and their role in it; and, thirdly, tasking them to prioritise generic strengths and weaknesses from the initial list produced by the senior managers for their area of work and to add those they thought more relevant.
3 *Team leaders' involvement.* The next step involved what we called 'CIT leaders'. All staff belonged to either a curriculum improvement team or, in the case of business support staff, a continuous improvement team. The former could constitute either a subject or a course team. The 'CIT leaders' were the staff who led these teams – they were not managers or in promoted posts. These team leaders were brought together in late October for a workshop (in practice there were about five such workshops because there were over 100 CIT leaders) to replicate the process that the middle managers had undergone earlier in the month.
4 *Lunch with academic board representatives.* One other important pre-meeting occurred in the week before the conference. That is, during each conference the staff met in boards of study in groups of about 10 to 20 staff, so there were about 50 of these groups, arranged according to what we called 'schools' and 'business support' groups. Each board of study was chaired by an elected representative and these sat on the academic board. I invited each of these 50 representatives to one of two working lunches a week before each conference to brief them on the issues that were to be debated at the conference. They then had the opportunity at these lunches to question me, to comment generally and to clarify any other matters.
5 *A special staff update.* All staff received notice of the content of the staff conference in a special staff update, which explained in accessible terms the background to the proposals, the changes proposed and the options for decision by all staff. There would therefore have been a great deal of preparation and consultation before the day of the November conference.
6 *Principal's briefing on the key issues.* On the day itself, I addressed the whole staff for about 30 minutes at the start of the day, reminding them about how the process that

was being followed that day fitted into the whole annual cycle and how what was to be decided would link to other stages in the cycle. I also briefed them on the issues for consultation and put these into the overall context of the college's plans.

7 *Faculty groups*. Following this presentation at 9.30, staff would then often split into faculty or other groups so that the issues could be 'customised' to their contexts by their respective senior managers.

8 *Boards of study*. Each member of staff would then go into one of the 50 groups, the boards of study, chaired by academic board representatives (it was agreed that managers should not occupy these roles).

9 *Academic board*. By 12 o'clock on the day of the conference, this stage of the consultation process was complete and then the 50 representatives joined me for a 2-hour working lunch with the academic board to provide feedback.

The same format as this November conference was followed for all five conferences. That is, the preparation process always consisted of workshops for senior managers, then middle managers, then CIT leaders and then the lunch with myself for the 50 academic board representatives, 25 at a time. A special staff update was always published for each to give staff the opportunity to read, digest, prepare, debate informally and generally be enabled to come into the conference with a sense of control and ownership. I always started each conference with a highlight of the key issues, an overview of how these fitted into the annual cycle and how the issues linked to decisions made in previous years. The 50 boards of study representatives met to consider the issues and the academic board came together at the lunchtime of each of the five conferences.

A new style of academic board

The conduct of the academic board on these occasions was also very important. In 1994, as part of the culture-change programme, the effectiveness of the academic board was evaluated. The conclusion was that it was widely regarded as a 'nodding shop', with representatives sitting around a board table at which senior managers dominated discussion. The former felt intimidated and were unable to contribute effectively, frightened that they would appear ignorant in debates about 'papers' that were dense, jargon-ridden and generally inaccessible.

On the basis of that evaluation, the way that the academic board operated thereafter was radically altered. Senior managers no longer attended. Representatives sat at cabaret-style tables in groups of six. All papers were simplified and made more accessible. Agendas were limited to three or four major items. At the meeting itself, each of these items was discussed by those at each table in the absence of any manager, a spokesperson was elected for each table and the three top priority concerns from each table were reported back for each issue as they were reviewed one by one.

The discussions at these tables were called 'buzz groups' and their purpose was to provide a safe, friendly, open environment for staff to give feedback. The whole style was very informal. There was a great deal of laughter. The tone was one of mutual respect, with the disagreements depersonalised and used as a basis for genuine debate. The quality and quantity of feedback was first class and management proposals for major policy and strategy changes were regularly challenged, changed, added to, overturned and replaced.

It was also agreed that the members should generally stand aside after 2 years so that other colleagues would have an opportunity to contribute, so over a 10-year period, several hundred staff experienced this consultative process. They met me in informal pre-conference lunches five times a year and participated in six academic board working lunch workshops each year (the sixth occurred in August each year when the Academic Board met to review the outcomes of the annual staff survey). Word spread that the college management genuinely valued what staff had to say, could be trusted to receive critical feedback as 'fair comment' or as a legitimate challenge, and were as committed to the students as staff were.

In 1994 the first evaluation of the academic board had revealed that no staff representative was satisfied with its workings and this led to the radical changes described above. Thereafter, there were annual evaluations of the workings of the academic board and, as a result, there were many additional developments to the way that it worked but none of these compared in significance to the original 1994 review. Instead, they were perceived by staff as 'continuous improvements'. For example, as the college grew in size it was agreed that two additional senior managers should join the principal in attendance at the academic board, one to engage in debates and respond to feedback about provision for the post-19 age group and the other to do the same for the 16–19 age group. The pre-conference lunches were suggested in about 1996. In 1997 it was suggested that full reports of the academic board's conclusions be made in the staff update. These were all incremental changes that aimed to increase the efficiency of the academic board's working rather than radically changing it.

The academic board operated like this between 1994 and 2004. It was incredibly open and it made a major contribution to the development of the college. It symbolised the new approach to staff consultation and empowerment. Overall, the tone and the substance of what the board did was crucial. In terms of substance, the contributions that it fed back from the conferences radically shaped college policy and strategy. With regard to the tone, it was one of mutual respect, openness, fun and freshness and there was a very high level of integrity in the debates on key issues about students, teaching and learning and the direction of the college. It had become recognised as a vital and central cog in the consultation process.

Its evaluations were not only contained to the working of the academic board; they also covered the workings of the whole consultation process. So, for example, we received feedback that staff wanted to use the afternoon session of each staff conference for 'CIT business' and, as a result, the afternoon timetable of most conferences was handed over to faculties to plan and organise curriculum-led staff development by teams.

The annual cycle of staff conferences

Each of the five annual 'stop-the-track' days had a designated role and the purpose of each was known by all staff beforehand. These were as follows:

1 *The November conference* enabled all staff to be involved in the self-assessment of their own team's performance in the way described above in this chapter.
2 *The December conference* focused on the college-level self-assessment of leadership and management. At these December conferences I also reported to staff the assessment by managers of the key strengths and weaknesses of the college's

leadership and management against the Ofsted criteria, having consulted managers in the usual stages that were used in the preparation for the November conference. Every year, the academic board would identify as least one additional weakness that staff perceived to be at least as important as those identified by the management. For example, in 2003 the key weakness identified by managers was our management information system and we proposed that we should create a new senior management post and a new infrastructure to address this weakness as part of our 2004 strategy, drawing upon significant scarce resources in so doing. The staff agreed with this but they identified a second weakness as equally important in terms of the college's strategy. That was, they argued that meetings were not as effective as they should be because there was a host of practical difficulties in arranging or conducting them effectively. This issue had not been mentioned by managers at any level as a significant weakness but large numbers of staff identified it. Managers had perceived it as a matter for continuous improvement but staff perceived the scale of it as so significant that it amounted to a strategic issue. This was typical. Real strategy demanding real resources regularly emerged from the December conferences.

3 *The January conference* was about agreeing the planned portfolio of courses, the student recruitment numbers and the admissions policy for the following September. This was about the heart of the college's strategic plan. It was about whom we would serve as a college and with what kind of provision. It was about selecting our strategic priorities. It was the occasion each year when, for example, we would formally agree to introduce new courses or new areas of provision, to expand recruitment targets in some areas and to reduce them in others and how we should change our admissions policy for specific courses. All of these issues were always controversial. None of them appeared for the first time at the January conference, having been discussed at team levels first, but they gave staff the opportunity to register their views formally and collectively. Once the decisions were made at this conference, everybody was clear that, for that year at least, the debate about these issues was over and everyone knew the outcome.

4 The agenda then switched to quality standards and how we could improve them in January and February in preparation for the *March conference*. At this stage in the year there tended to be a twin-track debate: one for teachers and a separate one for support staff. The former focused on teaching and learning and was used as a collective intellectual exploration of what was new in terms of educational theory. In 2003, for example, a consultant was employed to stimulate debate about what was the most effective way to achieve outstanding results for students. He led staff in a review of research by a New Zealand educationalist, Professor John Hattie, and at the March conference the teaching community at Runshaw decided that they wanted to adapt 'the Hattie factors' to form the quality agenda for 2003–4 and beyond. There were the usual preparatory workshops for managers and CIT leaders and, at the March conference itself, there were well prepared and detailed proposals for each subject and course team to consider about how they might address the implementation of 'the Hattie factors'. Business support staff followed a different quality track. They were much more interested in process management and how their problem-solving CITs could achieve quantum-leap breakthroughs in quality in the delivery of their processes. Again taking 2003 as an example, the March conference gave them the opportunity to agree a plan for introducing a new strategic approach within a process management project plan which involved intensive training for all support staff in new approaches to process management.

5 *The May conference* completed the annual cycle by focusing on the final strategic plan for the following year. A special staff version of the strategic plan was produced for this event each year and issued beforehand in the usual way. In truth, most of the key elements of the plan had already been agreed by staff at previous conferences. For example, the portfolio and student targets had been agreed in January but there was still always something of real importance to consider, even in May. Government documents appeared at regular intervals so the May conference provided an excellent opportunity to digest them and to think through their implications for our strategy. This whole conference had a sense of 'thinking-through' what the strategic plan meant for each staff team. Part of the consultation process for the day was for each CIT to respond to the question 'do you agree with the strategic plan?' Then each was required to respond to an equally important question, 'what does the strategic plan mean for your team in terms of your specific objectives and targets for the following year?' Indeed, each team was required to reach the end of the day of the conference with a list of concrete objectives and targets that were then reviewed by their respective manager over the following month. The May conference primarily produced concrete objectives but for each team there was also an opportunity, through the academic board process, to revisit values, vision and mission – to think ahead for the following year and beyond and to check that our sense of direction did not need to change.

Acting as way posts

In summary, all five conferences each year collectively acted as our way posts through the academic year. Evaluations showed that staff welcomed them, not only because they provided real opportunities for them to have their say about top-level policy and strategy but also because it brought the college together as a community to work collaboratively as a college rather than as isolated departments or sections.

There was also a real sense of fun about the occasions. They were interesting, intellectually satisfying, an opportunity for professional growth, a chance to gain a sense of control by gaining understanding of where the college had been, where it was and where it was going. They also acted as a relief from the day-to-day pressures of the classroom or routine business roles.

It should also be said that they served to reinforce all sorts of other strategies for managing the culture. For example, the preparation workshops provided opportunities for the management team to develop its approach to being 'one united team' in steering the formulation of major new policies and strategies through the staff consultation process. The conferences, the special staff updates, the academic board meetings and the workshops all provided a focus for the communication strategies. The conferences also presented excellent opportunities for the principal and other senior managers to be 'visible', to present themselves as people who were concerned with students, teaching and learning, values, vision, mission and quality standards.

A 'Runshaw person': conformism versus individualism

The process of creating 'one united staff team' and a 'professional learning community' as described above had implications for the role of staff at Runshaw. Staff had been invited to participate fully in the culture-change process; they had been asked what they thought about leaders and about what kind of leadership they needed. The outcome was the creation of a participative community in which all staff had ample opportunity to share in decision making and which, in return, required them to accept joint responsibility. As is obvious from Chapter 3, they seized both opportunity and responsibility with relish.

This changed their role fundamentally. For example, it was clarified that they should 'like students and enjoy being with them', that 'caring' should be defined in terms of 'not accepting low standards or acting in a patronising way that devalues students by accepting second-best', that they should act consistently, follow-through and 'not compromise our rules, standards, or expectations for the sake of comfortable relationships' and that they should 'challenge inappropriate behaviour'. Staff were required to be 'co-operative', to demonstrate a 'community spirit', to 'always seek to improve and learn', to have 'high expectations', to be 'non-elitist, egalitarian and inclusive', to be 'sensitive and responsive' and 'put teaching and learning first'.

It is interesting to note that these attitudes and behaviours are very similar to more recent research (Leithwood *et al.*, 1999) in North America about how teachers there perceive colleagues whom they regard as role models. For example, they prioritise qualities like 'being committed', 'holding strong beliefs', 'fairness', 'concern for the morality of decisions', being a 'good' person, 'openness and honesty', 'outspokenness', 'being non-confrontational', 'caring and sensitivity', 'listening and being approachable', 'being positive', 'even-tempered and modest', 'being responsible and hard-working', and being 'steady, conscientious and dependable'. These words and phrases overlapped with those used at Runshaw, as they probably would at any college in which staff were invited to define the beliefs, qualities, attitudes and behaviours of those they regard as role models.

Words like 'positive', 'friendly', 'supportive' and 'innovative' became part of the everyday language at Runshaw and, as we became increasingly aware of them, they started entering into informal and formal practices. One example of this occurred when, at a retirement ceremony for a member of staff, he was described by a colleague as a 'Runshaw person' and this was defined in the kind of terms identified above, like 'being positive'. The speaker said that, if you broke the person in half like a stick of rock, he would have 'Runshaw' printed right the way through him. This was intended and taken as a great compliment: the person retiring was proud to be called a 'Runshaw person'. By inference, it was assumed by those present that others should aspire to be so described and it was assumed, again by inference, that being the opposite, that is, being 'negative', was not the sort of thing that was expected of somebody who worked at Runshaw. It was in informal situations like this that the concept of a 'Runshaw person' became established. We began to use the phrase as a form of shorthand to describe the kind of person who was imbued with our core values and who 'lived' these values through their daily display of personal qualities, attitudes, beliefs and behaviours.

Aligning our human relations processes

It was then a short and natural step, initially unconscious, to start aligning our formal processes for selecting staff with this notion of a 'Runshaw person', assessing job applicants on, for example, their commitment to teamwork, their approach to challenging poor performance and their ability to balance 'tough and tender' approaches with both staff and students. Eventually, we began to use psychometric testing to ensure that those selected already had the attitudes and preferences that were believed to be needed to contribute effectively to the ethos of Runshaw.

This consciousness of what we considered to be crucially important attitudes and behaviours also crept into our induction and staff development processes, our performance management (and appraisal) processes, our person specifications and our criteria for rewarding staff through, for example, promotion. All of our personal and human resource policies and practices were gradually realigned around a clear view about the kind of person we wanted to work at Runshaw and to drive forward what became to be known as the 'Runshaw way'.

A conformist culture?

Some people suggested that this was potentially 'unhealthy', that it was like 'cloning' people along the lines of the *Stepford Wives* and that it created a mentality akin to a religious sect. It seemed to suggest to them that there was a profound distrust of individualism in a context that focused on building collaborative and trusting relationships, that individuals who did not buy into collective action would be seen as limiting or at least not contributing to the development of the college, and that they might be seen as a fragmenting the college's sense of direction by pursuing their own ideas.

Our response to that was twofold. First of all, staff at Runshaw were intelligent and principled individuals. There was no question of 'brainwashing' them or of imposing values of them. On the contrary, one of our core values was 'valuing the individual' and this applied to both staff and students. Secondly, we valued difference, including certain forms of individualism. We recognised the power of individualism in generating and pursuing ideas, innovations, creativity and initiatives. We wanted individuals to stimulate the many debates that we held, to create what Hadfield (2003) called the 'dramatic learning moments' in an organisation.

Distinguishing between different forms of individualism

It is important to distinguish between different forms of individualism. We did not want dysfunctional individualism that denounced core values like 'opportunities for all' in favour of elitist values, and we did not want what Hadfield described as 'crass and vulgar selfishness, narrow self-interest or mindless accumulation'. We wanted what Brooks (2000) called 'higher-selfishness' where self-cultivation is about individuals fulfilling their potential:

> *It's about making sure you get the most of yourself, which means putting yourself in a job that is spiritually fulfilling, socially constructive, experientially diverse, emotionally enriching, self-esteem boosting, perpetually challenging, and eternally edifying. It's about learning… it's about finding an organisation that can meet your creative and spiritual needs. (Brooks, 2000)*

Hadfield (2003) reports that 'this is described as "healthy" individualism in a "healthy" organisation'. Brooks argues that an organisation should therefore set out to support the 'higher selfishness' of individuals, their idea of self-fulfilment and development', and he warns that there are 'dangers in not sponsoring creative individualism and of overconformist cultures . . . a lack of creativity, variety in problem-solving and insufficient criticality.'

Hence, we valued individualism at Runshaw and there was ample opportunity for individuals to articulate their different views and to pursue their different interests in the myriad of debates, action-research projects and never-ending opportunities to innovate. What we did have at Runshaw was what Tom Peters (1989) called 'loose-tight' management: that is, a very clear and well articulated set of 'tight' core values that were explicitly translated and, within this value-driven culture, 'loose' delegation based on the belief that all staff at all levels shared the same values and would therefore act in a broadly similar way and make broadly similar decisions. These values, more than anything else, were therefore responsible for defining the 'Runshaw person'.

The outcome was eventually the definition of eight core competencies for managers at Runshaw, as described in Chapter 4. The explicit behaviours that are part of these definitions were scattered by words and phrases like 'trust', 'co-operation', 'concern for others', 'integrity', 'honesty', 'responsibility', 'ethical', 'setting exceptional personal standards', 'making others feel valued and appreciated', 'showing personal enthusiasm', 'taking difficult or unpopular decisions when addressing performance and being prepared to stand by them', ' being prepared to take ultimate responsibility when things go wrong', 'having the courage to confront issues or people where necessary', 'building relationships and partnerships', 'taking personal responsibility for meeting and exceeding customers' needs', 'remaining courteous and polite at all times', 'showing empathy and patience with others', 'showing respect', 'showing sensitivity and patience' and 'acting as a role model'. It was clear that the new management style at Runshaw college had become infused by a set of values which were clearly and explicitly translated into behaviours.

THE STRATEGIC PLANNING PROCESS

Key principles

From the processes of debating these key issues in 1994 and 1995, it became clear that strategic planning was not a purely rational, logical or scientific activity. We began to see it as a process that acted as a framework for creating a climate of optimism, of pride and of enthusiasm for the future. It was as much to do with creating the culture as about developing a more rigorous, disciplined and systematic way of going about the way we conducted our business. On this basis we identified a number of key principles that shaped our approach to strategic planning.

1 *It's the process not the product that matters.* We accepted that the actual product of this planning process would often be 'wrong' in the sense that it would be overtaken by events, would contain targets, goals and objectives that might not be met and might include strategies that would not work as planned. In many ways, we regarded the process as the most important aspect of strategic planning. We saw the plan as a motivator, a guide and a route map, not as infallible, inflexible or unchanging. We

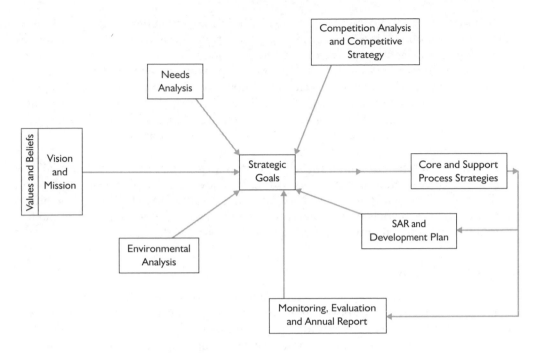

Figure 6.1 *Revisions to strategic planning*

believed that it should be dynamic and organic, developing constantly but at the same time giving us a sense of direction and keeping our vision, values and mission at the centre of our thinking about the long-term development of the college. As Preedy *et al.* (1997) said, 'strategic planning must become embedded in the culture of the organisation . . . (and) . . . is concerned with negotiating consent.'

2 *It is educative,* helping staff and all stakeholders see the 'big picture', in turn helping everyone involved in the college to face the future with confidence and to think long term. We believed that it should be communicated directly and explicitly as frequently as possible and in as many ways as possible to seek the alignment of everyone's efforts, energies and commitment.

3 *A control mechanism.* Although we assumed the plan would be 'wrong', it did still act as a control mechanism. That is, we set measurable targets that represented quantum-leap improvements in a range of key performance indicators like recruitment, student retention and achievement and financial surpluses. We also used it the basis for our annual budget, as the basis for allocating resources – 'plans with teeth' – and for detailed project plans, so all in all it acted as an effective management tool. It was also used to monitor progress thoroughly and regularly. We accepted that we would not necessarily – or even normally – achieve the planned targets and objectives, but we believed that it was important to understand why so that future planning would be properly informed.

4 *Top-led and bottom-up.* We believed that it should be a process that was top-led but which also involved significant bottom-up inputs. This chapter described earlier how the latter worked via the annual cycle of five 'stop-the-track' staff conferences. These

demanded a great deal of time and energy by both staff and college managers. So too did the preparatory workshops for managers at various levels which identified options and which formulated proposals for staff to consider.

5 *Quantum leap change.* We believed that strategic planning was about making things happen that would not occur by accident. It should be about quantum-leap change and it should be about the long term: we believed that a short-term focus would only reinforce the status quo. Nor should it be too detailed in case this created a smoke screen. We believed that the vision and mission should be simple and brief, that targets should be concrete, relevant and achievable.

6 *The basis for operational planning.* Below the top-level targets should be financial performance goals and business plans with milestones for the budget year and individual accountability for achieving measurable results. They should not contain opaque targets and goals that were written in terms that are so loose that they can be ignored or interpreted entirely differently by different stakeholders.

Being value driven

The driving force for Runshaw's strategic plan was its core values. These were described in detail in Chapter 3, which showed how they affected policy and strategy. They were important because they lent a moral tone to everything that we did. It was a matter of 'right' and 'wrong'. The constant repetition and revisiting of our core values, like 'valuing the individual' and 'opportunities for all', meant that they became our driving force and, consequently, inspired people and made them willing to be committed. I claim that what we were doing at Runshaw was incredibly worthwhile. It was not just a matter of belonging to a college community that was value driven – it meant that the personal goals of every individual member of staff became aligned with those core values and this motivated the behaviours that created high-performance standards.

What was also important at Runshaw was the way in which these core values explicitly infused the vision of what kind of place Runshaw should be. Many examples of explicit everyday policies and behaviours that shaped Runshaw's culture were described in Chapter 3, but one other is the way that senior managers constantly guided decisions about how we should manage students by saying that, for example, 'Runshaw is not a social club, it is a place for education, primarily for teaching and learning. We want students to be happy and to enjoy their experience at Runshaw, but most of all we want them to achieve examination results that will enable them to get on in their lives.' In a sense, this kind of down-to-earth articulation of what our values meant, what kind of place Runshaw should be, and how it should 'live' its values, meant that those who articulated them were the 'keepers of the values'.

Vision building

For several years we struggled with definitions of what a *vision* was. Eventually we came to understand that it explains a specific destination for staff at the college in the future. It had to be concrete and should paint a picture of the future that we sought to create. We also understood it to be linked to the concept of being 'visionary', providing a vivid and tangible picture that 'lights the flame', a 'clarion call' to excite, inspire and concentrate our minds. We found one definition particularly helpful: 'Visionary leadership engages in behaviours aimed at identifying new opportunities for his or her organisation – and developing, articulating, and inspiring others with his or her visions of the future' (Podaskoff *et al.*, 1990).

A second came from a book called *Visionary Leadership* (Nanus, 1992): 'There is no more powerful engine driving an organisation towards excellence and long-term success than an attractive, worthwhile, and achievable vision of the future, widely shared.'

Examples that we found helpful included BT's vision of a 'a phone in every home', Ford's 'an affordable car for every family', General Electric's 'number one or number two worldwide in our core businesses' and President Kennedy's 'a man on the Moon by 1970'.

The difference between vision and mission was illustrated for us by contrasting Kennedy's vision of a man on the moon with his more abstract, generalised mission 'to advance man's capability to explore the heavens'. Other examples that illustrated the difference between mission and vision were the mission of British athletes in 1952 to 'being the best we can' and the much more concrete vision of 'breaking the 4-minute mile by 1953'.

In terms of the process of producing them at Runshaw, both vision and mission were initiated by those at the top but, as can be seen from the description of our consultation process through the 'stop-the-track' days, we went to great pains to ensure that all staff shared and supported them. In line with our communication strategy, we also decided that both should be brief, concise, self-contained, specific, purposeful, realistic and feasible. Having said that they should be feasible, it should be added that we were informed by theorists that this should not stop people temporarily putting aside reason to look beyond the present to the future as they would like it to be when formulating their vision.

The actual outcome at Runshaw, in terms of our vision statement, may not seem inspiring to the reader but it did mean a great deal to Runshaw's staff and governors because it was the outcome of a long, intense, often funny and stimulating series of annual debates. Its origins owed a great deal to the vision for Pepsi Cola which 'beat Coca-Cola'! This struck a chord for us because our A-level provision – with 1800 students amounting to 25% of our college's work – tended to use Greenhead College, the best-performing sixth-form college in the annual A-level league tables, as its benchmark. Our relationship with Greenhead was friendly and respectful but nevertheless we would love to have 'beaten Greenhead' in A-level results and we aspired to do so. But of course it was absurd for a college whose values included collaboration to have a vision statement that appeared to be competitive.

That was one problem. Another was that 75% of our college was not about A-level and the majority of staff had never heard about Greenhead. As explained above, we had subdivided ourselves into 'three colleges in one', so whatever vision we created had to inspire these three separate entities and their respective staffs.

Nevertheless, we returned to explore the idea of 'beating Greenhead'! At one level, the debate about this was filled with humour but on a more serious level we explored what it was, apart from its league table position, that we admired about Greenhead. We concluded that Greenhead had become renowned and valued by its community for its outstanding levels of service that at least matched the best elsewhere. We realised that we wanted to achieve the same for each of our 'three colleges in one'.

Hence, our vision became: 'To be "three exceptional colleges in one", each of which is renowned and valued by its community for outstanding levels of service which at least match the best available elsewhere in the UK.'

I'm not sure that it would 'light the flame' for anyone outside Runshaw or, indeed, that it is particularly concrete, so it is not offered as a particularly good example of a vision statement. However, it did happen to be Runshaw's vision statement so I could hardly leave it out of this account. And, as I have already said, the process that produced it was very meaningful and stimulating to the staff who took part in it. We, at least, liked it.

But to be perfectly honest, and in mitigation, I should confess that we also had an 'in-house' vision and we did not want the world to know about it. Following our outstanding inspection reports in 1996 and 2001, we formulated a second vision which was 'to achieve a Grade 1 in everything' in the next inspection. In the event, it was very nearly achieved in February 2005. It was almost certainly an unattainable vision but it did act as a genuine goal for every curriculum area and for every business support service at Runshaw. It was inspirational and it could have been used as a public vision statement but for the fact that inspectors would probably have regarded it as a 'red rag to a bull', so it would have been a pretty spectacular case of 'shooting ourselves in the foot' had we publicised it.

One of the benefits of a vision statement like this was that it helped us avoid the danger of becoming immersed in detail and losing sight of the 'big picture'. This also explains the way in which we developed the concepts of 'annual themes'. The first of these had been the 'Three colleges in one', the second had been 'attract the top 5% . . .' and the third had been 'The New Beginning'. We continued with similar themes year after year, launching them each year at the March staff conference. These annual themes tried to encapsulate the primary emphasis that we proposed to give to the strategic plan in the following year.

The most striking thing about these themes was that they were rooted in the real issues of the college, as perceived by staff. It was the content of the themes and the vision – particularly the 'in-house' one – that attracted people to respond so positively.

There was also something about the tone as well as the content that inspired people. That is, it felt like we could overcome all the obstacles that external bodies put in our way. There was a sense of optimism among staff about the future and enthusiasm for tackling problems. There was also a powerful sense of trust among staff in their ability to achieve what had previously been unimaginable. This, in turn, generated a sense of pride and the annual vision-building process became a ceremony or ritual that symbolised success and accomplishment.

Mission statement

The meaning of the concept of 'mission' became clear to us in 1993 when we began to use a definition taken from an excellent book called *A Sense of Mission* (Campbell and Nash, 1992). On the basis of its definition, we decided that a mission statement should answer the question, 'Why does the college exist?' In other words:

• What is the college's purpose?
• Who does it serve?
• What does it serve?

In practice, we took this concept of mission to operate at a general abstract level, a desired goal rather than a specific performance like 'grade 1 in everything'.

Hence, our mission statement was much easier to formulate and agree than our vision statement. It spelled out and explained the concept of 'three colleges in one', it set out a broad outline of our strategic plan for the next five years and, perhaps unnecessarily, it included several statements that cross-referenced to our values. Although we had a separate value statement articulating our six core values, the staff felt strongly that our mission statement should also include reference to our values. Hence, our mission statement reads as follows:

> *At Runshaw, we believe that education is a profoundly worthwhile activity which has the capacity to change lives. Accordingly, Runshaw is a college where the needs of the learner always come first.*

> *We serve three groups primarily in South Ribble and Chorley through 'three colleges in one', that is:*

> *a Sixth Form College that seeks to match the best A-level provision and the best vocational provision and to provide all students with the skills required for progression; an adult college that provides inclusive learning opportunities, both academic and vocational, to meet personal and professional needs; and a Runshaw Business Centre that actively engages with the business community to meet the skill needs of employers.*

> *We aim to sustain the current size of our Sixth Form College to provide both a wide range of learning opportunities and a supportive environment where each individual feels valued. We seek to increase the number of adults participating in learning and to expand the services provided to the business community. We support all our learners with first-class facilities.*

> *In all that we do, we seek to:*
> * *instil a love of learning*
> * *set the highest possible standards*
> * *support individuals to fulfil their potential*
> * *achieve added value outcomes building upon learners' prior achievements*
> * *establish a climate of trust and mutual respect*
> * *promote equal opportunities.*

Goal setting

Our approach to goal setting was linked to our understanding of the concept of vision. We differentiated between the two in the time frame and the scope of the direction-setting activities. The vision was about our overall sense of purpose over a number of years: goal setting was about a shorter period, probably three years, and was guided by the vision. Again we found a definition by Podsakoff *et al.* (1990) particularly helpful: that is, goal setting 'aims at promoting co-operation among employees and getting them to work together towards a common goal'.

In 1995, Runshaw adopted a concept called Hoshin planning. 'Hoshin' is Japanese for 'clear shining light'. The idea behind Hoshin planning is that an organisation adopt one, two or three Hoshin goals to provide its long-term vision with shorter term steps towards that vision. The principle of Hoshin planning was that a small number of challenging but attainable goals should be set and that these encapsulate the vision. They should be tangible, measurable and exciting. They must not be trivial: they must be critical to the organisation's success. They must also be medium-term (three to five years) not short-term annual goals. Everyone in the organisation should have a sense of ownership of those goals and they should involve everyone. There should normally be a team to champion each goal, to establish baseline data, to create plans for achieving them, to communicate about them constantly and to monitor their progress. Each team in the college and each individual should set their own goals in relation to and in alignment with these Hoshin goals.

At Runshaw we always adapted three goals, reviewing them annually in May. One would usually address growth (for example, 'to recruit 50% more adult students within three years'), a second would usually address quality (for example, 'to improve student achievement to at least 10% above national benchmarks in all provision') and the third would normally address finance (for example, 'to become a Category A college'). On reflection, given that we used the Business Excellence Model and, with it, the concept of the balanced scorecard, we probably should have added a fourth goal covering staff satisfaction.

The 'vital few'

The use of annual themes partly defined our vision and partly defined our goals. To make them more meaningful, we underpinned them with what we called the 'vital few'. That is, when it came to developing annual operational plans, we recognised that there were so many ideas and opportunities for change and development that we might disperse our energies and resources and end up achieving little or nothing through initiative overload. Hence, we introduced the idea that three to five major projects could be launched each year, each with a project manager, a project team, ring-fenced resources and a detailed project plan that would be monitored and reviewed on a regular basis.

In 2003-4, for example, there were five 'vital few' projects. These were:

- a major new approach to staff development with the formal establishment of a professional development centre
- the relaunch of 'The New Beginning'
- the introduction of an assessment centre for management development for middle managers and team leaders
- a major new process management project involving all support staff
- the launch of a third centre of vocational excellence.

The inputs to strategic planning

The formulation of values, vision and mission generally operated at the conceptual, truly strategic level of the college's planning processes. On a more operational level, the college developed its plans on the basis of five annual reports.

1 The first of these was the *annual report* on the previous year's strategic plan, saying what had been achieved, what had not been achieved and why and what lessons there were for the future.

2 The second report was a *needs analysis*. This considered the inputs from various stakeholder groups as will be explained in Chapter 9. In 2003, for example, several of these identified that there appeared to be an unmet demand for construction courses. This led the governors to establish a research project looking into this issue, exploring whether local employers did actually have a skills shortage, whether neighbouring colleges were unable to cope with demand from students for places on their construction courses and the views of the Construction Industrial Training Board and other similar agencies. In the event, the report concluded that there was no justification for Runshaw introducing construction at that time. In this case, the 'needs' that were identified by stakeholders did not lead to a new strategy because, on investigation, it was found that this articulation of 'need' could not be substantiated. It was for this reason that we made an important distinction between meeting stakeholders' 'wishes' and 'needs'.

3 A third report was the *environmental analysis*. This examined the current and foreseeable changes, developments and trends that were likely to affect education and training. It explored the likely implications for the college of these and suggested what we should do in response. The most important changes were usually driven by government policy, especially those related to funding. However, other changes included the impact of new technologies, changes in the curriculum and changes to the demography, law and the political environment.

4 The fourth report was the *competitive analysis*. In this we reviewed what market we should serve, both in terms of geography and specific target groups. We looked at market share and the role of our competitors. This analysis covered the 'four Ps' of place, price, promotion and product. In our situation, these referred to issues like the location/place of courses (that is, which of our main centres or outreach centres should we offer particular courses); whether we should charge fees/prices for particular courses and, if so, how much and how fees should be paid (for example, whether they could be paid by credit card); how we should promote and advertise the courses and enrol the students; and what courses or products we should offer and for which markets.

5 The fifth and final report was the *development plan*, the outcome of our self-assessment process. This identified our strengths and weaknesses and suggested how we should build on the former and address the latter. In practice, this was a very important report and led us to focus on two or three key strategies for improvements each year. We were concerned at one stage that the concept of a development plan was being confused with that of a strategic plan, not least by our local Learning and Skills Council, which seemed to recognise only the outcome of the self-assessment process, the development plan, as significant or important.

To make things clearer, we identified five significant differences between the two, as follows:

- the key inputs into strategic planning were largely external (for example, the needs analysis, environmental analysis and competition analysis); the development plan was largely based on internal reflection
- strategic planning was about where we wanted to be in three to five years; the development plan was more concerned with annual improvement
- strategic planning focused on college-wide perspectives whereas the development plan focused on team-specific issues

- the strategic plan was built around business plans for large-scale cohorts of students, like A-level or higher education or Runshaw Business Centre, whereas the development plan was focused on the continuous improvements to be made by schools or curriculum improvement teams
- finally, the strategic plan emphasised top-down approaches whereas the development plan was essentially bottom up, based on the self-assessment process.

Learning from others

Other important inputs to the planning process were the outcomes of activities that we undertook to learn from others. Chapter 8 on staff development refers to most of these. They included the work of the professional development centre, especially its co-ordination of internal research projects, the dissemination within the college of external research and the cascading of what was learned by the staff who attended external conferences. It also included systematic learning derived from 'best in class' visits by staff to exemplary organisations, whether in the private or public sector. We also systematically benchmarked our processes – for example, a team visited South Cheshire College to explore its intranet set-up and another team visited Nottinghamshire to see an electronic registration system.

We were also founder-members of the benchmarking ALPs system for A-level; we systematically used the chief inspector's annual report and individual college inspection reports to identify excellent performance elsewhere in places that we could visit; we employed external consultants to lead our mock inspection process, asking them to tell us where we could find approaches that were better than or different from our own; and we used Ben Johnson-Hill's financial benchmarking service every two years to compare our various costs to those of other colleges. We also encouraged staff to become part-time examiners and inspectors so that they could bring experiences of other colleges' back to compare with our practices. In fact, all of these approaches were intended to identify best practice elsewhere so that we could challenge our own approaches and develop new strategies that would improve our quality.

A dynamic process

In addition to inputs from all these sources, the senior management team constantly identified the need for new strategies at its fortnightly meetings. The whole process of strategic planning was an evolving, dynamic process but the formality of producing annual reports and their injection into debates involving the senior management team acted as a disciplined approach to 'catching up', 'taking stock', 'thinking through' and making key decisions that could become central to our planning, budgeting and other resource allocation.

Competition and the environment never stood still, so the senior management team constantly had to gather information and use it to anticipate future developments. For example, the government constantly promoted major new strategies for quality improvement, for new 14–19 student strategies, for new higher education strategies and for new skills strategies.

To keep abreast of all these external drivers, we gathered information from innumerable sources. The most useful, of course, were publications by the Learning Skills Council or the Department for Education and Skills. Others included publications from the Regional Development Agency, skill sector councils, local councils' economic development departments, chambers of commerce, Businesslink, employer bodies like the Engineering Employers Federation, professional bodies like the Law Society and, very importantly, from the Association of Colleges, the employers' body for colleges.

Identifying critical success factors

On the basis of all the information that flowed from both external sources and internal performance reviews, we identified the critical success factors that would determine whether we would succeed. Put simply, we answered the question: 'In the light of all this information, what must we do to achieve our vision and mission?'

There were usually seven or eight things that we needed to do. These generally included something about marketing, improving teaching, improving student support, developing our accommodation, improving our use of IT, developing our efficiency and finances, developing our approaches to quality assurance and, finally, developing our approaches to human resource management. Hence, these critical success factors acted as the basis from which we derived our strategic objectives and targets.

Following this, the next step was to plan the detailed operational strategies that we hoped would deliver these objectives and targets. We wanted these operational strategies to be detailed, rigorous and structured, not vague expressions of 'good intentions' that raised expectations only to disappoint by failing because they lacked rigour and had been badly thought-through. Hence, we paid for three key managers to be trained in a formal project management process called Prince 2. In the event, this process proved to be far too demanding to be applied across the board at Runshaw. However, we did use its broad methodology for major, complex projects like those identified as the 'vital few' and we did adapt it for use by everyone else involved in strategic management.

Structuring the strategic plan

The structure of the strategic plan reflected the sequence in which it was built up:

- the first chapter included our deliberations that year on our top-level concepts: values, vision, mission, Hoshin goals and annual theme
- the second chapter included summaries of the five annual reports described earlier (for example, the needs analysis and environment analysis)
- the third chapter listed our critical success factors, goals, objectives and targets
- the fourth chapter contained our portfolio plans and student recruitment targets.

These first four chapters represented the heart of the strategic plan because they answer the questions: 'who did we want to serve and with what kind of provision?'

The remainder of the plan consisted of 10 chapters whose titles linked to our critical success factors and key processes; that is, marketing strategies, quality assurance strategies, curriculum strategies, student support strategies, human resources strategies, valuing diversity/equal opportunities strategies, knowledge management strategies, financial strategies, technology strategies and facilities strategies, the latter including our accommodation strategy.

The annual strategic planning cycle

The government's funding council required us to produce a strategic plan every three years so we produced a formal version that met this requirement. In practice, however, we believed that the discipline of producing an annual strategic plan was extremely useful. Hence, we developed a series of activities around the annual cycle of 'stop-the-track' days, which enabled us to respond quickly and fully to external changes and to internal evaluations and reviews of our own performance.

The outcome was a sizeable document, the annual strategic plan. It went to the governors in its final form for final approval each July. By that time, however, virtually nothing in it was new. For example, it included the portfolio and student recruitment plans and targets that were agreed in January each year.

Hence, the July version simply marked the 'end' of one cycle and the 'start' of the next. A written plan had to be agreed sometime during the year: in our case, this happened to be in July, but no sooner was it agreed than we began changing it and we did not feel concerned about doing so. One reason for feeling this was the fact that in the following August the examination results were published and, in September, recruitment numbers were known. Both of these events have a major impact on shaping future strategy so of course we should use them to revise our plans and to begin to develop future strategies.

The version of the strategic plan that was agreed by governors in July each year contained all the detailed analyses and plans that had been developed over the previous year. All had, at one time or another, appeared previously as discussion papers for the senior management team meetings and for governors' meetings. The strategic plan updated them and pulled them all together into a co-ordinated whole in July each year.

This version was not published to all staff. The reason for this was that the original papers were often technical, dense and contained confidential information. For example, the analysis of our marketing activities was included. It would not have been user-friendly or accessible and, as such, would probably have irritated most staff. For these reasons, it was inappropriate to provide staff with a copy of the full strategic plan.

Hence, we produced a staff version of the strategic plan. It went out to all staff one week before the staff conference in May so that they could prepare their feedback through their boards of studies. As already explained in the section on the consultative process, the May conference also provided them with the time to develop an action plan in their respective teams in response to the question, 'what contribution to the implementation of the strategic plan should your team make in the next year?'

As explained earlier, this conference also provided an annual opportunity for staff to review the values, vision, mission and Hoshin goals. Amendments could be made each year but in practice we arranged a major in-depth review of one of these concepts every three years or so. The mission statement, for example, would be the primary subject for a staff conference every three years.

When it was reviewed, there would be a series of pre-meetings for various groups to critique the existing statement: for example, external stakeholders would be consulted at a special annual meeting with governors, so by the time a special staff update was written for the staff conference, several criticisms and proposals for change would have been received and would stimulate debate. Normally, entirely new issues would then be raised by staff.

When such a review occurred, it always seemed relevant, appropriate and important. It was not a paper-exercise or a case of paying lip-service to a bureaucratic requirement. Consequently, it was interesting, engaged people in real debate and had an outcome that mattered and that made a real difference.

Cascading the strategic plan

The strategic plan covered the whole college's work and acted as a unifying tool. In addition, there were a number of appendices to it that cascaded and contextualised it into plans that directly addressed the student needs of our four faculties. From 1996 there was, therefore, a customised version of the strategic plan for the adult college, another for Runshaw Business Centre, a third for 16–19 vocational provision and a fourth for A-levels. The next step was to begin to produce additional subplans for specific areas of provision. For example, within the customised strategic plan for the adult college, there was a subplan for higher education, another for basic education and another for prison education.

Initially, we did not provide these subplans for every cohort of students. The guiding principle as to whether to have one or not was whether the situation for a particular area of work was distinctively different from those of others. In the example used above, it quickly became clear that there was a significant difference in the analysis of the environment, competition and needs for higher education, basic education and prison education, so a single version of the strategic plan for the adult college would have lacked sensitivity to these differences and would have been insufficient and inadequate.

By the late 1990s, we became increasingly convinced of the value in being disciplined, thorough and systematic in analysing the inputs into strategic planning and, once this was done properly, it became unequivocally clear that the plan for each 'programme' (we used this term from about 1987 to describe the co-ordinated provision for a cohort of students: for example, A-level students, access, higher education and so forth) had to be quite different. By 2002, we were beginning to complete these subplans alongside the college's strategic plan: it became difficult to know whether the subplans were shaping the college-level plan upwards or whether the college-level plan was shaping those below it.

Our focus throughout these years was primarily on how we served specific cohorts of students – 'client' groups like those on access or higher education or basic skills courses – but in 2000 we also began very cautiously to use a version of this planning approach for curriculum areas like IT or health and social care. This version focused on curriculum matters and not budgeting. The reason for our caution in producing full 'business plans' was driven by our concern not to burden our curriculum managers with such processes as business planning because we wanted them to focus their time and energy primarily on students and on teaching and learning. Hence, we never delegated budgeting to those middle managers who were in charge of curriculum areas (these were called heads of school at Runshaw), although we did so to middle managers who managed student programmes like higher education and access (these were called heads of studies at Runshaw).

During the May staff conference, after I had finished presenting the college plan, heads of faculties and heads of studies presented their customised versions for the respective student cohorts they managed, and then the heads of schools presented their curriculum plans to their respective staffs. Boards of studies would then meet to provide feedback through their staff representatives to me at the academic board and then teams (CITs) would meet in the afternoon to formulate team goals, objectives, targets and action plans. These would be reviewed and agreed in the following few weeks at meetings between the CIT leader, the respective middle manager and the respective senior manager.

In August or September, these agreed team goals would be further cascaded to the key goals for each individual member of staff as part of the performance management process (this process is described in Chapter 8 on staff development). This meant that there was alignment between the college's plan, 'programme' plans and curriculum plans at a school level, team goals and action plans for course teams and subject teams and finally, the key goals of individual staff.

Team goals were regularly reviewed at weekly meetings of each CIT and time was provided in the afternoons of all the 'stop-the-track' days for teams to monitor and review the progress of their action plans. We were very conscious of the need to provide such structured opportunities for teams to follow up the implementation of their action plans and, where necessary, 'close the loop'. Hence, we formalised this process by requiring action plans to be recorded on a computerised pro forma, and these included sections for recording monitoring activities and progress reports. These were formally monitored at monthly meetings of CIT leaders with middle managers and at an annual review with the respective senior manager.

Hence, we provided staff with a process through which they could establish 'local' team goals and regularly review these goals. We also established the expectation that teams and individuals should regularly engage in the processes of goal setting and reviewing progress. These processes and expectations were supported by a structured approach to creating consistency and alignment between the college's vision and the goals of teams and individuals. In summary, the whole consultative 'stop-the-track' approach provided the opportunity for people to work together towards the development of consensus about detailed goals and priorities.

Strategic management: the governors' role

The governors' role in monitoring the strategic plan was very important; indeed, it was their main task. The full governing body considered the five annual reports described earlier. Debates about top-level themes and goals were also considered there. So too were the portfolio plan and student numbers plan and our marketing strategies.

Each meeting of the governing body also included an in-depth review of one specific area of provision for one major cohort of students: for example, for A-level students, or for prison education, or for the Runshaw Business Centre, or for access, higher education and so on.

Apart from these top-level elements of the Strategic Plan, the full Governing Body did not do any more than approve the remainder of the Plan, delegating it for in-depth monitoring, review and development to committee level.

There were four committees and between them they shared responsibilities for monitoring respective chapters of the strategic plan and for formulating new strategies. The finance committee reviewed the financial strategy, the accommodation strategy and the most aspects of our IT strategy. The curriculum and standards committee reviewed the chapters on quality, curriculum, student support and equal opportunities (as far as it affected students). The remuneration and organisational development committee reviewed our human resources strategy, the staffing aspects of our equal opportunities strategy and any issues related to the management structure. The audit committee remained detached from the strategic plan, monitoring the way the college was conducted from the legal and financial perspective.

The senior management team's role

The senior management team met fortnightly as a strategic planning and management team. At the beginning of each year it agreed an annual schedule of policies and strategies to be considered in depth, fixing the dates in the calendar when each would be reviewed. Individual senior managers had responsibilities for these various strategies, so they then knew when they would be expected to provide detailed progress reports and proposals for future developments. Once approved by the team, these proposals would, in turn, feed into the schedule of governors meetings.

Once a month, the senior management team also met formally as a monitoring committee. Before the start of the year it agreed a list of in-year performance indicators for the various goals, objectives, targets, strategies, projects and so on. Some, like financial data, would be monitored monthly; some would be monitored half-termly or termly, and some annually.

All monitoring data were produced by an independent source. In most cases this was the quality unit. It would produce data about, for example, success rates, student absence, student progression, added value and student satisfaction. The finance unit would similarly provide monitoring data on business plans and the budget. The personnel unit would report on staff absence, staff turnover, staff satisfaction and so on.

The senior manager who was designated as responsible for the part of the strategic plan that was under review would provide an analysis of the data and propose actions to be taken in response to this analysis. Our general principle was that all data should be provided by independent and objective sources within the college, but that the manager responsible for the strategy that was being monitored should also be responsible for the analysis of the data and for formulating proposed action plans.

At the same monthly meetings, we also monitored stakeholder feedback about our performance and about any new needs that they had or that were emerging from our stakeholder meetings. Again, all this was done against an annual schedule of meetings with the stakeholders.

In practice, discussions about reports from these monitoring meetings overlapped with strategic planning business so it became the norm for us to consider the minutes of these monthly monitoring meetings at the fortnightly and strategic planning meetings, rather than waiting a whole month to follow-up actions agreed at the former.

Strategic subgroups

Below the senior management team level was a substructure of other groups that played critically important roles in strategic planning and management. For example, there were three strategic groups for each of the 'three colleges in one': that is, one for the 16–19 sixth-form centre provision, one for the adult college and one for Runshaw Business Centre. A fourth subgroup reviewed support staff issues. I chaired these and they were attended by the relevant senior managers and occasionally, by invitation, one or more middle managers.

CONCLUSION

Reflecting on what was really important at Runshaw in creating a shared sense of direction, there were probably nine key elements.

The first was the most obvious one: that is, we went to a great deal of trouble to create a strong and shared sense of direction and a sense of purpose. The decision to introduce a culture-change programme was the start of this. If one defines 'strategy' in terms of determining both the purpose of an organisation and the way that it conducts itself, then one can see that, with regard to the latter in particular, this decision to introduce culture-change represented a very significant strategic choice. The subsequent decision to build on this by the introduction of massive, time-consuming and permanent consultation processes was the second step. Without wishing to repeat all the other processes and developments described in this chapter – and in others like the chapter on communications – it is important to recognise that the senior management gave a very high priority, in terms of time, energy and other resources, to creating a shared direction and purpose. It was not left to chance and it was not easy. Any college that adopted similar approaches would have to recognise them as key leadership activities, occupying a great deal of their time and energy. Managers in colleges lack time but it was crucial that this whole approach should be unhurried. It was this factor that generated a feeling of collaboration. But we – and Leyland Trucks – judged it to be worthwhile. And academic educational research recognises it as one of the key elements in creating outstanding educational organisations.

The second element was the initiation of a range of processes that engaged staff in the collective development of a shared vision. The 'stop-the-track' days, the preparation meetings before them (usually occupying about seven days in all), the way that the academic board was organised, the use of boards of studies that included all staff – all were key processes and structures that created a strong feeling of involvement. It is interesting to note that what happened at Runshaw appears to be contrary to what theorists have found elsewhere: Lumby (1999), for example, found that involvement of staff was one of the two most significant issues (the other was securing adequate information) in hampering the development of strategic planning in colleges. She reported that 'Strategic decisions are taken at the centre and these are passed for local implementation to middle managers . . . this is one of the sources of the new managerialism in further education.' She added that the concept of 'ownership' was seen as 'unrealistic'.

The third element that contributed to effective direction setting at Runshaw was the sheer sense of excitement generated by its visions and annual themes. Staff shared a sense of pride that they could overcome obstacles, that they could accomplish remarkable achievements if they worked together to change the policies and practices. The New Beginning was a very visible and tangible example of this: people could see and feel the difference that it had made and there was a profound and widely shared understanding that the significant improvement in students' retention, achievement, attendance and behaviour had been the outcomes. Lumby's (1999) research on colleges reported that, 'the difficulties of involving staff in the formulation of the plan shade into the difficulties of motivating them to implement it once formulated', so once again Runshaw's experience seemed to be different from those of other colleges.

The fourth element is also illustrated by 'The New Beginning': it was the sense of clarity and meaningfulness about what we wanted to achieve. None of the annual themes, or Hoshin goals, or the 'vital few' projects that we created seemed at all 'managerial', 'corporate', irrelevant, abstract or obscure. They were all rooted in the staff's perceptions of the real issues and real problems. They were expressed in practical, hands-on, down-to-earth ways. They were explicitly interpreted into action plans and cascaded through the management structure to faculties, schools, programmes, curriculum improvement teams and, ultimately, into the goals of each individual in the performance management process.

A fifth key element was the way that this whole approach enabled staff to understand the relationship between external initiatives for change and the college's vision. The communications to staff via the five staff conferences each year – as well as the constant drip-drip effect through the weekly staff update and monthly briefing – meant that staff were extraordinarily well informed. And the presentations of this information included contextualised interpretations to make it meaningful for repeated staff discussions at the regular staff conferences. We went to great pains to remind people of how each new initiative fitted into both the government's existing strategy and our own. In due course, the high level of awareness that this created in staff itself created a sense of confidence that we could cope, that we would not be 'overwhelmed', 'bewildered' or 'knocked off course' as we had been between 1990 and 1993. Indeed, eventually it led to a feeling that we could turn external initiatives into opportunities for us to be entrepreneurial in furthering our vision. Hence, Runshaw became very successful at bidding for funds for new government initiatives: for example, we attracted over £500 000 to disseminate our culture-change programme, we succeeded in applications for three centres of vocational excellence within two years of the initiative being introduced, and Runshaw Business Centre developed a wide array of community and business partnerships to bid successfully for virtually every new economic regeneration initiative as they appeared.

A sixth key element was the way in which our whole approach to developing a shared sense of direction was rooted in core values. Through this, staff developed an understanding about the larger social mission of the college, of which our vision was a part. We raised our collective and individual consciousness and awareness of concepts like social justice, fairness, equality and integrity. It may, at times, have been uncomfortable to work at Runshaw but at least people did feel comfortable that what they were doing was worthwhile and how they did it was value driven.

The seventh element was the way in which this whole approach refocused the college back to student centredness. Runshaw had temporarily lost its way between 1990 and 1993, drowned by the plethora of government initiatives, but culture change provided the impetus to develop a new direction that gave us a strategic competitive edge to prosper in the new environment of market forces.

The eighth element was that this approach was, essentially, a social and cultural process, a total approach acting as a symbol to inspire organised action and 'speaking at an emotional level' to the staff.

Perhaps the most important element was the ninth and last one: that is, the whole approach generated high performance expectations. It was this, perhaps more than anything else, that linked the culture-change programme to the transformation of Runshaw from a 'good' college to an 'outstanding' one. This theme is developed further in the next chapter.

Summary

- Creating a shared sense of direction is one of the most important elements in creating an outstanding college.
- The essence of the culture-change programme at Runshaw was the introduction of a collaborative and consultative approach to this direction setting through the key process of strategic planning.
- Out of the culture-change process came a clear understanding of the key barriers to the future success for Runshaw and, with it, an understanding of the real meaning of 'strategy' in terms that addressed the real issues.
- Runshaw built on the consultative practices used in the culture-change process to construct a huge consultative infrastructure that provided staff with the information, time, structure and leadership to work together collaboratively to develop a consensus about their vision and goals.
- In all this, Runshaw radically altered the way in which the academic board worked, developing a structure that provide informed feedback in an atmosphere of openness.
- The role of staff changed significantly as they became part of 'one united staff team', sharing in decision making, goal setting and in joint responsibility.
- The strategic planning process moved from being a bureaucratic incumbrance to becoming a meaningful, positive and indispensable tool in helping Runshaw to identify its shared sense of direction, in clarifying the meaning of the issues that needed to be addressed and in developing a coherent approach to addressing them.

7 MAKING PEOPLE FEEL VALUED

The basic premise behind everything written in this book is that a college's success depends upon staff's commitment to improvement and change. Educational theorists argue that such commitment is derived from leadership that cares about staff, which involves staff in decision making and which creates a positive climate. To be 'outstanding', Runshaw needed staff to make an extra effort, to go 'the extra mile'. We believed that they would do so if they were engaged in developing the college's sense of direction – its vision and goals – as described in the last chapter, if they were motivated by the values to which they could personally relate, if they had the self-confidence, self-efficacy and self-esteem that we tried to create through the staff development processes described in the next chapter, and if the leadership of the college actively demonstrated that they valued staff by communicating with them, listening to them, recognising them through formal and informal approaches and protecting and sheltering them from overload.

Before 1994, we did not do this. Probably the strongest message from our culture-change programme then was that staff wanted, above all else, to feel valued. When they identified a prioritised list of 70 needs, the first need – the one that they identified as the most important and least satisfied – was the need to feel valued by senior managers. One of our key responses to this was embodied in the identification of the core value, 'valuing the individual'. It primarily applied to the student, of course, but we were also explicit in ensuring that it applied to relationships between managers and staff.

We realised that everything about the college – its structures, roles, policies, processes and routines – must be translated and applied by individuals. Their emotions, beliefs, values, behaviours and relationships would influence the way they did that. We believed that it was important that, as a basic precondition for a successful culture, we had to make people feel valued. Hence, we believed that it was important that we should demonstrate consideration for staff and that we should try to create a climate characterised by camaraderie, mutual respect and trust.

This chapter explains the approaches of managers at Runshaw to valuing its staff. The first section focuses on communications, explaining the three key principles and four key approaches that it employed. The second explains its seven approaches to 'listening' to staff. The third explains how we took a strategic approach to 'recognition', based on a new and profound understanding of the power of symbolism, developing a strategic approach that included six approaches. And the fourth section explains our responses to one of the central concerns articulated by staff in the culture-change process of 1993 to 1994, that is, the intensification of workloads created by the reduction in funding in the sector.

COMMUNICATIONS

Before the culture-change programme in 1994 we thought that we were very good at communication. At the end of the process we believed that we had been very weak at it, that the grapevine had 'ruled' at Runshaw, and that gossip and 'destructive spin' had distorted and miscommunicated our decisions and had presented them in the worst possible light. In short, we concluded that the culture at Runshaw was effectively unmanaged. Hence we decided to develop a new strategic approach to improving communications. During our culture-change process it became increasingly clear that we simply could not communicate enough. If the staff were to be expected to understand and appreciate what the college was trying to do they had to be involved as active participants and that meant that they had to be repeatedly informed on a massive scale.

Principles of communications

The first thing that we did was to agree three guiding principles.

1 *Every decision must have a communication strategy.* It would specify who would communicate what to whom, when and how. When we came to implement this principle, we found it surprising how long it took us to think through the best way to present information to staff and this underlined how negligent we had previously been in not having such an approach.
2 *Market to our internal customers.* We should apply the marketing techniques that we had used extremely successfully to recruit students – our external customers – for our staff, our 'internal customers'. For example, we had not thought twice about producing really professional documents for external customers but, for staff, our internal newsletter was shabby, unedited, *ad hoc,* haphazard and boring.
3 *Keep it simple.* The third principle was that all communications should be simple, accessible, meaningful, as brief as possible, avoid jargon or information overload and engage people by avoiding their business jargon.

Key approaches to communications

Staff update

A perfect demonstration of the third principle was the staff update, published each Friday for all staff. We copied the idea for it from a section in Tom Peters' book, *Thriving on Chaos,* where he describes *Stew's News,* an in-house journal in an American factory owned by Stew Leonard. It was a populist tabloid-style weekly newspaper that pulled together all the things that staff wanted to know about that week. It included, for example, the menus for the following week in the staff refectory, staff development events, job vacancies, features about the company that had appeared in the media in the last week and reminders about forthcoming activities like marketing events.

We decided that the simplest thing to do would be to replicate *Stew's News* as our new staff update and that is what we did. Subsequently, we developed the Runshaw version so that it increasingly included additional articles that reinforced our culture by celebrating its key elements: for example, we related stories about specific innovations, quality achievements and effective teamwork at Runshaw. It included responses to rumours and erroneous assumptions that were picked up from the grapevine. It intentionally reinforced commitment by trying to create a sense of pride, a sense of belonging, an awareness of shared success and it constantly reinforced our values.

It relentlessly raised awareness about the external environment, too, making sure that staff were fully informed about funding cuts driven by national policy and difficulties that these and other initiatives were causing in other colleges. It was deliberately educative as well as informative, explaining national policy developments in education, developments in teaching and learning (for example, ILT projects and initiatives) and government policy. It communicated policy and strategy, explaining these in terms that were relevant and intelligible. It also featured those parts of the college that might otherwise feel marginalised – the prison education units, the Business Centre, outreach centres and so on.

It also included a weekly page called 'The principal's diary', not a literal diary but an opportunity for me to be 'visible', to praise the successes of others publicly, to report on external meetings and governors' meetings, to answer the question, 'what exactly does the principal do?' and to present myself as a human being .

All other newsletters and memos were banned: we wanted to keep it simple and avoid a plethora of paper that nobody read. The staff update was edited by a senior manager and what went into it was discussed by a weekly group of senior managers. This was called the operations group and it was chaired by the editor of the staff update. It was printed and designed in-house, so it was not expensive, and it was evaluated frequently to find out whether people read it, which parts they liked best and how we could continuously improve it. The evaluations told us that it was very popular and very well received. People really appreciated the information flow. There is no doubt in my mind that this was an indispensable tool in creating the new culture.

Briefing

A second vital communication tool was 'briefing'. We had introduced this in 1993 before the culture-change programme. All senior and middle managers attended a two-day in-house conference centre at Matthew Brown Brewery where one of our governors was the Director of Human Relations. We received their training programme in briefing and introduced their process into Runshaw.

Essentially, briefing is a top-down process that enables the management to present information about its policies and decisions in the best possible way. It is monthly and all briefings take place at the same time so that rumours cannot spread from one group of staff, which has been briefed, to another which has not. It included both 'corporate' and 'local' briefings and we later introduced a question-and-answer session at the end of the briefing session.

One of the key ground rules was that all questions should be answered either at the meeting or within a few working days. The questions asked were recorded and reviewed each month by the senior management team at one of its monitoring meetings so that senior managers would be aware of the kind of things that people wanted to know about. It was an opportunity for listening.

The preparation for the monthly briefing had to be extremely disciplined. A great deal of time was being taken by staff attending these meetings so we did not want any briefing to be regarded by them as a 'waste of time'. Senior managers compiled the briefing as a group each month and then briefed the briefers, the middle managers, a week or so before the briefing took place at the monthly meeting of the college management meeting.

We believe that briefing was a very powerful tool in terms of communication. Some managers found it to be so effective that they went well beyond the college's basic requirement of a monthly event and had introduced much more frequent briefings. In one case, one manager introduced the 'daily shout', a 10-minute briefing, every day at 8.45 a.m. As a communication tool, briefing was powerful because it provided a systematic, structured and regular opportunity for the management to explain their decisions to staff in the most positive way possible.

But in some ways it was even more powerful as a means of making middle managers visible as 'the management'. It was middle managers who did the briefing. It was their job to explain the management's decisions, initiatives, policy and strategy and to do so in the most positive way, to 'sell' decisions as though they were their own in accordance with the ground rule of collective responsibility. In performing this new process there could be no fudge, no hiding. Nor could it any longer be said that 'middle managers don't manage!'

One of the most amusing and interesting parts of the training programme for briefing was a video showing John Cleese as a middle manager carrying out his first briefing. He starts well, authoritatively explaining management decisions but then he is slowly but surely dragged by persistent and hostile questioning by his team into stepping over an invisible line to join them in accusing the 'management' of incompetence and dishonesty.

Our managers thought that this was hilarious and completely unlikely to happen at Runshaw, especially to them as individuals. Nevertheless, we agreed that similar hostility might be forthcoming from staff at Runshaw and that it would be difficult for individual middle managers to hold the line initially, so it might be helpful for senior managers to attend briefings. Their role would be to observe the performance of the middle manager, and thereafter to provide 'individual critiquing' and coaching to him or her. Their presence would be explained in these terms. They would not, on any account, intervene in the process of the briefing. This was to be the responsibility of the middle manager. Notwithstanding the laughter about John Cleese's performance, in the first three months over 50% of middle managers behaved just as he had, some more blatantly than others.

This process really illustrated the truth behind the staff complaint that 'middle managers don't manage!' It also showed that the middle managers' response to this, that they were not enabled to manage because they had no significant role in the important processes involving staff management, was only part of the story.

Now, with briefing, they had had a very visible role but half of them could not perform it satisfactorily. It required a high level of skills, an ability to think on one's feet, an intellectual understanding and internalising of the rationales behind the decisions that they were explaining, the ability to sustain the justifications for these under questioning and to remain committed to their newly defined role of 'leader'.

For some it was all too much and it was this process that brought things to a head for them. Some needed to be helped to find a way out 'with dignity'. But at least those who replaced them knew exactly what was expected of them. Hence, there developed an improved management team composed of people who were committed to the concept of collective responsibility and who welcomed the challenge of a new staff management role.

Like everything else, this role needed constant maintenance. Briefing was part of the process that most visibly illustrated the new management style, the 'tough' and 'tender' approach that defined the role mostly in terms of 'tender' qualities like coaching, communicating, caring and supporting. However, it also included 'tough' aspects that required the middle manager to 'stand up and be counted' when necessary, to argue for change, to face down hostility, to 'stick to one's guns' and to assert high standards of behaviour, including the need for mutual respect in interactions during briefing sessions.

As ever, we evaluated the process rigorously, always checking that things were operating as they should be. The senior managers continued to attend briefings, observing different managers each month and providing confidential feedback and coaching to them on an individual basis. We also asked the briefer to evaluate his or her own performance and to evaluate the process itself, including the suitability of the contents of the briefing and the way that items had been presented.

Of course, we evaluated staff perceptions of each briefing. Initially, a common complaint was that it was 'a waste of time', that we could have communicated more efficiently in the staff update. We rejected this, believing that briefing should contribute more than the written word, and we compared the situation to that of a student who complains that all lessons are 'a waste of time' and that he or she could have read the lessons in a handout. This comparison struck a nerve for our managers, many of whom were teachers, so increasingly we began to say that a briefing should be 'the best lesson of the month', equivalent to an Ofsted grade 1 lesson. This concept set a meaningful standard for our managers.

The importance of professional documentation in communications

We did believe in the importance of professional documentation as another tool in our new approach to communications. It has already been said that the staff update was written in a populist, accessible, tabloid style. Similar characteristics applied to the production of a series of brochures produced for staff about a range of college activities which included governance, leadership, quality assurance, student support and teaching and learning. These eventually became the basis for *The Runshaw Way: Values Drive Behaviours,* a manual describing Runshaw's approaches to teaching and learning that was distributed to all Runshaw's staff as well to representatives of over 350 colleges who attended the LSC-sponsored conferences for its dissemination in 2002.

We took a similar approach to the development of our policy and strategy. Each of the five stop-the-track annual staff conferences, referred to earlier, was previewed in a staff publication that spelled out the issues to be addressed at the respective conference, the reason for the debate about the issues, the options available to staff, the advantages and disadvantages of each option and the process for decision making that was to be followed. For example, each May the staff conference was about the strategic plan for the following year. A staff version – about 10 pages long and written in tabloid style – was distributed to all staff about one week before the conference.

A more formal approach was taken to documentation of processes. Each team was required to produce several documents for all their key processes; these included a statement of policy, the description of the procedure, an induction pack for new members of staff who needed to know something about the policy and procedure, management guidelines that spelled out for managers what their role was in managing the process and the strategy to improve the process over the next year. For support services like finance, estates, health and safety, personnel and quality assurance, their processes were subdivided between those that only the support service staff needed to know and those (like, for example, travel expense claims) which everyone needed to know. By 2004, all these documents were being put on to the college's intranet. For teaching and learning, student support and other core processes, many documents were used across the whole college. For example, standard pro formas existed for schemes of work, assessment calendars, marking schemes and self-assessment. These helped to underpin quality assurance and quality control, they standardised quality across the whole college and ensured that best practice was spread efficiently and in such a way that it created a whole-college approach towards quality assurance.

But, overall, documentation was also perceived as a symbol. It was a way of visibly communicating that we knew what we were doing so people could be confident in their leaders; it demonstrated openness, clarity of thought and a sense of direction; and it communicated that we cared that people should know what was happening in 'their' college, thereby creating a sense of ownership, a sense of belonging and a sense of shared success.

Meetings

In 2001 the college hosted a research academic, Dr Margaret Wood, for several weeks so that she could identify the intangible elements of 'the Runshaw way'. She concluded that one of the most effective forms of communication that created the Runshaw culture was meetings. At management level, these included weekly senior management team meetings, a monthly college management team meeting, which all senior and middle managers attended, a weekly faculty management team meeting, centres of excellence, portfolio development groups and an infrastructure of process-management review groups led by process improvement teams. In addition, all the staff belonged to curriculum or continuous improvement teams, which met weekly.

CREATING A LISTENING CULTURE

The previous section describes the communication tools that we used to underpin our new culture but, as described in Chapter 2, one of the most powerful lessons that we learned from our culture-change programme was that it was the informal communications that were most destructive to our efforts to create 'team spirit'. Rumours seemed to take on a life of their own. They were usually very damaging and they sapped staff morale.

As has been said before, we developed as a guiding principle the belief that the management of a college had two choices: either the management could try to manage the culture or it could allow there to be an unmanaged culture. We had had an unmanaged culture until 1994, with gossip, rumour and destructive spin ensuring that 'the grapevine ruled!' As a matter of policy, therefore, we decided that we were going to put that right, that we would develop and implement a strategy for a 'managed culture', one that was based, firstly, on finding out what staff thought and, secondly, on doing something about it. We were determined to do both systematically and in a structured way, regularly and frequently and, if were really serious about doing this properly, then we agreed that all this had to be driven from the top. Hence, we adopted seven primary approaches.

1 *Finding out what was on the grapevine.* One of the first things that we did was to introduce several processes for finding out what was on the grapevine. The most simple and effective was to include on the agendas of a variety of meetings an item called 'what's on the grapevine?' As usual, we were open and candid about our approach. Everything written in this book has been explained to staff at Runshaw repeatedly. There was no sense of 'spying' on people. We simply needed to know what rumours and gossip were about so that we could either take them on board as 'fair comment' and change policies and strategies in a positive response, or we could challenge them as 'unfair negativity'. We said, clearly and loudly, that we needed to manage perceptions, whether they be fair or unfair.

2 *Staff focus groups.* We also introduced staff focus groups. We agreed that each senior manager would meet all their staff each term in small groups of about eight to 10. The outcomes of these were documented by the senior manager, circulated to other senior managers and relevant middle managers – probably those in the faculty – and reviewed at a monthly senior management team meeting that was dedicated to monitoring all such feedback.

3 *Staff surveys on the college's culture.* We also continued the annual staff survey that we first introduced in 1993, the trigger for the whole culture-change programme. That survey was mandatory for all staff and we administered it in July each year. In 1996, we began to ask staff to write the name of their middle manager on the questionnaires so that we could see whether expressions of dissatisfaction were clustered in localised sections of the college. They almost always were. We then did an analysis of all the data, identifying the managers in charge of those areas where there was most dissatisfaction, the main issues causing dissatisfaction and the ranking of their importance. We added to this a set of proposed actions and then consulted staff about the validity of both the analysis and the action plan. A special academic board met in August each year to receive the staff's response. One of the key subsequent developments in the process arose out of the academic board's request that a senior manager – initially the one responsible for human relations – should also present feedback to each group of staff in person, checking whether each group agreed with the data, the analysis and the proposed actions. The action plan for each part of the college became the basis for confidential feedback and coaching for individual middle managers and it informed the setting of their annual key goals.

4 *Staff surveys on management style.* In 1996 we also introduced a second annual staff survey, which specifically sought staff's views about management style. It was 'voluntary', unlike the other survey, but only about 50% of staff returned it. The responses that we received were very bland, what one might call 'happy sheets' because they produced very few critical comments. Hence, in 1999 we merged this survey with the mandatory staff survey that occurred in July, so we then received a much wider range of responses about both management style and other aspects of the way staff were managed. In 2002 we also began to benchmark it with the national survey conducted by the Learning Skills Development Agency and were then able to compare our responses with those of the sector.

5 *The SAR process.* The self-assessment review process was another way of finding out what people thought. This process allowed staff two separate opportunities to feedback their views on the college's leadership and management. The first was in

November when we 'stopped-the-track' to hold an annual workshop for all staff. They met in respective teams to assess their own team's performance, including the leadership of their team, the management support that their team received, the resources provided by their manager and so on. The second occasion was in December when a second 'stop-the-track' staff conference reviewed the concept of 'leadership and management' at the college level. The senior management team and the college management team, including all middle managers, completed their version of this self-assessment during a series of workshops in November so, in December, staff were then asked to review the outcome of managers' analysis and usually took the opportunity to identify additional major issues. For example, as explained in chapter 6, in 2003 the management had focused on the weaknesses of management information systems: the staff, on the other hand, identified a range of concerns about the logistics of teamwork, saying that the effectiveness of teamwork was being reduced by a host of organisational barriers. As a result of this feedback, both issues then became central to our development plan.

6 *The management of space as a communications issue.* This was perhaps the most controversial area. In 1995 the senior managers decided that, in all sorts of ways, the management of accommodation was critical to our new approach to managing the culture. This covered a range of issues, included relocating middle managers from individual offices to the workrooms occupied by their staff. We believed that if we were really serious about finding out what people thought and about making middle managers manage then we should place middle managers at the heart of the grapevine, the staff workrooms. Middle managers predictably resisted this fiercely. It was one of those rare occasions when we 'informed' them of our decision: we did not 'involve' or 'consult' them. At the same time, we demanded collective responsibility from them as part of 'one united management team', requiring them to communicate the decision and implement it positively. They argued against the decision, not on the grounds of their conditions of service but on the grounds that they needed somewhere private to coach individuals, to give staff feedback about their performance and to counsel their staff. We acknowledged that their arguments had substantial validity so we provided them with access to small rooms in which they – and others – could arrange meetings with individual staff for short periods. Did the strategy of relocating them to workrooms work? In my view, it has been extremely effective but, more to the point, we evaluated it with middle managers in recent years and they were unanimous that it was a good decision, that they should be in workrooms, supporting, coaching, communicating, guiding and challenging their colleagues, all as part of a hands-on exercise in managing people on a daily basis. So what about managing the space of the senior managers? We had been together in a management suite. We learnt in the culture-change process that this was seen as a symbol of out-of-touch, invisible, remote and ivory-tower management. So senior managers too were relocated to various different buildings around the campuses. We did discuss the possibility of senior managers, including myself as principal, relocating out of offices and 'hot desking' into workrooms. One, the director of human relations, did so for a period before ending up in a small and very modest office. The deciding factor against senior managers' relocation was not comfort or conditions of service but the probability that our action would have seemed absurd to external visitors like employers and parents.

7 *Management-by-walking-about.* The final strategy to counter the dangers of informal, unmanaged communications was management-by-walking-about. We wanted this to

be structured and purposeful so, for example, we introduced what we called 'management patrols'. These were patrols around the college sites at lunchtime by pairs of managers – including senior managers – to demonstrate to staff and students that managers were prepared to 'get their sleeves rolled up' in managing student behaviour in public areas. We had various other mechanisms for doing this, including a team of 'zone supervisors', with one for each area of the college, but the fact that managers would prioritise their time and energy to do a difficult task that we were asking all staff to do – to take responsibility for the behaviour of all students inside and outside the classroom – was a symbol of management's commitment to high standards. It also provided an opportunity to chat informally to staff, to give support to refectory staff and to the zone supervisors and to build relationships with students.

RECOGNITION

During the culture-change process, staff did not actually complain specifically about poor formal communications or inadequate structures for listening. For example, they did not ask for the staff update or briefing or focus groups. What they appeared to be obsessed with were the symbolic actions and behaviours of leaders, which seemed to indicate that the latter believed themselves to be 'superior'.

The feedback that the senior managers received from the consultant was riddled with anecdotes that illustrated real pain, anger, hurt and frustration by staff, almost always generated by informal actions which symbolised insensitivity, lack of care and respect, and the feeling by staff that they were not valued. We came to realise that 'boss watching' was a powerful part of our culture and that we communicated something every time we had contact with someone – that 'every contact left an impression'.

There were obvious examples of symbolism that irritated people – for example, the fact that we had reserved car parking for senior managers. Another was the 'ivory-tower' suite of offices for senior managers. But the most offensive symbols were often much more subtle than these. For example, one senior manager was severely criticised because he walked past staff in the corridor without acknowledging them, without saying 'good morning' to them or smiling at them. Staff felt that he was not friendly, that he did not value them, and this was important to them.

Other senior managers were accused of being ' the grey suits', speaking the jargon of the business world, posturing as 'corporate', 'strategic', 'executives' or 'directors', clothing themselves in an impenetrable mystique of expertise about funding units, 'MIS', marketing and finance. Students, teaching and learning, educational values – all seemed to have little relevance or importance to the new breed of senior manager in the new world of incorporation in which senior managers increasingly seemed to 'talk down' to staff.

Nor did staff feel valued in the way they were treated in terms of their pay and conditions of service. Obviously, the dominating concern was pay and the new contracts that formed a central part of the incorporation agenda. But it was more than that: it was the feeling that somehow the culture of the public sector implied that staff should not benefit from the kinds of comfort and support that had become commonplace in 'blue chip' private companies. For example, at Runshaw the staff lounge was small, full of boxes and files, uncomfortable and generally unused. It had fallen victim to a circle of decline in which the more unpleasant it became the less it was used, and so it was neglected even more. It was really unmanaged space and, symbolically, this sent out the message to staff that management did not care about their comfort.

So symbolism covered a vast range of behaviours and actions. These communicated far more than speeches, exhortations, declarations of support or anything else. Actions spoke louder than words. So if the leadership of the college was really serious about culture change, about communicating to staff that they were valued, about developing team spirit, a sense of commitment and a sense of belonging, then symbols had to be managed properly.

In a review of educational literature, Leithwood *et al.* (1999) recognised the power of symbolism and linked it to a model for transformational leadership that included 'providing individual support'. He quoted Podsakoff *et al.* (1990) in defining this as 'a dimension of transformational leadership that encompasses behaviours indicating the leader respects followers and is concerned about their personal feelings and needs.'

At Runshaw, we rather simplistically called this our 'recognition' strategy. In this section, the principles and approaches that we used to 'indicate' that leaders 'respected followers' and were 'concerned about their personal feelings and needs' are described.

Recognition principles

We derived five guiding principles from this core value. They were:

- everyone should feel valued
- recognition should be *true*, meaning that it should be timely, responsive, unconditional and enthusiastic
- developing the same theme, recognition should be spontaneous, individual, specific and unique
- effective coaching should be regarded as the best form of demonstrating that we value people and we should define 'effective coaching' as having a focus on the celebration of success, not on failure or blame
- the criteria for deciding what to recognise should reflect whatever we valued most, so recognition should be about teaching and learning, student success, meeting the needs of students of all abilities, teamwork and other tangible illustrations of our core values.

We were never convinced that we implemented these principles particularly effectively but, after 1996 at least, there was never any tangible evidence to the contrary in the staff surveys.

Recognition strategies

Like everything else, if we were to be serious about recognition then we had to introduce systematic and structured approaches to ensuring that it was achieved. Hence, we adopted five general approaches:

- we created a number of scheduled recognition events
- a strategic approach towards staff facilities and staff benefits
- a distinctive approach towards the management of part-time staff
- a formal and disciplined management process for planning recognition.

Recognition events

The first approach focused on the deliberate, systematic and structured attempt to introduce formal recognition processes. One of these was 'team of the month'. We introduced it in 1995 after a visit to Leyland Trucks where it worked successfully but we were very uncertain about whether it would transfer to our environment. It involved receiving nominations each month from managers or staff about teams that had performed exceptionally. In practice there were always several obvious candidates – the exams team or the estates team or particular subject teams whose students had achieved extraordinary results the previous month. The prize was a free meal in the college's training restaurant for each of the members of the winning team; this was often taken by the team together at Christmas. In addition, they attended a ceremony held before each governors meeting.

In the event, despite our uncertainties, this whole process was well received by staff. It was popular and generally regarded as the public way for the whole college to say 'thank you' to a wide variety of teams. It was also an opportunity to spread good practice by publicising the outstanding activities of the respective teams. It acted as a reinforcement of the core value of 'working together' and 'striving for excellence', and it made a significant contribution to the creation of a 'feel-good' factor, a feeling of shared success.

We also introduced long-service awards for those who had been at the college for 15, 20, 25 or more years. At Christmas each year there was a staff meeting that included 'fun' activities like very participative carol singing. One of the activities included the presentation of these awards. We would invite the staff to identify a photograph of each person (there were usually about 15) who was receiving an award; the photograph had been taken at least 20 years earlier so it would be greeted with laughter; the individual, once identified, would then come to the front of the audience to receive a bottle of champagne, a bunch of flowers, a cheque for about £80 and a framed certificate for long service. He or she would then have a photograph taken shaking hands with me – all to applause and laughter from the audience. All this was arranged by a staff committee. They paid great attention to detail in the ceremony – for example, they decided that the certificate for long service should be framed and this, in the event, made a real difference to the status of these certificates and the occasion.

We also organised a series of free social events to thank staff. These included a Christmas dinner dance, a summer barbecue, a day out on the Mersey ferry, another to the Lake District, visits to Chester each year in early August for support staff, and a variety of working lunches.

In addition, we recognised the special role of the role of the principal in celebrating collective and individual successes on every possible occasion, especially at social events like those described above, at staff conferences and in the 'principal's diary'.

Lavish staff facilities

It took one minute to decide to abolish reserved car parking for senior managers. It took a little longer to build a beautifully furnished new staff lounge with easy access to an excellent refectory and, initially, to free coffee and tea.

This latter had a more powerful impact than almost anything else we did. It communicated very visibly that we valued staff, that we appreciated them, that their comfort mattered to us and that we believed that we should prioritise support for staff over other pressing demands. At that time, Runshaw was a category C college with the lowest financial status, and we were very overcrowded so we could not easily afford the staff lounge in terms of space or in terms of the cost of furniture or renovation and we certainly could not easily afford the £10 000 a year that we spent on free coffee and tea.

Staff knew that we were overcrowded and they knew that we had financial problems so they were all the more appreciative of the fact that one of the first things that management did in response to the drubbing that we had received in the staff survey of 1994 was to provide a lavish staff lounge. It was, symbolically, our way of saying we were sorry, that we had taken on board most of the things staff had said about us, that we would try to do better and that here, on account, was one symbolic action that demonstrated our new approach.

We also provided staff with the new workrooms, with more and better furniture, computers, telephones, photocopiers, access to interview rooms and to upgraded, well-maintained classrooms. The icing on the cake was the provision of what we called 'staff havens', a number of rooms around the campuses in which staff could retreat to get away from students or other staff or from telephones or from other distractions – places of peace and quiet where they could relax or work without interruption. Again, we were symbolically saying that we cared, that we understood and appreciated staff's needs and that we sympathised with them.

The creation of subject suites was also important. Between 1993 and 2000 we constructed new buildings and extended or modified existing buildings so that, in effect, the college was 'rebuilt'. So each subject team had a workroom, a staff haven, store rooms and easy access to a cluster of subject-specific classrooms, laboratories and workshops in which they taught. They were able to create their own ethos, decorate and furnish 'their' part of the college as they saw fit, create special relationships with support staff who worked in their area, establish clubs, societies, drop-in facilities, displays and exhibitions – all contributing to the creation of an intense sense of pride, ownership and a sense of belonging for their part of the college. As Runshaw became very big this enabled students and staff to identify with their base area. This sense of pride, ownership and belonging describes staff's emotions and feelings but, on a practical level too, it was also much easier and more comfortable for staff to access their rooms, to carry resources to them, to start classes on time, to recognise their students in 'their' corridors and to form relationships with 'their' cleaners, all of which, on a practical level, made life easier. This approach was appreciated by staff because it demonstrated consideration by managers and an awareness by them of the realities of day-to-day working life for staff and students.

A strategic approach to benefits was aligned with this approach to facilities. For example, when staff lost some of their August holidays as part of the new contractual work arrangements we provided free childcare so that those with children would not be too inconvenienced.

We also operated a system whereby staff would receive a £100 subsidy for any course on which they enrolled. This meant that they could attend non-vocational as well as vocational classes that were unrelated to their jobs. The social events described earlier also fit into the category of benefits.

Changes in behaviour

More subtly, managers discussed how we should change our behaviour. Autocratic management styles were to be used very rarely, only in a few situations when firm directiveness was necessary. Managers were to stop using business language and deliberately to try to create situations in which they could show that, in common with other staff, they primarily valued students and teaching and learning. They were expected to take every opportunity to demonstrate that they shared staff educational values and vision. They were to reinstate the language of the 'leading professional teacher' instead of that of 'grey suits'.

We also decided that senior managers should, as a guiding principle, always behave in a way that would be perceived as equitable, humane and considerate. This involved treating everyone equally, not showing favouritism; having an 'open-door' policy; being approachable, accessible and welcoming; protecting lecturers from excessive intrusion on their classroom work; giving personal attention to colleagues who seemed neglected by others; and being thoughtful about the personal needs of staff.

The senior management team also decided that, as a policy, senior managers should teach, if only for a few hours a week. This demonstrated that they valued teaching and teachers, it kept them in touch with the reality of the classroom and the students, it enabled them to evaluate and experience curriculum developments in things like ILT, personal tutoring, target-setting for individual students and other curriculum developments. More than anything, it communicated to staff that teaching and learning was the college's priority – it visibly demonstrated that it was our first core value.

Senior staff also increased and formalised their meetings with student focus groups. These were minuted and the records of them were reported to other senior managers and other relevant staff. They were then reviewed at the senior management team meetings. These proved to be incredibly helpful in generating actions that improved the students' experience. It was an entirely 'customer-focused' approach but it also signalled to staff that senior managers were prepared to put their time and effort into the things that really mattered to staff and students and that they shared with staff the values of student centredness.

Caring for part-time staff

Our fourth strategic approach to 'recognising' people concerned part-time staff. In all our surveys we identified that part-time staff had a much greater level of dissatisfaction than full-time staff; there was a qualitative difference between the two. This partly led us to prioritise the appointment of a larger number of full-time staff: we believed that this was a very effective, if expensive and inflexible, quality strategy.

Nevertheless, we still employed over 300 part-time staff and we decided that there had to be a step-change improvement in their morale if they were to be effective. It is a platitude but still true to say that the student is only interested in receiving the best possible teaching, irrespective of the status of the teacher, so it was important that part-time staff were as motivated to 'go the extra mile' as full-time staff. Hence, it was the managers' job to ensure that all teachers, whether full or part-time, experienced the same levels of support, staff development, commitment and sense of belonging. It was difficult to do this and we never fully achieved it but we did significantly improve the attitudes, feelings and relationships of part-time staff and, with these, their performance.

Firstly, part-time staff were, as a matter of policy, employed by Runshaw, not by an external agency. Secondly, we included them in all communications with staff. For example, the staff update was posted to them. Thirdly, they were invited to all consultation events, including staff conferences. Fourthly, they were paid to attend staff development events. A special mandatory programme of training was provided for them. They were also paid to attend team meetings because we regarded them as curriculum-led staff-development occasions. Fifthly, a special staff manual was written specifically to address their issues and concerns. Sixthly, there was an annual survey of part-time staff morale, taken separately from full-time staff, to enable us to benchmark the difference and to identify their special concerns.

We also included them in two additional very time-consuming but very effective processes that offered individual coaching and support. These were lesson observation and performance management. So each part-time member of staff was observed three times a year and received individual feedback linked to his or her individual training plan. And each met his or her line manager twice a year on a one-to-one basis so that they could agree key goals and review progress.

In terms of facilities, we introduced a version of 'hot desking' at Runshaw, which ensured that part-time staff had somewhere to sit between their teaching sessions, somewhere to leave their books, their coats, their bags, and so forth, acting as both a practical and a symbolic way of saying that they were valued.

Finally, the management structure was designed to ensure that each team had a 'critical mass' – that it had sufficient full-time staff to give the proper level of support to its part-time staff. We also gave some team leaders time and 'management' responsibilities for supporting, appraising, coaching and communicating with part-time staff.

A *disciplined approach to planning 'recognition'*

As part of our efforts to bring the same amount of rigour and discipline to the implementation of the 'soft Ss' as we did to the 'hard Ss', we required that all middle managers submit a written recognition plan each year for their staff. We gave each manager a book entitled *One Hundred and Twenty Ways to Manage with your Heart,* so that, if they ran out of ideas, they could identify new ones.

Eventually, after six years, word spread on the grapevine about this approach and some staff perceived it as mechanistic and even cynical, so we stopped requiring a written plan. However, we did review the role of the middle manager in terms of our recognition strategy each year in order to try to find new, imaginative and creative ways to make people feel valued. In 2003, for example, we created a fund for middle managers to resource social events for their respective teams. Of course, like everything else that we did, these were all monitored to check that we did what we said we would do to ensure that we put our 'ethos into action'.

REDUCING WORKLOADS

Our fourth approach to 'making people feel valued' was related to the intensification of workloads that had occurred following incorporation. In 1994, this was identified as a major concern by the culture-change staff surveys. Staff felt that senior management in particular did not care about staff workloads and that they did not appreciate how difficult it was for the staff to meet the standards of performance required. There was clearly an appreciation that changes to workloads was part of a government-driven strategy, but senior management was blamed nevertheless.

We decided that we had to address this issue in collaboration with staff if we were ever to change the culture or to improve staff morale or to gain their commitment and convince them that we shared their values, especially that of 'valuing the individual'. Hence, we established a workloads committee, composed largely of staff representatives chaired by the deputy principal.

The strategic options

It quickly established that there were limited options for tackling this issue, given that any college spends up to 70% of its funds on staffing and has little scope to find spare resources from the remaining 30%, which was spent mostly on accommodation and other physical resources. With regard to the 70%, it was quickly established that there were three key variables that could determine the way that we allocated workloads: pay; the hours that teachers teach; and class size. It was acknowledged that there may also be some scope to change the amount spent on support staff and management staff but the benchmarking studies that we commissioned from external consultants showed that there was relatively little real scope for saving in these areas at Runshaw.

With regard to pay, the college's policy was to pay as much as possible, always at least matching the national guidelines and often exceeding these, thereby ensuring that our staff's pay matched that of neighbouring sixth-form colleges. So there was an immediate consensus that we could not reduce workloads by switching resources from pay rises. The second option was to increase the hours that teachers teach but, since we had established a workloads committee to reduce this kind of workload, this was clearly not a real option.

That left the third option, class sizes. It seemed that the only way we could release significant resources to reduce workloads was to increase class sizes. And this was the option that we chose. Class sizes for provision in our sixth-form centre eventually averaged 18 with courses at level 3 (for example, A-level) starting in year one with an average of 25 students. The national average of class size, according to the annual chief inspector's report, was around 11. We were able to achieve our average of 18 partly as a result of economies of scale. That is, we were recruiting over 3700 students aged 16 to 19 each year so we could fill all our classes. But we also retimetabled classes at the end of the first year to ensure that group sizes remained high. And we reduced dropout dramatically with year-on-year intensive strategies to improve student retention. We introduced the same approaches in the post-19 adult college, although, in addition, we reduced the curriculum range significantly to eliminate small classes and eventually ended up with an average of about 15 students per class for post-19 provision and retention rates about 20% above the sector average.

Staff-led problem solving

Increases in class sizes could also have exacerbated our workload problems, irretrievably damaging our staff morale and destroying their commitment. It was for the workloads committee to find ways around this. The fact that it was a staff-driven problem-solving team was key to its success in doing this. They produced ideas which, had they come from 'command-and-control' leadership, would have been unacceptable and would have inflamed resistance. In the event, they produced a stream of innovative ideas, four of which are described below.

1 *External markers*. The committee realised that teaching 25 students was not the source of the workload problems. Rather, it was marking the coursework produced by such a large number of students, especially for A-level teachers who marked large amounts of essay writing. Hence, the committee considered how the marking workload could be reduced. Eventually, it proposed that one subject team be invited to pilot a new approach – appointing an 'external marker' to mark their course work. The team could appoint a former colleague, somebody perhaps who had retired, or a part-time member of the team, or anybody else whose ability and judgement the team trusted, and that person could act in a similar way to an external examiner, marking some pieces of coursework almost as though they were examination scripts and providing written and verbal feedback. The team that carried out this experiment found it to be a great success. Not only did it reduce workload but it also introduced an element of quality control because the external marker provided feedback about the way that different teachers appeared to have taught the same topic in markedly different ways, with some disadvantaging their students by so doing. On the basis of this successful pilot, the members of the team then disseminated the concept to other teams, enthusing about it and reassuring others that it could work. This approach is now standard practice at Runshaw.

2 *'Joint classes'*. A similar process of piloting a timesaving innovation was a that of 'joint classes'. That is, two classes of 25 students, taught by two teachers for four or five hours a week each, were brought together to form a class of 50 students for one of the four or five hours per week, saving 10% of the cost of teaching time. In 1997 we invited 15 of our most successful teachers to pilot this approach. We spent about £10 000 on each of five rooms in which we installed 50 seats in rows and equipped the rooms with excellent audio-visual resources. We required that the one-hour 'joint class' become the 'lead lesson' for each weekly block of four or five hours. This proved to be an outstanding success and the 15 teachers who piloted it disseminated it the following year to the rest of the staff. Like the 'external markers' experiment, this pilot proved to have unexpected quality assurance benefits, which improved standards. For example, every student began to experience contact with the best teachers, the concept of a 'lead lesson' led to much greater integration of teamwork and the students had a taste of life as it would be in higher education in lectures.

3 *'Free teachers to teach'*. This kind of approach became the theme of our workload strategy. We constantly sought to 'free teachers to teach', releasing them from duties that took them away from their primary focus in the classroom. Hence, we changed the process of reference writing, employing others to do that; we employed supported self-study 'authors' to work with each team in writing study packs for students; we employed pastoral support tutors to 'chase' students, to phone home in the evening if the student had been absent; and we changed our approach to marketing, separating teachers from the process of visiting schools.

4 *Timetabling as a workload issue*. The workloads committee also identified a source of the problem of workloads in timetabling procedures. Uneven, unbalanced timetables and long travelling distances to teaching rooms contributed significantly to the workload problem. So did teaching too many different subjects to too many different levels and to too many different classes in the same week, week after week. In fact, an

American exchange teacher told us that in her state, Florida, the trade union debate was not about how many hours a week a teacher taught but how many different preparations they had to make each week. She and her colleagues had no problem with teaching, for example, 26 hours a week as long as it did not involve more than five prepared lessons a week. This represented a whole new way of thinking about the problem and, consequently, we produced a set of timetabled guidelines that limited the number of preparations that teachers were required to make each week. These were agreed with staff and administered by managers.

Did we solve the workloads problem?

These strategies allowed us to release vast amounts of money, enabling us to acquire grade A financial status, even after spending over £10 000 000 on accommodation strategies, a massive investment in information technology and an equally massive investment in all the staff-focused strategies described in this book. Hence, at Runshaw we could afford to significantly reduce class contact hours for teachers of students aged 16–19. For example, we reduced the class contact hours for A-level teachers to 18 hours per week, resourced from our strategy of increasing class sizes. But we retained 828 annual contact hours as before for such lecturers so that they could be formally required to provide subject-specific individual and small-group additional support. In effect, this was formalising what they did anyway.

When I left in 2004, the workload problem was not solved at Runshaw but it had been transformed from the situation that had existed in 1994. Workloads had been reduced significantly but, more than that, the staff had seen management joining with them in collaboratively recognising workloads to be a major concern and collaboratively trying to find a solution to the problem. At the very least, managers had demonstrated that they cared about staff and that they valued them.

CONCLUSION

The importance of the approaches described in this chapter is that, as part of an overall approach to creating a positive culture at Runshaw, we believed that we should try to demonstrate one of our core values, that is, that we 'valued the individual' member of staff and thereby made him or her 'feel valued'. By doing this, we wanted staff to become predisposed to collaborate in improving standards, to making Runshaw a better college, and to be committed to change. Without that predisposition we did not think that staff would have fully engaged in making the changes and improvements embodied in, for example, the consistent and whole-hearted implementation of 'The New Beginning', described in the previous chapter. Everything that we did – every new policy, process, strategy, expenditure on equipment and accommodation and all the other 'hard' Ss – depended upon the willingness of staff to go the 'extra mile'. As Leithwood *et al.* (1999) said:

> *The dispositions, motivations, emotions, bodies of knowledge and skills of people who belong to the school are the lenses through which the 'non-people' part of the school are interpreted. Policies, resources, structures and the like exist only to shape or influence the thoughts, decisions and eventually the behaviours of these people.*

An evaluation of the success of our approaches can be informed by the evidence of very high ratings of satisfaction year after year in the staff surveys after 1996, particularly in response to questions about feeling valued, communicated with, listened to, recognised and individually supported. After 1996, staff feelings about 'feeling valued' never registered as a significant concern in annual staff surveys, always obtaining satisfaction ratings of about 80% to 90%, but when we reviewed it with middle managers they always identified it as one of the key staff concerns. That is, each year at one of our two-day management development workshops, the college management team collectively reviewed our approaches and, no matter how much we tried and no matter what we did to address this issue, it always remained a significant concern.

The staff survey also constantly provided specific feedback about facilities – for example, the computer rooms were too hot; there were insufficient staff toilets in a particular teaching block; the staff lounge in one centre was not as good as those in others; the computers in staff workrooms took too long to start – all in themselves legitimate concerns but also always tinged by a sense of irritation by staff that such inadequacies demonstrated a lack of care by managers, keeping us constantly aware of the need to maintain the perception that we did care for staff. The social events were appreciated, although not greatly valued in themselves, and there was a feeling by managers that they were being 'taken for granted'. As already explained, there was also a degree of staff cynicism about the managers' 'written' recognition plans.

Interestingly, the staff surveys after 1996 did not express concerns about management style, pay, or about the way that the college was trying to tackle workloads – in other words, they did not express concerns about the 'big' issues. Nor were the staff facilities taken for granted – they were positively relished and enjoyed by most staff. Part-time staff, many of whom still worked in other colleges or had recently done so, really appreciated the benefits that they received by working at Runshaw and their performance in, for example, lesson observation significantly improved. And staff really did appreciate the fact that they were amongst the best-paid and most well-accommodated, well-equipped and well-informed staff in the sector, and that they had significantly fewer weekly teaching hours than staff in other colleges.

Overall, staff could see for themselves that, over a period of 10 years, it was clear that governors and managers at Runshaw had prioritised the need to make staff feel valued when they planned the college's long-term quality improvement strategies. Runshaw was an example of what the 2002 Hay Report described when it said: 'we found that many of the barriers to success claimed to operate in the education sector – such as initiative overload, poor pay and esteem – can be, and are being, addressed with the right sort of leadership.'

Overall, leaders at Runshaw tried very hard – at a personal, operational and strategic level – to create and maintain a powerful 'feel-good' factor that reassured staff that they worked in a successful college in which they could thrive. With such a feeling, staff became predisposed to engaging with and supporting the implementation of change and improvements enthusiastically. There was a real commitment to change that provided the energy for capacity building and that was one of the main reasons why Runshaw became 'outstanding'.

SUMMARY

- Educational theory recognises that it is important to the success of the institution for individual staff to feel recognised, valued and supported.
- We developed three guiding principles for our approach to communications: the need to develop a communications strategy for all decisions; marketing to staff as 'internal customers'; and keeping it simple.
- We introduced four key approaches to communications: a weekly newsletter; briefing; a professional approach to documentation; and recognition of the importance of meetings as a means of communication.
- We purposely created a 'listening culture', thereby creating a 'managed' as opposed to an 'unmanaged' culture.
- 'Listening' involved seven key approaches, including regular staff surveys and staff focus groups.
- We developed a strategic approach to 'recognition' based upon a new and profound understanding of the power of symbolism.
- This included particular approaches to recognition events, staff facilities and management behaviours.
- It also prioritised the needs of part-time staff, introducing a range of approaches that significantly improved their feelings of belonging and the standard of their teaching.
- As part of our strategy, Runshaw invested significantly in providing lavish staff facilities.
- By far the most radical recognition strategy at Runshaw was its approach to workloads. A collaborative problem-solving group of managers and staff continuously reviewed this over a period of years, constantly producing innovative approaches and sustaining a strategic focus on the issue.
- The aim was to protect and shelter lecturers so that they could focus on what was really important: students and teaching and learning.
- Class sizes were increased to reduce lecturer contact hours, and innovative ways were found to avoid increasing the burdens of marking whilst improving quality.
- The outcome of all these efforts was a significant strengthening of staff commitment to improvement and change, and this gave Runshaw the capacity to sustain its efforts to improve.

8 STAFF DEVELOPMENT

One of the central themes of this book is the creation of a 'professional learning community'. Along with new approaches to leadership, this is the key element in capacity building, the condition that produces outstanding performance in colleges. Theorists argue that there are three dimensions to creating a professional learning community:

- the personal (that is, the individual's knowledge, skills and capabilities)
- the interpersonal (that is, the team)
- the organisational (that is, the whole college).

This chapter primarily explains Runshaw's approaches to developing the personal capacity of each individual. The first section focuses upon the nine principles that underpinned our approaches and shows how these were in synergy and alignment with all the other approaches. The second section describes the infrastructure for staff development, primarily our professional development centre. The third explains the key process – performance management – that provided a systematic and structured approach to identifying and meeting individuals' development needs. The fourth specifically focuses on the importance at Runshaw of lesson observation as a developmental process. The fifth section explains the role of the professional tutors. The sixth describes the way in which we structured approaches to learning from others outside Runshaw.

THE PRINCIPLES OF STAFF DEVELOPMENT

This section identifies nine principles, all linked to our leadership approaches and to the concept of a professional learning community. Five of our six core values suggest what these principles should be. 'Valuing the individual' clearly includes the development of each individual member of staff as well as of students. 'Working together and with others' is about collaboration as a powerful learning opportunity. 'Teaching and learning is our first priority' gives a clear focus to the knowledge, skills and capabilities needed. 'Striving for excellence' underpins the notion of development and improvement and 'putting our ethos into action' demands that whatever we do, it should be relevant, practical, purposeful and properly implemented.

These values were not just seen as moral or ethical or emotionally intelligent: they were all of these but they also helped us to develop the level of adaptability and flexibility that we believed we needed to ensure that we competed effectively. We saw staff development as a competitive strategy as much as anything else. The principles that we applied were as follows.

1 *Staff development as empowerment*. The first was linked to the concept of dispersed leadership, the belief that the acquisition of personal capability is essential for individuals to be able to participate meaningfully in decision making, vision building

and goal setting, and that it is an equally essential precondition for expecting individuals to accept joint responsibility. It argues that there would be no point in inviting individuals to take on 'dispersed' leadership roles if they lack the capability of fulfilling those roles. As Hopkins (2003) argued, 'the acquisition of a range of learning skills allows the learner, whether they student or teacher, to take control of their world. Becoming more skilful and more competent is the basis of empowerment.'

2 *Focusing on teaching and learning.* The second principle was that our staff development resources, efforts, energies, processes and structures should prioritise the development of teaching and learning capabilities. This was the essence of instructional leadership. Theorists argue that, ultimately, for an educational organisation to improve itself significantly it has to improve what goes on in the classroom: 'Creating the conditions for growth in teachers' professional knowledge and skills assumes the need for significant change in classroom practice . . . those changes invariably require additional knowledge and skills on the part of the teacher' (Leithwood *et al.*, 1999). Hence, lesson observation, both by line managers and by peers, became a central element of our staff development processes, feeding into a continuous programme of training modules about teaching, provided by our professional development centre.

3 *Learning through collaboration.* The third principle is that individuals learn through working with others. We believed that 'Collaboration is at the heart of teacher development . . . there is shared understanding and shared purpose at its core. It engages all those within an organisation in a reciprocal learning process that leads to collective action and meaningful change' (Harris *et al.*, 2003). Leithwood *et al.* (1999) argued that such co-operation 'deepens intellectual stimulation' and that the route to knowledge is 'through significant deliberations with others about "what" needs to be done and "why" it is important.' Hence, action research projects, ILT projects, centres of excellence, portfolio development groups and many other structures like curriculum improvement teams, provided systematic and structured opportunities for people at Runshaw to learn through collaboration.

4 *Investment in an infrastructure is essential.* It may sound like a statement of the obvious that 'conditions most likely to foster teacher development did not emerge without substantial efforts' (Harris *et al.*, 2003) but most research at the school level suggests that such investment is not made to the degree that is necessary. At Runshaw, investment in staff development was lavish and not because we were wealthy: in 1993 we were in the bottom 10% of colleges in the published league table of average levels of funding (ALF) inherited from pre-incorporation local authorities. In one sense, we could not 'afford' the investment we made but the culture-change programme created in us a profound conviction that we really needed to invest in staff development. The process itself would not have been credible or effective if we had not provided the infrastructure, commitment and resources to deliver the training identified by the 800 individual training and development plans. Overall, we committed 3% of our annual budget to staff development. One of our key policies was that every individual member of staff was entitled to 16 days training and/or development each year. These days included the five 'stop-the-track' conferences that we provided each year for all staff.

5 *The best learning is in-house.* Whilst we did believe in attending external conferences and using external trainers, coaches and consultants, we also believed that much of the most effective training was entirely in-house. For example, our twice-yearly

management conferences, our whole-college 'stop-the-track' staff conferences, and our staffing of our professional development centre were all organised and run by our own staff. We believed that our own staff were most 'in tune' with our own needs and that they would provide well-conceived, authentic and relevant experiences for their colleagues. Having said that, I should emphasise that, on occasion, inputs from external speakers acted as remarkable catalysts for change by generating real enthusiasm and commitment from staff to new ideas and, of course, our culture-change programme was entirely facilitated by a consultant.

6 *Aligning staff development with the role of line management.* We had a professional development centre staffed by specialists and we had professional tutors – both described later in this chapter – but, fundamentally, we believed that the people primarily responsible for staff development of individuals should be line managers. They implemented a process called performance management (described later in this chapter) which defined and integrated the roles of staff manager as, amongst other things, coach, developer, communicator and trainer. We believed that individual learning could occur most powerfully through reflection on everyday experiences on-the-job and that, therefore, the people best placed to support that learning through ongoing interactions about the improvement needed were line managers. Such learning optimised the opportunities for practical thinking embedded in authentic activities and supported the high-performance culture. People could naturally develop capability by applying their knowledge to real-life problems. We saw the facilitation of this by line managers as one of their key leadership roles. This implies that each individual staff member is an active participant in their own development, that each will engage in collaborative work and each accept joint responsibility for their own development.

7 *Development as multidimensional.* We clearly believed that 'stop-the-track' staff conferences, management conferences and team structures were important ways of organisational learning but we also believed that there was an educative purpose to many other processes and structures. For example, the staff update was deliberately educative, constantly making staff aware of external developments and disseminating good practice. So too was briefing. The annual cycle of five 'stop-the-track' conferences developed staff understanding of the 'big picture' of where the college was positioned in the broader context of developments in further education. The self-assessment process enabled them to analyse their strengths and weaknesses in the context of the Ofsted criteria for excellent provision, so they learned about themselves and they learned about external perceptions and external definitions of excellence in all the key processes that they managed and for which they were responsible. The teamwork structure enabled them to spread best practice, to learn from each other, to share ideas and resources and to learn through structured reflection of their shared experience. Even within our more specifically focused staff development approaches, we believed, in principle, that some learning occurs better off-the-job whereas other kinds of learning occur better on-the-job. For example, our professional development centre provided the infrastructure for staff to receive presentations, to observe demonstrations and modelling of best practice and to try things out in simulated situations that were entirely unthreatening. But our lesson observation process was regarded as an extraordinarily powerful process for learning about how best to transfer skills and how to apply them in real situations. As explained in Chapter 4 in the context of management development, we regarded feedback through what we

called 'individual critiquing' as a very powerful method for learning. It had become the 'way we do things around here' in the 1993–4 culture-change programme so feedback and subsequent coaching became one of our norms.

8   *Co-ordinating action research.* Action research projects. These grew from the concept of piloting new curriculum initiatives. Each year, all teams were invited to bid for resources for experimentation and innovation. About £1000 was available per experiment and the money could be spent on either time or physical resources. We also provided a separate fund for ILT pilots and occasionally we provided other funds to encourage staff to develop specific strategies that had worked particularly well in other parts of the college. Two examples of these were supported self-study packs and 'external markers', the latter described in Chapter 7. The first was an approach that some curriculum teams had developed to add structure to their students' learning outside the classroom: they used the resources for which they had successfully bid to spend on materials and to employ somebody from outside the college – often a former colleague who had retired or a part-time teacher – to write the pack. The second was the development of processes to structure the use of external people to mark coursework. A separate fund was available to pay such people and many curriculum areas used this approach once it had been successfully disseminated. In 2001 we formalised all these approaches into action research projects. Each year we would identify about 20 curriculum issues that we wanted to explore. These would be researched and developed by staff in teams. They were drawn from academic and theoretical debates by educationalists outside Runshaw and we identified the issues in a dialogue with external consultants. The professional development centre proposed the 20 research topics to staff, invited them to bid to experiment with them and also invited them to suggest other potential experiments of their own. Formal criteria and processes for selection, monitoring, evaluation and dissemination were agreed. At the end of each year, it arranged a 'showcase' event for staff to attend dissemination events in which the outcomes of the experiments were demonstrated. Compared with college-wide strategies like 'The New Beginning', these research projects had a limited impact. They have, however, provided the opportunity for some staff to experiment and to develop their specific ideas. Perhaps more importantly, they contributed to the idea that teaching and learning is a respectable academic discipline, that continuous improvement does not carry a stigma and that failure is acceptable as long as it is within the limits of a controlled experiment with carefully defined and managed boundaries. The 'showcase' events also presented the opportunity for a structured approach to spreading best practice.

9   *'Just-in-time' staff development.* These arrangements were insufficient to deliver our strategic objectives. To do that, we developed the key principle that staff training had to be 'just-in-time' and, to support this concept, we needed a permanent infrastructure in the form of a professional development centre for staff development. The concept of 'just-in-time' first arose when we employed an evaluator from Lancaster University to review our information learning technology strategy. We had collectively reviewed it in 1996 with the help of a consultant from BECTA and we then concluded that our IT strategy should primarily be a human resources strategy rather than a technical strategy. We believed that we had made a mistake in leaving technologists to develop and implement it because the key issue in the development of its widespread use was enabling all staff to use the technology. It had to be a 'people' strategy involving communications, consultation, training and teamwork. It had to integrate with

mainstream processes like teaching and learning, student support and assessment. It had to be implemented and managed primarily by curriculum managers, supported by technical managers and their staff. So in 1996 we switched track but staff were still slow to take up the opportunities to implement ILT. It was then that the evaluator made a significant impact on our approach by reporting that the way staff learned was by incremental experimentation, trying out new techniques when they had the time, inclination and energy. Massive training programmes at the end of the year were, he reported from the evaluation, ineffective because staff quickly forgot what they had learned, lacked practice and consequently lost interest and enthusiasm. The evaluator argued convincingly that what would make a real difference would be a permanent infrastructure, easily accessed and user-friendly to staff whenever they asked for help – 'just-in-time' for their individual development. Consequently, we established an IT learning centre, permanently staffed with a staff IT trainer and located in a staff-only room. We also provided easy access for staff to computers, including laptops for home loan. All this had a breakthrough impact on staff development so we were then keen to explore whether we could extend this whole approach further to other skills areas other than IT, through the creation of a professional development centre, described in the next section.

A PROFESSIONAL DEVELOPMENT CENTRE

This second section explains the purpose, organisation and activities of our professional development centre, how it addressed the two key issues that threatened to impede its effectiveness, that is, access to it by staff and the quality of training it provided, and how it then widened its scope.

We regarded the creation of a professional development centre as critically important to our success as a college. We believed that our competitive strength in a fiercely competitive marketplace depended upon delivering outstanding teaching and learning and, with it, excellent standards of student achievement, retention and student satisfaction. We also recognised that lesson observation grades were a critical performance indicator – along with success rates – for the award of high grades in an inspection. In terms of our mission, the quality of teaching and learning was one of our critical success factors.

Consequently, a deputy principal was put in charge of the new professional development centre and her staff included a middle manager whose primary function was to manage it. A base for this centre was provided and this was furnished in a comfortable and user-friendly way.

One of the most important things that it did was to provide a programme of short courses on specific aspects of teaching and learning. These included courses on student management, a range of teaching methods, how to construct an effective lesson plan, the use of differentiation, effective questioning of students, setting goals for individual students, tutoring, coaching, setting and marking coursework and teaching study skills. These short courses were offered at several times of the week, including evenings and occasionally on Saturdays.

Access for staff

The first of two major problems that we had in operating it successfully was access for staff to attend. We took the view that, in principle, staff should be prepared to commit some of their own time to attending courses. In particular, if a person had been observed teaching and had received a grade and feedback that indicated a need for significant improvements, and had agreed an action plan that showed how training could support such improvement, we believed that this member of staff should welcome the opportunity to attend courses. In the event, such staff did generally choose to attend courses in their own time, possibly because the lesson observation process was experienced as a positive activity that contributed to the concept of the professional learning community.

We also recognised that there was a valid issue about conditions of service in asking staff to attend for more than their contractual hours. We did not want to create a situation where somebody could refuse to attend training because such attendance was beyond their working hours. Hence, we offered all teaching staff the option of taking three additional days leave in the summer on condition that they attended at least the equivalent time at the professional development centre during the year over and above the normal weekly attendance. In truth, we were also keen to match the summer holiday entitlements of four neighbouring sixth-form colleges as a staff recruitment and retention strategy so, in all sorts of ways, it suited the college that such an arrangement be agreed. All but three teachers accepted the offer.

Quality of delivery

The second issue was staffing the delivery of in-service short courses. In principle, we wanted to align this issue with our wish that senior managers be very visible to staff and that they be perceived as 'leading professional teachers' rather than 'grey suits' who were concerned only with 'business' matters. As already explained, we also saw our core 'business' as teaching and learning and we wanted staff to perceive senior managers as people who were in touch with the day-to-day realities of the classroom and of managing students.

Hence, it was natural for senior managers to play a leading part in delivering these short courses. This also supported the concepts of consultation and listening because staff would then have an additional opportunity to talk to senior managers about their concerns. The fact that four of the senior managers were trained and experienced as part-time Ofsted inspectors was very useful; it gave them credibility, confidence and the opportunity to draw upon their experiences of other colleges, but their time was limited so we needed other help. Some of this came from the contributions of some middle managers but it also came from that of some of our serving teachers. At Runshaw we had talked about 'sparkle' as a key ingredient in the way some teachers lit up their classrooms with enthusiasm and excitement. We later came to amend our use of this word to refer to students who 'sparkle' because we recognised that it was the impact on the students that really mattered and that some teachers could create 'sparkle' without necessarily 'sparkling' themselves in class. Whichever definition of 'sparkle' one chooses to use, in any college there are some teachers who become recognised as truly outstanding teachers; we chose to use some of these teachers at Runshaw to teach other teachers and in so doing to demonstrate their skills and knowledge.

They also provided the intensive training programme that was provided for teachers at the start and end of each academic year. This was highly focused and co-ordinated. We identified specific themes from the strategic plan and used these days to deliver training in these themes. It should be said that our strategic plan included chapters or sections on 'teaching and learning', 'student support', information and learning technology, equal opportunities and health and safety, so there was never a shortage of important matters to be addressed.

Each year we also revisited the 1996 approach to staff–student relationships embodied in 'The New Beginning' in a cycle of workshops held between April and May, so these too were included in the entitlement to staff development.

Widening the scope of the professional development centre

The professional development centre was widely regarded as an outstanding success. It had pulled together all the *ad hoc* in-house teacher training activities that had previously existed. It created a co-ordinated, holistic structure. It linked lesson observation to performance management and ensured that the training outcomes of both were followed up with high-quality training. It was not surprising, then, that we began to extend its role as soon as it had proved itself a success.

The first of these new roles was responsibility for our existing initial teacher training unit. We had operated a policy since the 1980s that all new full-time teachers should be qualified teachers and that all part-time teachers should, on appointment, agree to become teacher-trained within two years. Hence, most of the staff were teacher trained and we were not at all concerned when 'Success For All' set national targets for teaching qualifications for lecturers in colleges.

Nevertheless, each year we enrolled about 50 people – mostly our part-time staff but also external applicants – on initial teacher training courses and all of these needed extensive and time-consuming observation and visits. We constantly debated whether we should merge this activity with our professional development centre. On the one hand, there was obvious synergy in what was being delivered but on the other the logistics of visiting 50 new teachers were very demanding and might distract from the quality of delivery in an already complex rolling programme of in-house short courses. In the event, we did merge the two functions but we were never certain that this was the right thing to do.

Part of our reservation was because it was far more obvious for the professional development centre to expand its roles into a range of other in-service activities. These included the annual cycle of five staff conferences and the two intensive training programmes at the start and end of the year.

But it was also more obvious that we should extend its role to managing our approach to research and development. Part of our overall approach to research and development was, of course, the role of teams in learning from reflecting on their work. Curriculum improvement teams were required to review the effectiveness of their schemes of work and assessment plans and we even explicitly renamed the former as 'active schemes of work', reflecting their dynamic nature and the fact that constant evaluation should produce 'active' continuous improvement. But we never asked the professional development centre to co-ordinate such teamwork: this would have been too much of a burden and would have taken a key responsibility from curriculum managers.

We did, however, ask it to co-ordinate all other forms of research and development.

So the professional development centre integrated our approaches to research and development with in-service courses for our own staff and with initial teacher training, but perhaps its greatest contribution was to provide the infrastructure for a range of other training programmes that existed in *ad hoc* or piecemeal fashion for purposes other than teaching. These included a special programme for business support staff, another for part-time teachers, another for governors, an induction programme for all new staff, a management development programme for middle managers and a second for team leaders, a mentoring programme for newly qualified teachers and eventually we integrated the information technology learning centre into it.

Its scope became massive. It consequently increased its level of communication through the weekly staff update, taking up two or three pages each week. In evaluations of the staff update, this section was found to be the most widely read and the most popular. It not only listed courses about what was being offered that week but it also provided feedback on the evaluations by staff about courses they had attended. It also reported on progress of the action research projects. It described new external developments in educational theory and practice that came into the college from such sources as the Learning and Skills Development Agency, the Centre for Educational Leadership, and from articles in the *Times Educational Supplement* or the *Guardian*.

It also became increasingly active in co-ordinating staff involvement in external courses. For example, it developed the processes used to determine which staff could attend external conferences, how they should report back, how they should disseminate what they had learned and how they should evaluate the events. Pro formas covering all these processes were devised and compliance with them was monitored. For example, expense claims by staff for attendance on these external courses were linked to the completion of feedback and evaluation processes, so the claims would only be paid after the latter were completed.

PERFORMANCE MANAGEMENT

The culture-change programme between 1993 and 1995 changed our approach to staff development a great deal but the single most important approach – and in some ways the backbone of our entire approach to staff development – had been introduced in 1991 before the culture-change programme: a performance management process. The context in 1991 was the introduction of staff appraisal. This section seeks to explain its origins, the way it worked, how over time it integrated other human relations processes into it, the difficulties we encountered and how we overcame these, and the role of managers in implementing this process.

The origins of performance management

Like most other colleges in schools, we had struggled with the implementation of staff appraisal. Part of the problem was staff resistance to the increased accountability that it implied but just as important were the technical and administrative difficulties. People were sceptical about appraisal and did not trust what was going on, so they sought cast-iron guarantees that the judgements that were to be made by managers would be 'objective' and 'fair'. The whole initiative also seemed to be detached from other staffing practices. It seemed bolted-on. It seemed to have little to do with the general organisation or development of the college.

In 1991 we happened to come across a review of a process called performance management. It explained how this process could be transferred from the private sector to schools in such a way that it would integrate with strategic planning, target setting, training, development and coaching, appraisal and recognition processes, and by so doing would contextualise appraisal within a supportive framework. We were very impressed by the review so we bought a copy of the manual and implemented it quickly and in exactly the way suggested by it. It was an immediate success: it reduced fears and tensions and was received as a wholly positive way to support and develop staff.

How the process worked

The process itself consisted of several stages. The first was the completion of the college's strategic plan: in Runshaw's case this occurred in time for the fifth of the five annual staff conferences at the end of May. On the day of the conference, each team set itself key goals derived from the college's strategic plan and these were verified and agreed by the line manager in the following few weeks.

In the following September, each individual member of staff would sit down for an individual interview with his or her line manager to agree three or four individual key goals for the following year. These might be derived from the respective team's goals or they might be personal, taken from student feedback, examination results or other aspects of the individual's performance during the previous year. The individual would come to the meeting having completed a pre-meeting self-review pro forma to ensure that he or she had a sense of control and ownership over the process and its outcomes. Ultimately, the line manager could override the goals identified by the individual but, in practice, this rarely happened. If it had done so frequently then it would have been in breach of the spirit of the whole process.

In the same meeting, the individual and the line manager would complete a pro forma entitled 'Individual training and development plan'. This had to be subsequently agreed with the staff development manager if it implied a need for resources, as it usually did.

Incidentally, the existence and effectiveness of such plans and of the performance management process meant that Runshaw became one of the first colleges in 1995 to receive the Investors in People Award. This was reawarded every three years thereafter. We believed that, if the college operated the performance management process effectively, it would have been virtually impossible not to achieve this award.

Six months after the September meeting to fix the key goals, each individual met his or her line manager for a second time. On this occasion, the meeting focused on conducting what was called a mid-year review. This was a formal opportunity for coaching and for checking that what had been agreed was being implemented. Informal coaching occurred constantly as part of the normal relationship between manager and staff but this gave a structured, quiet, protected time for them to sit down and reflect on how things were going, what barriers to progress had arisen and what needed to be done to overcome these.

In September the cycle was completed with an appraisal. The key principle at this meeting was that there should be no surprises. It was not an opportunity for the manager to offload stored-up complaints and concerns. These should have been expressed as they occurred during the year. So the appraisal should have been an opportunity to take stock, to reflect, to thank the individual and to praise him or her. It was primarily intended to offer a positive experience for the person being appraised.

The appraisal occurred at the start of the same September meeting that generated the individual's key goals and individual development and training plan for the following year, so there was a natural opportunity for follow-through. Initially, in 1991, we had arranged three separate meetings each year for all staff and their line managers but the demands on time meant that we had to reduce these to two meetings a year.

Integrating other human resource processes into performance management

Over the years we subsequently integrated virtually every other human relations process that applied to the individual member of staff with the performance management process. These included job and person descriptions, updated annually and jointly during the September meeting, the action plans that emerged from lesson observation processes and the action plans developed by each team from the self-assessment process. We also added to the process constantly: for example, we introduced a professional development record for each individual member staff, borrowing the idea from records of achievement for students.

We also used performance management to implement many of our annual staff development strategies by asking managers to be proactive in promoting certain kinds of training when agreeing individual development and training plans. A classic example was IT skills. Others included personal tutoring skills, team leadership skills and counselling skills.

The process also offered the opportunity to use performance management as a way of targeting specific strategies. It enabled us to take a systematic and structured approach to the implementation of new college policies or strategies. For example, we used the process to ensure that all staff were trained in equal opportunities. Similarly, when we introduced a new teaching and learning strategy in 2003 – called 'the Hattie factors' – we were able to use this process to check that every individual was involved in planning to implement it in one way or other, depending on how each individual team had chosen to tackle its implementation.

Performance management was operated for all staff, including all support staff and all part-time staff. We thought it was really important for all members of staff to have the opportunity to discuss their own development and their individual contribution to the college's goals. We also thought it important that they receive the support, coaching and recognition that one-to-one meetings could offer.

Problems in managing performance management

There were real difficulties in implementation across the college in this way. The catering manager, for example, had well over 70 staff, most of them part time, so there was a simple logistical difficulty in meeting all of them twice each year. The same applied to those who managed prison units. Indeed, it was a problem in any programme – usually, in our case, in adult education – where there were large numbers of part-time staff.

We overcame these difficulties in a range of ways. The most common way was to involve team leaders. These were not 'managers' as such so normally we would not expect them to operate any formal staffing process that involved the potential for conflict, as performance management did at, for example, the appraisal stage. Where this could not be avoided, as in this case, we tried to avoid any ambiguity of role by saying that, if conflict did arise, the manager would then be involved by either party to resolve matters. In practice, because performance management was perceived as a supportive mechanism, this issue never became significant.

Nevertheless, where logistics permitted, we always preferred the manager to operate performance management. We regarded it as the single most important vehicle for managers to manage individual relationships and the process underpinned the key role of the manager as a developer of staff.

The role of managers in performance management

In some cases, especially in the performance of some business support managers, this role was resisted because people did not want to do it. Some cited logistical problems but in reality many used such arguments as an excuse to avoid the difficult job of managing staff. They claimed to be technical specialists, knowledgeable in their specific discipline, and not generalist managers of people.

We did not accept this position. If they were in charge of a team of staff then they had to manage people effectively and this meant that they had to operate the performance management process along with other key human-relations processes like briefing. Moreover, they were required to do it with a high level of competency, meaning that they had to be knowledgeable about how to motivate, support and develop people. They also had to be skilled in listening, setting goals, coaching, giving feedback, making people feel valued and they had to have the positive, enthusiastic attitudes and dispositions that demonstrated that they cared about the performance and development of people.

Often, they were genuinely afraid that they lacked the skills to do their job properly or they were afraid that they would get into situations of conflict and accountability that might jeopardise their popularity. But such fears equally affected curriculum managers. It was true that the latter's teaching experience would have given them more experience of managing people – in their case students – but it was essentially the same fear or lack of confidence that had contributed to the pre-1993 role which was described by staff in the culture-change programme in terms of 'middle managers don't manage!'

Having said all the above, we did come to the conclusion that it may be that a specialist manager is so valuable for his or her specialist contribution and is so poor at managing people that we had to decide to allow him or her to manage the specialist processes only. In such a case we believe that it was essential that such people did not carry on managing people.

We had at least one such case at Runshaw. The manager in question was dedicated, hard-working, committed and first class in his specialism but absolutely hopeless in communicating, in being assertive, in clarifying priorities, in delegating or in developing people. We tried very hard to develop him but failed to meet the minimum standards. Eventually, we simply let him get on with managing his specialism.

Ironically, although he admitted his weaknesses in managing people, he protested that he should be allowed to carry on managing people because, firstly, he liked to be perceived as a team leader and, secondly, he believed the loss of a team leader role would be perceived as a demotion by others. He wanted his cake and halfpenny too and this was just not acceptable.

Had we accepted his point of view, we would, firstly, have had a team of dissatisfied, demotivated staff on our hands and, secondly, we would have signalled to everyone else – managers and staff – that we would accept low standards of performance in managing staff. In a college whose core values included 'striving for excellence', we would never have signalled to anybody that we would ever accept low standards for anything.

Performance management as a case study in managing compliance

Because performance management operated for 800 staff and was managed by about 80 people at various levels, there were constant problems of compliance. People were genuinely very busy doing other really important things in September and February so finding the substantial amount of time needed – about one hour for each individual meeting – was a real problem.

We supported the process in all sorts of ways: for example, pro formas were created, staff were trained in the operation and benefits of the process and our communications processes constantly reminded people of the procedures. Nevertheless, significant number of managers did not operate the process on time for one reason or another. Nobody ever argued that it was not worthwhile or important: it simply proved to be too much of a burden for some in terms of the time required.

So we had to decide whether we would require 100% compliance. We were saying that the performance management process was the 'backbone' of our staff development and management processes, that it was one of the key ways in which we implemented our core value of 'valuing the individual' and that it was the vehicle that supported our entire approach to developing individuals, aligning their efforts with their team's goals and the college's goals. If it was so important, there was really no question about whether we would require 100% compliance. Of course we would.

The alternative would be to say 'do it if you want or if you can', effectively making it voluntary. It was a very demanding process, both in terms of time and emotional energy, so there was no doubt that many managers would have taken the option to ignore the process. We believed that this would have offered an opportunity for those managers who did not like some of the more onerous responsibilities of managing staff or who would shirk the difficulties of doing so whenever possible, to opt out of this role and responsibility.

We also believed that making it a 'voluntary' process would produce massive inconsistency and a sense of unfair treatment by many staff, perhaps even a breach of equal opportunities, and it would have undermined the efforts of all those who welcomed the process as a positive and supportive mechanism to managing individual performance and development

Consequently we did require 100% compliance. Each month the senior managers met to monitor a wide range of performance indicators. These included examination results, retention, absence and finance. It also included the monitoring of compliance of key processes, including performance management.

We would receive from the personnel unit a list of names of managers who had not returned completed pro formas. The list would be circulated to senior managers a week before our meeting so that they could check with their respective managers as to the reason for non-compliance. They would then plan to take action with the manager and reported this to the senior management meeting for the action to be noted and followed up the following month. Often these reports claimed that personnel had 'got it wrong' and had produced an inaccurate report. We spent a great deal of time ensuring that personnel did not 'get it wrong' so the onus was firmly placed on the respective managers to follow up and ensure that compliance was met.

In practice, there was a clear correlation between this non-compliance and the general effectiveness of the manager. That is, non-compliant managers would often be struggling to perform their general role as a manager: often, for example, non-compliance illustrated a general tendency to be disorganised, to be weak at planning their time or completing paperwork in an orderly way. In some cases, it highlighted that the manager could not cope with the scale and complexity of the role and was being overwhelmed. Non-compliance was not a deliberate cry for help but, in effect, it often acted as such.

LESSON OBSERVATION LINKED TO STAFF DEVELOPMENT

We had operated compulsory lesson observation processes since the 1980s, believing that the most important thing that we could do to improve as a college was to increase the effectiveness of the individual teacher in the classroom and that the most effective way to do that was by individual critiquing, providing feedback on performance and identifying specific ways to improve.

Over the years this process was constantly evaluated and continuously improved. Our policy was that there should be two forms of lesson observation, one led by managers and the second based on peer observation. Both were compulsory in the sense that all teachers had to engage in them.

The first meant that managers should observe all teachers at least once a year. The managers should be trained to operate like Ofsted inspectors. Four of our seven senior managers and one middle manager were part-time Ofsted inspectors, so they cascaded their training to all curriculum managers. The latter then operated our internal lesson observation process in the same way as inspectors observe and grade classes. They graded staff in the same way and to the same standards as Ofsted inspectors.

We were concerned that our quality assurance approach should address the issue of standardisation of grades, knowing from Ofsted reports that college managers are usually more generous in the grades they give than were inspectors, so we also operated a 'mock' inspection process called curriculum review to ensure that grades were properly standardised. This involved employing part-time external inspectors to grade lessons and to report on specific curriculum areas. This process operated continuously in such a way that all curriculum areas were reviewed every three years.

The internal lesson observation process included an action-plan stage for each observation. This was supported by a pro forma, which was used to record the grades awarded, the judgements made and the actions agreed, including all the staff developments that were needed. This was fed into the performance management process and specifically into the individual training and development plans of the individuals concerned. As was mentioned above, the observation occurred at least once a year, but this frequency was limited to those who had previously scored grades 1–3 on the 1–7 scale. For others it was more frequent and for some it could be three or four times a year.

The second form of lesson observation was peer observation. There was always a debate about whether management-led observation was 'better' or 'worse' than peer observation. The advantages of the first was that, in terms of quality assurance, it provided a reasonably reliable and valid measure of teachers' performance in the classroom, upon which we could build college-wide curriculum strategies for improvement in teaching and learning. The disadvantage was that it could create stress, it could distort our judgement about individuals and it could demotivate people.

Peer observation avoided the latter because it would be confidential, no grades were involved, the feedback might be 'gentle' and individuals could select somebody they liked and trusted to conduct the observation. The disadvantage was that this process could have lacked rigour and could therefore have misled the person being observed. It might generate complacency and fall into the category of a 'cosy and comfortable' relationship. It also did not provide grades or a performance indicator that could inform the college management about where resources and efforts should be focused for improvement.

We never seriously considered the option of not conducting management-led observation. We considered it absolutely critical to quality assurance. But we also recognised that many teachers really valued the more informal, relaxed approach of peer observation. The latter was more about reflective learning than about quality assurance. In practice, we saw outstanding examples of real learning and improvement on the basis of peer observation, especially when staff asked one of our professional tutors to conduct this form of observation. We were so impressed by the benefits of it that we began to encourage peer observation, then we began to encourage it 'strongly' and it was by then a small step to say that all teachers should participate in peer observation as a standard practice within the concept of a professional learning community. By the time this happened such a step was completely uncontroversial and went without comment by staff.

Hence, a constant stream of training needs was being identified by both processes. Sometimes patterns could be identified. For example, we noted a widespread weakness in questioning technique on the part of many teachers. On other occasions, specific needs identified by individuals were relatively unique. In both circumstances, however, there was a need for immediate follow-up, for 'just-in-time' training that covered a wide range of aspects of teaching and learning theory and skills.

THE ROLE OF THE PROFESSIONAL TUTOR

Part of our infrastructure for responding to such needs was the creation of a new role of professional tutor. This role included the delivery of short courses but it was much more than this. The professional tutor was also a mentor, providing confidential guidance and coaching to any individual teacher who asked for help. When we evaluated this role we found that it was extraordinarily popular. Many people had used it and could point to concrete benefits and improvements.

It also added to the notion of a learning community in a very overt and explicit way. It underlined the feeling that there was no stigma in asking for help. The way that this help was given was neither remedial nor patronising. The focus was on skills and knowledge, not personal qualities. It made the concept of mentoring seem very 'above-board', 'open', 'honest' and symbolic of a truly 'professional learning community'.

Consequently, we extended the model, adding three more professional tutors. They then formed a team, supporting and stimulating each other, generating ideas for new developments. One of these was for curriculum middle managers to meet informally once a month without any senior manager present and with no formal agenda or minutes. The purpose of it was to talk informally about curriculum management issues. It was to be a 'learning set', with individuals learning from each other in discussion. Themes for each meeting were usually agreed beforehand and somebody – often one of the professional tutors – would agree to lead the discussion by presenting an outline of a specific development, often drawn from outside the college. Quite often these referred to current teaching theory by academics like Professor Hattie, referred to earlier.

'BEST IN CLASS'

Another form of learning was what we called 'best in class'. This was a scheme that enabled staff to attend other institutions or organisations, which could demonstrate best practice in specific disciplines or processes. In July each year two days were identified for staff to be able to attend these places. For example, some staff would visit colleges that had achieved grade 1 in their subject or vocational teachers might visit places like Marks and Spencer to study business practices or the catering manager might attend a fast-food enterprise like McDonald's to see how it managed its catering processes. In one year, a team of physics teachers visited a research centre in Switzerland. In another year, engineering teachers visited Saab in Sweden and British Aerospace in England. On average, about 50 staff went out of college each year on 'best in class' visits and, at its height, over 200 staff went out in one year.

A similar approach guided our policy on encouraging staff to be active participants in external networks and professional associations. One specific policy was that at least one teacher from each subject team should be an external examiner or verifier in that subject. Another policy was that we strongly encouraged people to become part-time inspectors.

Having said all this, Runshaw was also characterised by an absolute belief that 'teaching and learning was our first priority' so staff absence for any reason – including external activities like attending courses – was only permitted within manageable limitations that avoided disruption to the students' learning. Our policy was that all lessons must be covered by a teacher and preferably by the teacher who was timetabled for that lesson.

A similar approach operated at management level. Whilst, in principle, we agreed that people should learn from external contacts, in practice we strongly managed and limited external activities to ensure that they did not interfere with the smooth running of the college. There was undoubtedly a balance to be struck in this, but at Runshaw the balance was weighted firmly in the direction of hands-on management in the college rather than outside it.

CONCLUSION

Staff development focused on creating a professional learning community at Runshaw. The specific approaches used illustrate the general commitment to creating such a community. Other colleges probably use approaches that are equally effective in doing this. The purpose of this chapter is not, therefore, to argue that a college should adopt the specific approaches that Runshaw used. Rather, it argues that the competitive strategy of any college should include staff development as a critical success factor. We believed that, to survive and prosper, a college needs to develop a very high level of capacity, meaning collective competence, if it is to tackle its problems and to control its development effectively. The development of that capacity and competence cannot be left to chance. There has to be a systematic and structured approach to invest heavily in the development of its staff.

This chapter also argues that the staff development programme must focus primarily on the individual as well as on the team. At Runshaw, performance management was a process linking goal setting at various levels, including the individual level, with coaching, training, development, appraisal and recognition. It met our cultural needs because it provided the structure for positive relationships, it removed the threat from appraisal and it emphasised concepts like dialogue, listening and coaching. There may be alternatives to performance management that work equally well in other colleges but, ultimately, every college needs an approach that focuses on individuals and that links their development needs to the college's goals and to the individual's own performance.

Such a systematic and structured approach to identifying individuals' needs implies that there should be an equally structured approach to responding to those needs. Resources have to be committed and focused. Flexible arrangements need to be made in providing a wide range of training programmes to a range of different staff groupings. Each group has a different set of needs and every college should practise the concept of differentiation for these staff groupings as professionally as it should practise it for students. A professional development centre may be or may not be a good idea for individual colleges but the way that it was operated at Runshaw does illustrate the kind of resource provision, commitment and infrastructure that is needed in any college if it is to turn the concept of a professional learning community into reality.

Finally, lesson observation and related processes like that of curriculum review, as practised at Runshaw, illustrate that learning occurs in several different ways. For example, people learn through structured reflection on their experience as well as by attending courses. At Runshaw, we provided opportunities for people to learn in a simulated environment with 'micro-teaching' in the relative safety of the workshop, but we also recognised the power of learning by individuals on the basis of feedback and individual critiquing. If presented in a supportive, positive, caring and coaching way, with specific actions identified that will lead to improvement, we believed that this is the most effective way for people to improve. In our case, we operated both management-led lesson observation and peer observation but we saw no fundamental difference between the way that feedback should be given: in both cases, it should emphasise praise and identify improvement opportunities, precisely the same way that a teacher should provide feedback to a student.

We did not experience the tensions and conflict that some colleges experience with lesson observation processes. We would explain this by referring to the reduction of disagreements and conflicts that occurred as a result of our culture-change programme which is described in earlier chapters and about the importance of developing positive relationships based on trust and mutual respect.

We also believed that achieving this requires a high level of competence on the part of managers.

SUMMARY

- This chapter focuses on the development of individual staff, noting that the ways that team and organisational learning occurred are described in other chapters.
- There were nine principles behind our approach to staff development.
- We invested significantly in creating a professional development centre.
- Two key barriers to its success needed to be overcome – providing easy access for staff and ensuring that the delivery of staff development was the highest quality.
- We widened the scope of our professional development centre to cover support staff, managers, governors, whole-college conferences, part-time staff and action research.
- The backbone to our entire approach to develop the individual was a process called performance management.
- We integrated virtually every other human resource process into it.
- There were major problems in implementing it, the most significant of which was the role of middle managers in staff management.
- Lesson observation was a critically important link to staff development.
- We created a number of professional tutors' roles and these were significant to our overall approach.
- We purposefully learned from external sources, deploying, for example, a process called 'best in class' in which over 200 staff went out of college in one year to visit other organisations.

9 QUALITY MANAGEMENT USING THE BUSINESS EXCELLENCE MODEL

One of the most puzzling things about the development of further education since about 1990 has been the almost complete absence of debate about the most widely recognised and commonly used quality management framework in both the private sector and the rest of the public sector – the Business Excellence Model – and, in particular, its focus on the concept of 'processes'. This is especially puzzling when one considers that concerns about 'quality assurance' have, along with finance and growth, occupied the greatest attention of successive government ministers and officials over the last decade.

By the mid- to late-1990s it had become very clear that some colleges achieved very high quality standards with relatively low financial resources and that, conversely, some achieved poor quality with relatively high funding. Hence, the annual reports of the chief inspector throughout the 1990s constantly argued that there was little correlation between quality standards and levels of funding. Runshaw's experience is an example that substantiates this. We achieved a grade 1 for quality assurance in all inspection cycles but we had been the tenth worst-funded college in the sector in 1993 with an average level of funding (ALF) of £14.43 compared to many colleges with over £30 or even £40 that achieved much lower standards. This kind of example enabled the inspectors to underline the fundamental weaknesses in 'quality assurance' in many colleges and to focus on this – not lack of funding – as the explanation for poor performance in many colleges. Even when compared with other aspects of management, quality assurance was clearly very weak. For example, the results of the first and second cycles of inspections of the 450 colleges in England produced only a handful of grade 1s for quality assurance (there were, in fact, about 14 in each cycle) whereas there were 50 to 60 grade 1s for each of the other cross-college elements like student support, resources, responsiveness and leadership. Ironically, the one element – quality assurance – that really seemed to make a difference to quality standards and financial wellbeing was by far the weakest element in the college sector. What really mattered was done least well.

Why were there such differences in performance? Essentially, the answer is the same as for any system where things are left to chance and where there is no systematic or consistent approach to create and achieve high standards. The same would apply to a college – as it did to Runshaw in 1984 – in which some individual managers and some individual lecturers excelled, whilst others, perhaps a majority, provided weak or inconsistent performances.

This chapter seeks to explain Runshaw's approach to 'what really mattered' – to quality management and to quality assurance. In doing so, it explains the background, fundamental concepts and the key elements of the Business Excellence Model, why and how Runshaw adopted it in 1995, and how the five 'enablers' helped to shape our approaches to quality management. Three of these – our approaches to 'leadership', 'strategy' and 'people' management – have already been explained in previous chapters. Two have not: they are our approaches to 'customers' and to 'processes', so this chapter focuses on these in subsequent sections. This chapter explains our approach to continuous improvement at the grass-root level through a permanent structure of teams involving all staff in measuring, reviewing and planning improvements to their everyday tasks and the processes they own.

THE BUSINESS EXCELLENCE MODEL

Origins and background

In Japan in the 1950s, Dr W. Edwards Deming, an American statistician, was appointed advisor to the Japanese government with the remit to help the country repair its economy. He is widely credited as the founder of the continuous improvement movement and his teaching instilled principles of improvement, quality, productivity and service, leading to Japan hitting its peak in the 1980s, forcing many US industries to their knees and prompting Americans to rediscover Deming's ideas. In response, the Baldridge Award was created in the US in 1988.

In the footsteps of the Baldridge example, the European Foundation for Quality Management (EFQM) was formed in 1988 by the heads of 14 of the most influential companies in Europe. They created what was then called the EFQM Business Excellence Model, building on the best of the US and Japanese models. The EFQM created the first European Quality Awards in 1992 and 1993 and supported the formation of the British Quality Foundation (BQF) as licensed custodian of the model in the UK, with the first UK Awards being made in 1994.

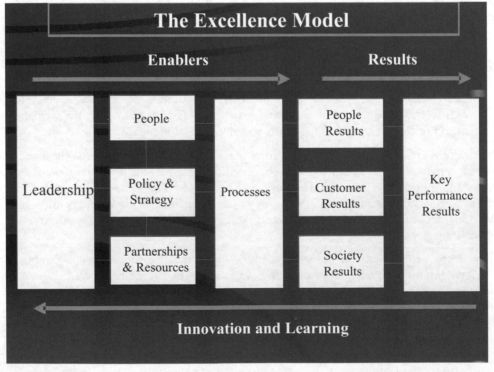

Figure 9.1   *The excellence model® The EFQM Excellence Model is a registered trademark of EFQM.*

During 1999 the model was improved and renamed the EFQM Excellence Model, the word 'business' being dropped in recognition of the increasing number of not-for-profit and public sector members. In fact, much of the recent growth in the model's use in the UK and the rest of Europe is in the public sector. America has taken the lead in the education sector in so far as the Baldridge Model began its pilot stage there some five years ago, with notable success.

From its birth in principle with Deming to the present day, the use of the excellence model has brought spectacular success for some organisations and saved many. Its following in the private and public sectors, and in government, continues to expand. There are certainly tens of thousands and probably hundreds of thousands of European organisations using it today.

When asked why they use the model, the answer many people give is that it is simply a great way to bring people together to run an organisation and is one of the best approaches to self-assessment. It is internationally acclaimed, growing in recognition, trusted, and its use produces results. The model has been described as 'Looking into a mirror, and being prepared not to like everything you see' and, if applied in that way, it is self-assessment with rigour. The assumption behind the model is that, regardless of sector, size, structure or maturity, to be successful organisations need to establish an appropriate management system. The EFQM Excellence Model is a practical tool to help do this by assessing how the organisation is doing, helping to understand what can be improved and stimulating ways forward. The EFQM researches and updates the model with the inputs of tested good practices from thousands of organisations both within and outside Europe. In this way the model remains dynamic and in line with current thinking.

There are many indicators pointing towards the increased use of the model in the public sector. For example, the Higher Education Funding Council for England (HEFCE) strategic plan in 2000 describes the model as an 'internationally recognised framework for high quality management practices' and it was HEFCE's aim to 'be among the top 20 per cent of public sector organisations as measured by the Excellence Model' by 2004. Around half a million government employees in hundreds of departments and agencies are actively engaged in using the model.

The project was run from the Cabinet Office and it declared two priority sectors for the model's implementation: the health sector and the education sector. In the schools sector, over 4000 schools use it as the basis of their self-assessment framework and it has been formally endorsed for use in schools by the Secretary of State for Education and Skills. As part of a project at Runshaw College in 2003 to disseminate the use of the excellence model in further education, the Minister of State for Lifelong Learning and Higher Education gave her endorsement as did the Chief Executive of the Learning Skills Council. Notwithstanding this, very few colleges actually use it.

The fundamental concepts

The EFQM's espoused route to better management through the excellence model involves rigorous self-assessment against a framework, defining 'excellence' as 'outstanding practice in managing an organisation and achieving results, all based on a set of eight fundamental concepts.' These eight fundamental concepts are the distillation of what the 14 founding companies of the EFQM decided were the most important and basic principles on which they ran their organisations. To put it another way, they are the underlying values of their philosophy of excellence. They are:

- leadership and constancy of purpose
- people development and involvement
- partnership development
- corporate social responsibility
- continuous learning, innovation and improvement
- results orientation
- customer focus
- management by process and fact.

The concept of 'leadership and constancy of purpose' suggests that the behaviour of an organisation's leaders should create a clarity and unity of purpose within the organisation and an environment in which the organisation and its people can excel.

The concept of 'people development and involvement' is about releasing the full potential of an organisation's people through shared values and a culture of trust and empowerment that encourages the involvement of everyone, thereby helping to create a motivated workforce with good morale and the competence to do the job well. Runshaw's approach to these two concepts were explained in Chapters 3, 6, 7, and 8.

The concept of 'partnership development' is about the notion that an organisation works more effectively when it has mutually beneficial relationships that are built on trust, sharing of knowledge and integration with its partners. Runshaw's approach to this is described in Chapter 3 in the section on 'working together and with others'. The concept of 'corporate social responsibility' argues that the long-term interests of an organisation and its people are best served by adopting an ethical approach and exceeding the expectations of the community at large. This is essential for the long-term sustainability of an organisation as it provides credibility, safety, trust and confidence. The public sector is especially reliant on the trust of the public, with reputations for responsible and ethical behaviour being hard won and easily lost, so this concept is particularly relevant for our sector. Runshaw's approach is described in Chapter 3.

The concept of 'continuous learning, innovation and improvement' is related to the concept of the 'professional learning community', which educational theorists argued to be (along with transformational leadership) the key component of building the capacity for long-term sustainability of excellence. This concept suggests that organisational performance is maximised when it is based on the management and sharing of knowledge within a culture of continuous learning, innovation and improvement. One of the 'big ideas' that Deming introduced so successfully was that of continuous improvement – a focus on many small day-to-day changes that keep improving the way you work, in addition to making the bigger step changes that are needed less frequently. He argued that by working preventively and proactively in this way, it is possible for an organisation to avoid the development of problems that gradually build up to lessen its effectiveness. Runshaw's approach to this is partly explained in Chapter 8 and partly in a later section of this chapter.

The concept of 'results orientation' suggests that excellence depends upon measures that:

- anticipate the needs and expectations of an organisation's stakeholders

- monitor their experiences and perceptions
- monitor and review the performance of other organisations
- balance and satisfy the needs of all relevant stakeholders and
- thereby achieves a balanced set of stakeholder 'results', including favourable student and staff perceptions as well as more traditional measures like financial performance or student achievement.

'Stakeholders' here include employees, customers, suppliers, partners, society in general and those with financial or regulatory interests in the organisation.

This concept of 'customer focus' argues that the 'customer' is the final arbiter of product and service quality. Therefore, it is argued that customer loyalty, retention and recruitment are best optimised through a clear focus on the needs, expectations and opinions of current and potential customers. Runshaw's approach to 'results orientation' and 'customer focus' is described in the next section.

The eighth fundamental concept – 'management by process and facts' – is the one that resonates most with Runshaw's sixth core value, 'putting our ethos into action' and encapsulates Runshaw's distinctive and unusual approach to quality management. That is, this concept suggests that organisations perform more effectively when all interrelated activities are understood and systematically managed through 'processes' and when decisions about planned improvements are made on the basis of reliable information that includes stakeholder perceptions. It implies that an organisation should develop a systematic and structured approach to process management in addition to or instead of traditional hierarchical management structures. Runshaw's approach to this concept is described below.

The application of the excellence model at Runshaw

One of the most powerful benefits of using the excellence model at Runshaw was the way that it helped us to clarify, make sense of and understand the meaning of fundamental concepts like 'quality', 'quality policy', 'quality management', 'quality assurance' and 'quality control'. Our definition of 'quality' was as follows: 'The achievement of high levels of satisfaction for all of our stakeholders, including learners, staff and the community'.

Our 'quality policy' was as follows:

> *We aim to*
> - *do the 'right things' to meet the needs of our learners and other stakeholders;*
> - *do them 'right';*
> - *and continuously seek 'right things' to do and better ways to them.*

The 'right things' were determined by what our 'customers' wanted. We then had to do these things 'right', meaning that they should be done effectively and efficiently, and we then had to explore how we could go further, become better, become more effective and efficient, and serve the needs of other 'customers' whose needs were unmet or met unsatisfactorily elsewhere.

Our interpretation of 'quality management' was that it was about 'how good the leadership and management of a college was', not about the more specific management of quality which we took to mean 'quality assurance'. We defined the latter as: '. . . putting the systems in place to ensure that high standards are achieved: as little as possible is left to chance in ensuring "right first time"'. This is generally termed 'feed-forward' because it is about anticipating and preventing potential problems. 'Quality control', on the other hand, is usually described as 'feedback' because it is about checking outcomes to identify problems or weaknesses and then taking action to remedy the situation.

IMPLEMENTING THE CONCEPT OF 'CUSTOMER FOCUS' AT RUNSHAW

As explained earlier in this chapter, this concept asserts that 'the customer is the final arbiter of product and service quality so customer loyalty, retention and recruitment are best optimised through a clear focus on the needs, expectations and opinions of current and potential customers'. The questions that arise from this are:

- Who are the customers?
- How did we organise ourselves to identify and respond to their needs?

In further education, the first of these is a particularly complex question because, whilst the taxpayer pays for the service through the funding bodies like the Learning and Skills Council, the learner receives it – so, in a sense, both are 'customers'. Debates about this question sometimes seek clarity by introducing concepts like 'consumer' or 'client' (the learner) as well as the 'customer' (the government agency responsible for funding) but, ultimately, one is required to identify and prioritise all those served by the organisation. At Runshaw we had endless debates about these issues and finally settled on establishing a stakeholder framework in which we identified and prioritised the needs of six clusters of stakeholders. These were, firstly, learners ('the student comes first'), then the funding and sponsoring stakeholders (the funding bodies, parents who sponsor and support 16–19 year olds and employers who pay for the courses attended by their employees), staff, partners, the community (for example, the Commission for Racial Equality, the representatives of local churches, groups representing learners with disabilities and learning difficulties, neighbours, local councils, and economic regeneration agencies), and suppliers. These were our 'customers' in that priority order.

With regard to the second question, we 'responded' by using six key approaches:

1 *Stakeholder liaison structure.* In 1993, the governors established a formal structure for liaising with all stakeholders. That is, they identified a number of committees to enable stakeholders to identify their needs and their levels of satisfaction in meetings with senior managers of the college. An annual schedule of meetings – each with agreed terms of reference, composition, frequency and lines of reporting – was agreed each year. The stakeholder reports that were produced by these went first to the senior management team and then to the governing body. They were then integrated into such strategic planning mechanisms as the needs analysis, the self-assessment report and the annual report, each feeding into the planning process a review of our performance and the identification of new needs that needed to be addressed.

2 *Developing a 'customer-focused' faculty structure.* Our primary 'customer' was the learner and one of the most powerful perceptions expressed by staff in the culture-change process of 1993–4 was that, by developing a new management structure in

1990–3, which enabled us to create new responsibilities for such matters as finance, human relations management, marketing, and strategic planning, we had inadvertently sent out a strong message that students were no longer our central focus. Moreover, on reflection managers felt that we had fragmented responsibilities for quality, staffing, planning and finance by introducing separate corporate roles at senior management level. Hence, in 1995, partly in response to this and partly in response to the need to strengthen lines of communication and accountability, we restructured the college into a federal structure as described in Chapter 6. That is, we created 'three colleges in one' with a sixth-form centre, an adult college and Runshaw Business Centre, each focused on delivering a coherent and co-ordinated experience for respective client groups. The first was so large that it was subdivided into two faculties. Each was led by a senior manager so there were four senior managers for these roles. We then began to reduce corporate roles, eventually reducing these to three, that is, my role as principal, another for resources and the third for student services, seven senior managers in total, four of whom were 'customer-focused' heads of faculty. Linked to the 'three colleges in one', there were three marketing units for the three key client groups, that is, school-leavers, adults and employers. They used different techniques for such marketing activities as advertising, distribution and for market research, but all three underpinned a customer-focused approach within the respective faculties.

3 *The role of head of studies.* In each faculty there was a traditional level of middle management posts called heads of school, responsible for delivering the curriculum in subject areas like business studies and information technology. At Runshaw we also created a second middle management 'customer-focused' role called heads of studies. Such positions existed for each main cohort of students so there were 11 such posts – that is, for A-level, advanced vocational studies (16–19), foundation, entry, higher education, access, prison education, basic skills, Runshaw Training (that is, work-based learning), Runshaw Business Centre and for part-time vocational provision. Their role was to act as the 'champion of the student'. It was their job to ensure that the experience of their respective cohort of students was excellent in every way. They had an overview of the students' whole experience, from pre-enrolment to post-course advice and guidance. They tracked individual students' progress, managed a base in which students could drop in for individual counselling and guidance, monitored student absence, designed the curriculum to meet the needs of their cohort of students, administered discipline beyond the levels conducted by heads of school and managed a budget to 'purchase' whatever services they needed to meet 'their' students' needs. This included the purchase of subject delivery from heads of school, including the amount of provision needed in terms of hours and class size. They set high standards for delivery on behalf of their students requiring, for example, that all classes be covered in the case of staff absence. They learned from students about questionable performance of individual teachers and took this up with the respective head of school. These roles and responsibilities gave them a great deal of insight into what was going on in the students' experience and it was their responsibility to act upon what they learned. This created real tension between heads of studies and heads of schools, both middle managers – so much so that there was a real danger of conflict and negative relationships. Until 1995, the heads of studies operated from student services, a central unit led by a senior manager but, in 1995, as an outcome of the culture-change process, we relocated heads of studies into respective faculties to work

alongside heads of school. This treated a much more collaborative spirit, sharing more responsibility for student discipline, the student experience and the students' progress with those responsible on a day-to-day basis for academic delivery and managing staff–student relationships in the classroom. Interestingly, when a deputy-principal from Runshaw became principal of another college in 1999, he immediately introduced the role of head of studies and thereafter claimed that, of all the ideas that he brought from Runshaw, this particular one had the single most immediate and dynamic impact on raising standards, with middle managers demanding higher standards from other middle management colleagues on an everyday basis in a way that had never been done before.

4 *Student services.* Heads of studies operated 'student services' within each customer-focused faculty, offering a drop-in 'base' for students to resolve their problems and concerns. Runshaw also operated a central unit called student services led by a senior manager. It provided a wide range of specialist services like counselling, careers guidance, additional support and the learning centre, but it also pulled together heads of studies to collaborate in setting cross-college standards and sharing approaches to areas of provision like personal tutoring, key skills, enhancement and enrichment. It also co-ordinated the provision of a range of processes like student tracking, diagnostic assessment and study support. Overall, it provided a safety net for students, set high standards for those areas of provision – like personal tutoring – which are often neglected in colleges, and served to act as a dynamic force to ensure that our focus should always primarily be on the student.

5 *Finding out what students need.* Within the roles and structures described above, there were several important mechanisms for systematically finding out what students needed. The key principle behind these was that those on the front line who interacted with students should be the key players in the process of obtaining, analysing and planning responses to feedback from students. The rationale for this was that such front-line staff had most control over the degree to which quality, service and efficiency could be improved and they had the potential to make the greatest impact. The role of managers in this process was to facilitate it, acting in partnership with the front line, demonstrating that they were listening to and acting upon what the front line reported. For example, as is explained in Chapter 6, the culture-change process at Runshaw resulted in staff working with managers and students in 1996 to create 'The New Beginning', described earlier as a redefinition of our student culture. This new approach engaged our front-line staff in a key market research activity – measuring what matters most to customers. When asked, students said that they valued order, safety, high standards, high expectations, discipline and a structured approach. They also wanted to be treated like individuals, with good access to individual support. They wanted rules that were clear, fair and consistently applied, and they wanted an environment in which people could focus primarily on teaching and learning in a friendly, positive atmosphere. The dialogue between staff and students that identified this new form of culture was an excellent form of market research but it also strengthened staff–student relationships. That is, students were sometimes cynical about questionnaires and activities involving market research but they felt valued and relevant when asked their opinion by front-line staff – lecturers and relevant support staff – because they believed, quite rightly, that they could make a difference.

6 *Student charter.* In terms of the scope of our interest in student satisfaction, we took the view that 'customer research' should be about the total relationship of each

student with Runshaw College, including all contacts with all of its people and its services. Hence, we developed a student charter that covered all stages of the students' experience. Whenever we talked about students' 'rights' at Runshaw, there was always an immediate assertion by staff that we should also articulate what was expected from students. Hence, a list of 'expectations' was also placed alongside our 'promises' in the student charter. This charter was posted around the college and was deliberately limited to 10 short 'promises' in order to be readable, intelligible, memorable and accessible. However, we felt that it was insufficient and inadequate for staff to understand what was required from them, so we produced a second, longer version which was agreed by staff and students and used in personal tutor discussion groups. All these lists were developed through a lengthy consultation process that fully involved students and staff. They were communicated in student assemblies, on posters, in the student diary and in personal tutor groups, and they were reviewed on an annual basis.

RUNSHAW'S APPROACH TO 'PROCESSES'

Using processes to address the problems with the traditional culture in colleges

In practical terms, the excellence model asserts that managing any strategy – including student culture and staff morale – must be delivered through 'processes', defining a 'process' as 'the sequence of activities that gets your work done'.

Without effective process management, it is argued that a college cannot deliver its strategy effectively. Our key processes included teaching and learning and student support, as well as marketing, financial management, quality assurance, facilities management, so they were at the heart of the college's work. 'Process management' was not some obscure concept misapplied from the jargon of the private sector. It was fundamental to the management of our performance.

Adopting such an approach challenges the traditional weaknesses of many FE colleges:

- the danger of initiating too many changes, failing to prioritise and creating initiative overload and a consequent failure to see things through
- making false promises and raising unfulfilled expectations, with consequent disillusionment
- a lack of systematic and structured measurement, review and continuous improvement
- a failure to recognise that processes cut across college's management structures, requiring staff from across the college to link together to work systematically
- a culture in which the 'academic' puts his subject first, regarding 'management' as a necessary evil and 'systems' as unnecessary bureaucracy.

At Runshaw we challenged these approaches fiercely. We believed that processes were our 'ethos in action'. Without them, we would be guilty of empty rhetoric. We believed that processes empower staff to implement their values and beliefs. Minimum target grades (MTG) and performance management, for example, were processes that enabled staff to implement our culture. That is, when members of staff wanted to sit down with a student to agree targets, review progress or make an action plan, the MTG process told them exactly what to do, how and when. Similarly, when managers wanted a one-to-one meeting with individual staff members to agree goals, review progress, coach, agree training, show recognition and appreciation, the process of performance management explained exactly how to do this, when, where and so forth.

Runshaw suffered to a degree from all the traditional FE problems listed above, but we were acutely aware of them and we addressed them through process management at a strategic level since we adopted the excellence model in 1995. Process management has been by far the most challenging element of the excellence model for us, as it is for most organisations. However, it is not recognised by most colleges as an important concept. Nor is it is understood and few colleges have a formal process management model in place. Between 1990 and 1993, further education colleges and managers were urged to become 'businesslike'. Pressures were created to encourage them to look at best practice in the private sector so that they could improve standards, achieve growth and become more efficient, all at the same time. If they had looked at the private sector, they would have found there a justifiable obsession with process management. Many recent books, like *Command and Control* by John Seddon, reveal an irritation with endless debates about leadership, values, mission and vision: he argues that energy and attention should be spent primarily on process management, with senior and middle managers working closely with front-line staff to improve those processes that directly impact on service to customers.

Why is the concept of 'processes' little used in colleges?

So why has the concept of 'processes' not entered the language of further education? Why has there been no significant management training in process management for further education managers? Why is the word 'process' absence from Ofsted's criteria for assessing 'leadership and management'? And why is there no established consensus about the kind of process management model that every college should adopt?

These are good questions to which the answer may be that there is no tradition in the world of education for research and development about the concept of 'process' as such. In this context, it is worth repeating that the concept of 'process management' is not mentioned in the Common Inspection Framework. If one accepts the dictum that 'what gets measured gets done!' and that inspection is one of the most important ways of measuring the performance of colleges, then it is little wonder that colleges are not focused on process management.

What we have had, however, is a focus in most schools and probably in most sixth-form colleges and in some general further education colleges on what would be described, in the language of process management, as education's 'core processes' – teaching and learning, assessment, curriculum design and student support. As long as schools and colleges focus on such things, they are doing 'the right thing' without needing to recourse to the jargon of the private sector's 'businesslike' approaches.

The problem is that not everybody has been doing that. In fact, as already explained in Chapter 1, most research on the management of further education over the last decade has pointed to the spread of 'managerialism', and especially to senior managers becoming 'distanced' and 'estranged' from the concerns of students and lecturers and from teaching and learning. It is argued that they have become preoccupied with finance, marketing, MIS, strategic planning, accommodation strategies and so on, losing all sense of touch with teaching and learning. If that is the case, then they have lost touch with their 'core processes' and that would be regarded as poor management by the best practitioners in the private sector. It is also suggested that many principals have moved from being 'leading professional teachers' to becoming chief executives but, ironically, a successful chief executive in the private sector would probably be the 'leading professional' in whatever core processes his or her organisation focused upon, whether it be retail, manufacturing, financial management or education.

Although Runshaw achieved four out of five cross-college grade 1s in its 1996 inspection and was therefore judged to be an outstanding college, privately we did not believe that it was. The reason for this was that, in 1995, we had begun to use the Business Excellence Model to assess ourselves and scored only about 400 points out of 1000. By that time we had gone through two phases of management development, the first in 1990–3 when we had focused on the 'hard Ss' – strategy, structure and systems – only to achieve very little. The second phase was in 1993–5 when we immersed ourselves in a culture-change programme – the four 'soft Ss' of staff morale and commitment, shared values, skills and (management) style, which had a very significant impact in improving our quality.

It was the Business Excellence Model that brought us back in 1995 to appreciate the importance of the 'hard Ss'. Without it, we would have assumed that it was the culture change, the 'soft Ss', that were entirely responsible for our improvement. The Business Excellence Model challenged this and made us appreciate that the 'soft Ss' must be implemented by the 'hard Ss'. Without processes, all our talk and good intentions would have amounted to 'hot air', raising expectations only to have them dashed by disappointing performance.

Using the Business Excellence Model, we had scored well in 1995 on 'leadership' and on our approaches to managing staff but we scored very poorly on 'processes'. In truth, we had no process management model, we did not know what our key processes were, we had no systematic way of measuring or reviewing their performance and our structures for managing processes were piecemeal and *ad hoc*. We did not even really understand what a process was. Nevertheless we achieved a grade 1 in quality assurance in our 1996 inspection. So much for the relative standards of quality assurance in the sector at that time!

By the time that we won the UK Business Excellence Award in 2002 and the European Award in 2003, we had developed a process management model. We had also integrated it with our strategic planning model, our approach to performance measurement, self-assessment performance management and staff development, as Figure 9.2 on the next page illustrates.

So how did we identify our key processes and what were they?

The answer to the first part of the question links back to our strategic planning process. This involved identifying our critical success factors – the things that we had to do in order to achieve our vision and mission – and it followed that we then had to say how we would achieve these things. For example, if we said that it was 'critical' to market effectively, then this suggested that 'marketing' would be a critical process. Using this approach, we believed that we – and, of course, every other college – had to provide

Figure 9.2 *Process management model*

excellent teaching and learning, assessment, curriculum design/management and student support. We identified these as our four 'core' processes. As such, our core processes were aligned with our core values: for example, 'teaching and learning is our first priority' aligned with the fact that teaching and learning was a core process and 'valuing the individual' aligned with the notion of student support.

What was important here was that the identification of these core processes asserted that the most important activities performed at Runshaw were about how we served the student. We did have other less important debates about whether there should be one, two, three or four core processes – for example, originally we included the core process of 'assessment' as part of 'teaching and learning' and only made it a separate core process to align with Ofsted's Common Inspection Framework – but such debates were not really important. What *was* important was the explicit assertion that the principal, senior managers, middle managers, support staff and, of course, lecturers, should all focus their time, energy, resources, creativity and innovation primarily on creating the conditions for these four core processes to be implemented effectively.

It would be inconceivable for a college to identify anything other than these as its core processes. Assuming it did, it would be equally inconceivable in a rational world for senior managers to become preoccupied with anything else. This very first elementary step towards process management would, in itself, send a powerful message within the culture of any college and would challenge the activities of senior managers who spend an inordinate amount of their time on other things. As such, it would make a big difference to the standard of quality assurance in a college. The identification of these four core processes as our 'core' processes did make a big difference at Runshaw: there was never any doubt about what our jobs were and what we should spend our time doing. We saw our roles quite clearly as 'leading professional teachers' and, as such, we believed that our behaviour was compatible with that of outstanding chief executives. Our 'business' was teaching and learning, assessment, curriculum design/management and student support and we decided to spend the majority of our time developing these.

We distinguished between these four 'core' processes and nine other 'support' processes to clarify our priorities. Identifying the support processes was not always straightforward. The obvious ones were strategic planning, quality assurance, human resource development, marketing and financial management and we never had very much debate about these. We did wonder if 'quality assurance' should be part of 'strategic planning' and not a separate process but there was never much appetite for pursuing this particular debate energetically. We also occasionally questioned whether 'marketing' should be regarded as a 'core process' and we would not have disagreed strongly with someone who believed that it should. There was also a debate about whether 'accommodation management' should include health and safety, catering, cleaning, grounds maintenance and a host of other aspects of managing our facilities. In the event, we finally decided to identify 'facilities management' as a sixth support process encompassing all these 'subprocesses'.

More contentiously, over subsequent years we added three more support processes. One was the 'management of partnerships', another was the 'management of equal opportunities' and the third was 'knowledge management'. The last one, in particular, caused a great deal of concern because it included student tracking and MIS, and several of us felt that these should be separate support processes.

The debate about all of these could fill a book but such debates are not particularly important. Nor am I suggesting that Runshaw has produced the definitive process management model for further education colleges. The really important point being made here is that the Business Excellence Model argues that every college and, indeed, every organisation should identify the key processes that it will use to deliver its strategic plan. It is these key processes that will put its 'ethos into action'.

Runshaw's process management model

Having identified its key processes, a college should then reconstruct its management system in such a way that it can effectively manage, review and improve these key processes on a continuous basis. If it does so it should then have achieved true quality assurance by establishing the systems and infrastructure that anticipate and prevent problems.

The management structure at Runshaw has been described in terms of four 'customer-focused' faculties, one for A-level, one for vocational provision for 16–19 year olds, a third for the adult college and a fourth for Runshaw Business Centre. This was described as 'the dominant structure' and as such it enabled the college to integrate the management of staff, quality, accommodation, funding and planning into four customer-focused 'businesses'. A second tier of heads of studies, each of whom specialised in one specific cohort of students, reinforced this. Below them, a tier of course leaders and course teams reinforced it further.

The creation of process improvement teams

The danger in all this was that other cross-college perspectives would be lost, that competing and contrasting policies and practices might spring up in each faculty, and that standardisation and sharing good practice across the college might be impeded.

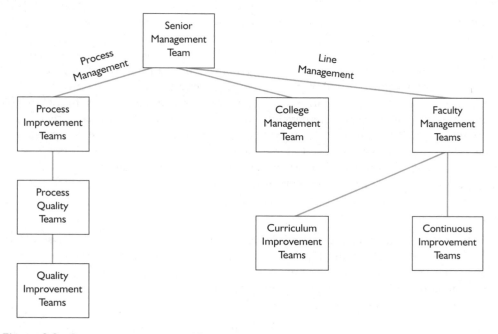

Figure 9.3 *Process management and line management teams*

So, a second kind of management structure was superimposed on the faculty structure. Each of our 13 key processes was allocated to a structure of cross-college process improvement teams, each chaired by a senior manager. Three of our four core processes – teaching and learning, assessment and curriculum design/management – were grouped together under the auspices of one process improvement team (PIT) chaired by me and composed of the four faculty heads and the head of student services – in other words, six of the seven senior managers. It held 'away days' on a regular basis, exploring best practice outside Runshaw, reviewing policy and practice within it and developing plans for future strategic developments like the creation of a professional development centre, a new process for lesson observation, a strategy called the 'Hattie factors', and a new self-assessment checklist based on Ofsted's criteria for outstanding teaching and learning. Another PIT existed for student support. It was chaired by the senior manager responsible for that function and it was composed of heads of studies.

Process improvement teams also existed for seven of the nine support processes – one each for the management of finance, technology, facilities (all three chaired by the director for resources), partnerships (chaired by the senior manager for Runshaw Business Centre), the management of knowledge (chaired by the head of student support because it focused so strongly on student tracking), human resource management and marketing (both chaired by me). Two other support processes, quality assurance and strategic planning, came under the auspices of two separate existing structures, the quality council (established in 1991 to meet monthly and steer our approaches to quality management, chaired by me) and the fortnightly meetings of the senior management team for strategic planning.

The terms of reference of the PITs were to define and map the respective key process and its subprocesses to four levels. These were designated as 'key process', 'process', 'subprocess' and 'task'. It would identify the 'owner' for each – the person responsible for it. It would arrange for standards to be set for each level and for the assessment and reviewing of these standards, measuring their effectiveness and monitoring compliance of their implementation. They would then plan improvements, prioritise these, ensure that these improvements were implemented and, finally, evaluate them.

Process quality teams (PQTs) and quality improvement teams (QITs)

When a process improvement team identified that a significant development was needed to improve a specific subprocess, it would establish a second temporary kind of structure, a process quality team (PQT), to carry out the improvement. This would be chaired by somebody from the parent process improvement team to maintain the link but its composition would depend on the identification of those who held significant roles and responsibility for managing each specific step in the subprocess. It was not composed of 'volunteers' or 'representatives': it was composed of a group of people who collectively managed all the steps in the subprocess. They would carry out the assessment and review of the subprocess, make the necessary improvements without reference upwards and then evaluate these. Usually, the process quality team would then cease to exist.

As part of the process quality team's review process, it might identify one specific step in the flowchart of a subprocess that was causing difficulties. In such a case, it would then establish a quality improvement team (QIT) to resolve the concerns about that step. Like process quality teams, these would be chaired by someone from the parent body, and they would be composed of those staff directly responsible for the step or steps in question.

An overelaborate structure?

Although this might sound overly elaborate and unnecessarily complex, in practice, whilst the jargon caused laughter, it was a very simple system. The simplicity was in the fact that all of the people who were responsible for the various stages in a process were brought together from across the college. They had an interest in being there. It was not a talking shop: they made decisions and they made improvements that affected the way they did their job. It drew upon their knowledge and experience, gave them an opportunity to express frustrations and, ultimately, enabled them to get things done.

At any one time, there could be 30 or 40 of these structures busily improving things across the college, bringing together people who would normally never have had the opportunity to meet or collectively review the processes they managed. In practice, therefore, these structures were welcomed and perceived generally as an invaluable mechanism in making the college work smoothly.

Expanding the role of process improvement teams

Over a period of years, the roles of the process improvement teams were expanded beyond their initial remit. It became increasingly clear, for example, that the process improvement team was very close to policy formulation as well as to managing the process, so each became responsible for this. The process improvement team for financial management, for example, became responsible for formulating financial policies, though ultimately the senior management team and then the governors made the final decisions.

Process improvement teams also became responsible for documenting both policy and processes so that everybody could have access to definitive statements on both via the corporate intranet. Although they were technically necessary for those operating a process to know precisely what to do, these documents were generally not very readable, so each process improvement team then became responsible for arranging the production of more accessible management guidelines that could then be used to train managers in their role in managing the respective process. It was then a short step to add to the process improvement teams' responsibilities that of producing induction training materials for staff. These materials would tell the staff what they needed to know about each process.

This was not documentation for its own sake. The process documentation was used to empower people by helping them to understand how to do their jobs properly and to know what was expected of them in promoting values. For example, newly appointed staff may start their careers at Runshaw full of enthusiasm for these values but, without the support of training and written guidance in the processes that implement those values, they would be likely to become frustrated and disillusioned.

By 2004, Runshaw had developed a mass of documentation. Figure 9.4 demonstrates what had been achieved in one key process, that of human relations management.

There were 13 key processes at Runshaw, each of which could be represented by diagrams similar to Figure 9.4. Process improvement teams used the documentation to organise measurement and evaluation, and to plan improvements. Diagrams like this facilitated a thorough, structured and systematic quality management system, marching forward like a well-organised Arm, achieving both incremental and 'breakthrough' improvements across the college in 13 dimensions.

Performance measurement and the quality unit

In our quality assurance model, the process management model was followed by the concept of performance measurement. For lecturers, three kinds of measurements were critical:

- lesson observation
- student satisfaction surveys
- data, especially data on student attendance, retention and achievement.

All these came from one source, the quality unit. We established this unit in 1999 after the quality council identified concerns that lecturers were using their own versions of examination results for self-assessment. Their versions were different from those used by external inspectors so this was unacceptable. There would certainly have been significant difficulties in future inspections if they had continued to use what would be regarded as

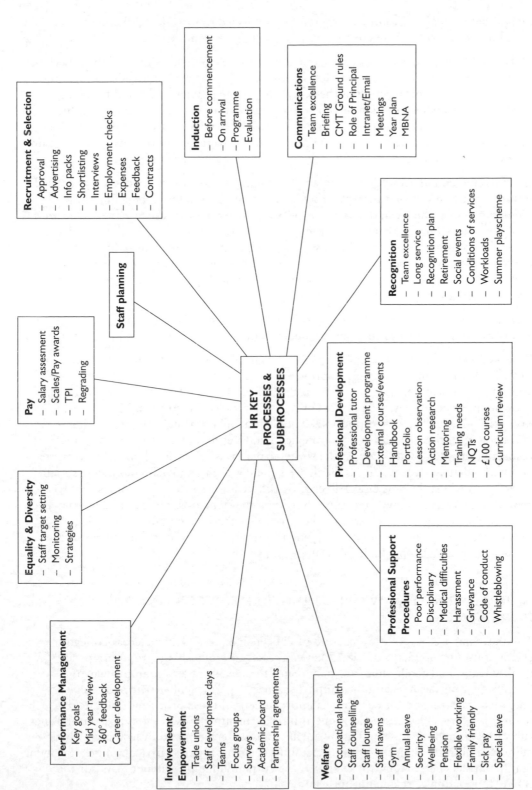

Recruitment & Selection
– Approval
– Advertising
– Info packs
– Shortlisting
– Interviews
– Employment checks
– Expenses
– Feedback
– Contracts

Induction
– Before commencement
– On arrival
– Programme
– Evaluation

Communications
– Team excellence
– Briefing
– CMT Ground rules
– Role of Principal
– Intranet/Email
– Meetings
– Year plan
– MBNA

Staff planning

Pay
– Salary assesment
– Scales/Pay awards
– TPI
– Regrading

HR KEY PROCESSES & SUBPROCESSES

Recognition
– Team excellence
– Long service
– Recognition plan
– Retirement
– Social events
– Conditions of services
– Workloads
– Summer playscheme

Equality & Diversity
– Staff target setting
– Monitoring
– Strategies

Professional Development
– Professional tutor
– Development programme
– External courses/events
– Handbook
– Portfolio
– Lesson observation
– Action research
– Mentoring
– Training needs
– NQTs
– £100 courses
– Curriculum review

Performance Management
– Key goals
– Mid year review
– 360° feedback
– Career development

Involvemeent/ Empowerment
– Trade unions
– Staff development days
– Teams
– Focus groups
– Surveys
– Academic board
– Partnership agreements

Professional Support Procedures
– Poor performance
– Disciplinary
– Medical difficulties
– Harassment
– Grievance
– Code of conduct
– Whistleblowing

Welfare
– Occupational health
– Staff counselling
– Staff lounge
– Staff havens
– Gym
– Annual leave
– Security
– Wellbeing
– Pension
– Flexible working
– Family friendly
– Sick pay
– Special leave

Figure 9.4 *Human resources – key processes and subprocesses*

invalid data. The quality unit was therefore established to provide valid and reliable data on all measures for all assessments, including self-assessment by staff.

Once established and seen to be very effective, its role expanded significantly. It became responsible for the secretariat function for the senior management team's monitoring committee, a monthly meeting of the senior management team dedicated to monitoring all the 'results', which we identified using the concept of 'results orientation' in the excellence model. The quality unit supported this by producing a constant stream of monitoring reports against an annual schedule that covered every performance indicator for every internal or external service that was delivered by our processes.

It conducted an annual student survey, which supplemented the regular surveys carried out by front-line staff and thereby provided a standardised internal benchmark. It conducted our in-house staff surveys on 16 support services, measuring the satisfaction of 'internal customers' (that is, the other staff) with the level of service they received from, for example, MIS, cleaning, custodial services, finance, reception, library, marketing, etc. It also acted as the secretariat to the quality council, supporting the implementation, assessment and review of a host of quality assurance subprocesses like lesson observation and curriculum review.

The next logical step in developing its role would have been to give it responsibility for acting as the secretariat to the senior management team's strategic planning meetings.

Process improvement teams had become the college's 'engine', identifying and driving through 'breakthrough' strategic improvements in the college as well as day-to-day continuous improvements. Each was engaged in top-level policy and strategy. Each had become intellectually engaged in the concepts that underpinned the policies and processes for which it was responsible. These became increasingly aligned to the titles and content of the chapters in our strategic plan, so each took charge of 'its own' respective chapter. That is, whilst the strategic plan was primarily about who we serve and with what service – which students we should recruit and what courses we should offer – and whilst this was best delivered by the 'customer-focused' faculties that were geared to deliver these, when it came to guiding the standards, policies and cross-college strategies for these services it was the key processes that shaped our cross-college 'teaching and learning' strategy, our 'student support' strategy, our 'human resources' strategy, our 'equal opportunities' strategy and so on.

A PERMANENT TEAMWORK STRUCTURE FOR CONTINUOUS IMPROVEMENT

The permanent cross-college structure of PITs enabled us to achieve cross-college continuous improvements of the 13 key processes by establishing temporary process quality teams and quality improvement teams for specific tasks and improvements. Within the four faculties and the support services, a permanent structure of CITs provided the structure for continuous improvement of those processes operated by such teams on a day-to-day basis. Continuous improvement teams were composed of business support staff and curriculum improvement teams were composed of lecturers. The latter embraced both the subject team (for example, the mathematics curriculum improvement team) and the course team (for example, the curriculum improvement team for the BTEC foundation course in business studies).

Origins of the team approach

The team structure existed at Runshaw before the culture-change programme. It was introduced in 1984 when the college changed to tertiary status and when I was appointed as the new principal. Previously there had been no teams and no teamwork. Individual teachers did not meet together formally to consider their work collectively. They each taught and assessed as they saw fit. There was no standardisation process and no sharing of approaches or materials. There was no collective evaluation or reflection. Indeed, the concept of teamwork violated the concept of professional autonomy as practised by most staff.

In 1984 I introduced a new structure of teams, primarily as a form of curriculum-led staff development. I had studied curriculum management for an MEd. degree at the University of Liverpool between 1974 and 1976 and learned then that a great deal of resources, energy and effort had been wasted in the late 1960s by the attempts of the Schools Council – the major research, development and dissemination body in English education at that time – to impose centrally-devised curriculum projects as 'idiot-proof' teaching packages on teachers in schools and colleges throughout the UK.

I studied one specific example of curriculum innovation in the college in which I was then working. It was the York Project, a general studies pack developed at York University. The college in which I worked had bought it but I found the box of materials unopened, gathering dust on a shelf in a storeroom. The materials themselves were superb but nobody in the college had used them. This, apparently, was typical of what was happening elsewhere. Excellent developments were produced centrally but they made little or no impact on the front-line teacher because the latter felt no sense of ownership or involvement in their development. Often they simply did not know about them or, if they did, they did not understand them or how best to use them.

By the time I began to study curriculum management in 1974, the late Professor Stenhouse had emerged as the leading critic of this whole approach. He argued that resources should be redirected to enable teachers, working in teams, to design, develop and innovate new approaches to teaching and learning. Their actual product might not be as impressive as centrally-produced materials, but they would at least be implemented. Teachers would 'own' them. Teachers would be committed to them. Hence, there was a much greater chance that real improvement would occur in teaching and learning.

All this struck a chord with the approach which Geoff Melling and Geoff Stanton brought to the new Further Education Unit, formed in 1976 to support curriculum change in further education. It produced a superb document called *Experience, Reflection, Learning,* whose title encapsulated a view about the way people learned, 'people' including both students and staff. This led to the concept of 'curriculum-led staff development', the idea that teachers learned by working collaboratively in a team, sharing resources, spreading their best practice, energising each other and raising standards.

This is the approach that I had used as a teacher in the 1970s and then as a manager prior to becoming principal of Runshaw in 1984. It was the single most important organisational change that I made when I started there. It was also very unpopular. Most teachers who were at Runshaw then did not want to share their resources. Nor did they want to reflect collectively on what worked and what did not work. They perceived the concept of 'staff development' as an imputation that there was something wrong with them and resented the notion of spreading good practice. Many did not think that they had anything to learn from anybody else. The whole idea of teamwork smacked of a kind of peer accountability that many did not want.

Teamwork as the implementation of a core value

Nevertheless, teamwork became a standard approach at Runshaw and one of six core values became 'working together and with others'. When we later developed the concept of 'the Runshaw person' to guide our selection and development of staff, we included 'team skills' as a key attribute. When we developed a list of eight core management competencies in which we trained Runshaw managers, we introduced 'team membership', 'team leadership' and 'interpersonal skills' as three of the core competencies.

By 1995, all staff at Runshaw belonged to at least one team. Teaching teams were required to share schemes of work, assessment calendars, assignment schedules and marking schemes: this ensured that the approaches of each team and of each teacher met a minimum standard – it contributed to the assurance of quality.

It also enabled the college to work more economically and efficiently. For example, the 'joint classes' that saved 10% of our teaching costs could not have existed without these shared approaches. Cover for staff absence would have been less effective without them. We could not have merged classes when we needed to if we had not had shared approaches. For example, we regularly merged classes to maintain large class sizes at the end of the first year or at the end of the first term or when a teacher left suddenly and could not be replaced quickly.

There is copious evidence that teamwork in colleges is often very ineffective. Some staff either resisted teamwork or used it for mutual support to complain about students, the 'management', resources, the timetable or curriculum initiatives. To ensure that teamwork at Runshaw was effective we defined very clearly the purposes of different teams and we clarified their role in terms of quality assurance and curriculum-led staff development.

We also developed templates for the agendas of different meetings. For example, the template for curriculum improvement teams clearly suggested that teams should primarily focus in a structured way on monitoring students' progress, on reviewing student feedback and on evaluation of teaching and learning. We also developed a set of ground rules for the conduct of team meetings, including what was expected in terms of preparation for meetings, for their conduct and for the kind of rigour of follow-up that was expected after a meeting. And all staff were trained in all of the above as well as in the skills of team membership. Team leaders, for example, were required to attend a team leadership training programme.

We also provided a calendarised schedule of meetings to ensure that different groups could meet on a regular basis, avoiding clashes with other groups. We provided times for meetings: for example, we decided to close the afternoon session at the sixth-form centre at 4.30 p.m. each day rather than at 5.00 p.m. so that teachers could meet regularly.

Self-assessment by CITs

These weekly meetings were supplemented by the more intensive opportunities for CITs to meet during the five annual 'stop-the-track' days when they carried out highly structured activities like self-assessment, target-setting and action planning. This was a very structured form of empowerment in which each team completed an analysis of its strengths and weaknesses and then produced an action plan which formed the basis for its progress reviews throughout the year.

The process was 'facilitated' by the use of college-wide detailed pro formas that listed questions that were derived from the Ofsted inspection handbook and that provided a scale for each team to score its performance against each question and the related inspection criteria. Examples of 'excellent performance' and 'poor performance' were provided against each criteria and question to guide that scoring process. The team leaders were trained in the process of completing this pro forma.

They and the whole team were provided with data and other forms of evidence from the quality unit. They then analysed the evidence given to them and interpreted it to form their judgements. In some cases, as in the interpretation of student achievement data, they were told how inspectors would use the data to define their grades. In other cases, like student feedback, much was left to their judgement for interpretation as to what grade the evidence justified.

All this meant that, within a college-wide process in which they were provided with pro formas, evidence, training and time, each team developed a powerful sense of ownership, understanding the problems that it faced and devising solutions to them.

CONCLUSION

This conclusion seeks to answer two questions that arise from our experience of developing a quality management approach based on the excellence model. The first is 'what were the benefits for Runshaw of using the excellence model?' The second is, 'what lessons have we learned from this experience?'

With regard to the first question, there were five main benefits. They were as follows.

1 *A management framework.* We first came across the model in 1994 and used it as a simple self-assessment mechanism at a management conference in February 1995. By that time we had used total quality management as our management philosophy for four years. We had become completely disillusioned with our experience of process management between 1991 and 1993, and by 1995 we had become extremely excited by the power and value of culture change. Without the excellence model, we almost certainly would have concluded that managing the culture was the only thing that really mattered and that process management had nothing to offer. The excellence model challenged that. Its eight fundamental concepts include 'management by processes', meaning that organisations perform more effectively when inter-related activities are understood and systematically managed. This then led to the creation of the process management structure described above and this, in turn, enabled us to sustain excellence and build upon it through continuous improvement. So the first benefit was that it provided us with a quality management framework.

2 *The 'enablers'.* Within the quality management framework, we were constantly stimulated by the questions in the five 'enablers' of the model – leadership, policy and strategy, people, partnerships and resources, and processes, the five elements that the excellence model suggest create the 'results' that constitute excellence. Often we did not fully understand the question, triggering a review of literature or attendance on courses or the use of consultants to help us to understand and to develop new approaches to leadership and management. Even when we did understand the question, we often found that our responses were weak, that our approach was virtually non-existent and that we had not really thought about the question before. The most frequent examples of this were when we were faced with questions arising from the fifth enabler, 'processes'. So the second benefit was that it provided us with a checklist that stimulated and directed our search for 'best practice' in excellence organisations.

3 *The value of external support.* A third benefit is that we had a sense of certainty and confidence about what best practice business approaches we should adopt. For example, whilst many in the college sector pursued the principles of macho management throughout the 1990s, we felt secure that our focus on culture was shared by the 'best and the brightest' in the private and public sector. We also found the submissions by winners of the UKQA very enlightening and we unashamedly plagiarised many of their approaches. If we ever needed further sustenance, the support provided by the British Quality Foundation and European Foundation for Quality Management, the associated training and consultancies that are available and the networks of enthusiasts who are eager to disseminate the model, all provided a huge infrastructure to support, guide and encourage us.

4 *A quality assurance framework.* A fourth benefit is RADAR. This is where the model requires an organisation to:

- identify and monitor its performance indicators – its Results (R)
- similarly identify its Approaches (A) to achieving those results
- Deploy (D) these approaches throughout the college, in every area and at every level as appropriate
- Assess (A) its approaches in a systematic and structured way
- Review (R) its approaches, to continuously improve them.

There could hardly be a better definition of quality assurance in further education. The chief inspector's reports over the last decade have repeatedly criticised colleges for failures to make effective use of performance indicators, to analyse trends, to carry out self-assessment with rigour, or to monitor and evaluate effectively. Runshaw obtained a grade 1 for quality assurance in both its 1996 and 2001 inspections because it used RADAR as its framework. It required us to set targets and standards, benchmark them, analyse trends, identify our key performance indicators, measure the processes that delivered targets, review all processes and approaches systematically using schedules, a highly structured self-assessment process and management structures whose remit was to arrange these reviews. Consequently, we invested heavily in management information systems and we established a quality unit to arrange objective measures and to co-ordinate and support the review process. The RADAR system helped us do all this in 1995, long before the Further Education Funding Council (FEFC) and now the LSC required target-setting, trend analysis, benchmarking or self-assessment. In many respects, FEFC and LSC have been introducing RADAR piecemeal over a number of years. A college that adopted the excellence model, as we did in 1995, would have had a head start and would have been helped to understand how quality assurance and quality control should be implemented in the context of an overall management framework.

5 *Acting as an umbrella model.* The excellence model is completely compatible with other quality initiatives is, of course, no accident. When the model was introduced in the UK in 1992, it was called the 'umbrella' model because it absorbed all the other different quality initiatives. For example, Investors in People (IIP) overlaps with the two enablers 'leadership' and 'people'; Charter Mark overlaps with 'customer'; ISO 9000 overlaps with 'processes'; and ISO 14001 overlaps with aspects of 'society'. There is, of course, also a huge overlap between the model and the Common Inspection Framework (CIF). 'Leadership', 'resources', 'policy and strategy', 'partnerships' and 'people' have many similar elements. 'Processes' can be interpreted to focus on teaching and learning, student support, curriculum organisation and other key processes that are central to the CIF. 'Results', of course, align very easily with student achievement and retention. However, there are differences and these are quite fundamental. Using the CIF alone as a management framework – and I appreciate that it is not intended to act as such – a college would simply fail to appreciate the importance of culture management or process management. 'Leadership' in the excellence model means much more than the CIF explicitly suggests. Staff management and staff surveys do not feature in the CIF to anything like the same extent as in the excellence model. Unlike the CIF, the model does argue that the approaches are just as important as the outcomes and it offers a clear set of linkages between 'enablers' and 'results', suggesting what you must do if you wish to achieve your required outcomes. Hence, I would argue that the excellence model offers a significant and substantial enhancement to the CIF. In a time when colleges are crying out for a reduction in bureaucracy, the danger is that colleges design their self-assessment processes to address only the CIF, failing to recognise that if they do so they may be in danger of neglecting the self-assessment of such critically important aspects of management as staff culture, process management and performance management. Having said that, however, it should also be emphasised that the CIF was never offered as a self-assessment framework. It is an audit checklist: it simply tells us what will be inspected. It explicitly does not attempt to prescribe all the approaches that colleges should develop to achieve the required results. The clear implication is that colleges should self-assess those approaches that they identify as appropriate, although it includes some strong indications of some of the approaches that should be included in colleges' self-assessments. For example, strategic planning, staff development and appraisal, lesson observation, quality assurance, curriculum design and delivery all feature in the CIF. But it never pretended to offer a comprehensive framework; it left colleges to develop their own approaches to the way they manage themselves and, in our case, that was helped by using the quality management framework in the excellence model. All in all, we have found that EFQM has provided a significant enhancement to CIF in devising our SAR process. It has posed challenging questions and introduced us to fundamental concepts that have stimulated us to identify significant areas for improvement. Even in 2002, despite winning the UK Award, the 50-page 'feedback' provided by a team of eight assessors, based on a week's visit and assessment of the college, provided us with a long and substantial list of 'areas for improvement'. Similarly, in 2003 when we won the

European Award, we received the benefit of a 'free' consultancy by six senior quality managers from leading international companies who assessed us for a week.

What lessons have we learned?

1 A map and a guide really are crucial, but great care has to be taken in finding the right ones, possibly by being mentored by an organisation that has successfully used the model.

2 Start with culture, not processes. In our case, we did the opposite and all our efforts to change processes failed because staff did not have shared values – including customer focus – or an understanding that effective management style, teamwork, communications, involvement and making staff feel valued were all essential before commitment to the continuous improvement of processes that served customers could be achieved.

3 Make it relevant. Focus on results that are our 'bottom line' in colleges, such as student achievement, retention, recruitment, staff morale and financial strength.

4 Present the model to staff as a way of implementing the fundamental concepts on which it is based. These are very user friendly in our value-driven world of education. Avoid using business jargon. Throughout the 1990s there was an underlying resentment by many staff of the need to copy private sector businesslike language and concepts. We recognised in the 1993–5 culture change programme that most staff are inspired by values that focus on students, teaching and learning and a mission that asserts that, by changing people's lives, what we do is incredibly worthwhile. The wholesale adoption of business jargon would have been uninspiring and demoralising in our context. Hence, we did not want to fall into the error of allowing the language in the excellence model to distract us, so we simply did not use it outside management development conferences.

5 Focus on your core processes: teaching and learning, student support, curriculum management, and assessment and student monitoring.

6 Integrate RADAR into your existing self-assessment and quality assurance processes, so that it is integral to the way you manage, analyse and improve performance.

7 Do not worry about awards initially. Writing a winning entry is a different activity from self-assessment that generates improvement. The strength of a self-assessment is in the identification of 'areas for improvement' and the action plan that follows. A submission for an award is about presenting yourself in the best possible light to earn high scores.

8 In our case, IIP rolled naturally out of our work on 'leadership' and 'staff', Chartermark rolled out of 'customer satisfaction', ISO 9000 could roll out of 'processes'. The Common Inspection Framework overlaps completely with the model, so use it as an umbrella model for other useful quality models like IIP.

9 Use it to understand management theories and how to implement total quality management. The wealth of literature, the networks of quality management professionals, the strength of academic research on the model, and the availability of training all provide a supportive infrastructure to assist in the creation of a 'professional learning community'.

10 Resource the 'quality journey'. This might mean:
  • a quality council to steer the whole process of organisational development that the model requires

- a quality unit to gather all the statistical data and surveys to support the assessment and review of all your approaches, and to co-ordinate the analyses of trends, benchmarks and targets for all your 'results'
- consultants and trainers to guide you
- documents like a policy manual and process mapping, possibly on a corporate intranet as at Runshaw, to record your approaches and to support reviews
- time for managers and staff to meet for continuous improvement.

We have found the excellence model to have been a superb framework with which to manage and develop our college's organisation. We believe that our most important outcomes – student recruitment, achievement, retention, satisfaction, our finances and so on – have all improved at a pace and to a level that would not have occurred without using the model. We believe that if there was one simple message to the government about how to improve quality rapidly in FE colleges, it would be to encourage colleges to use the model as a management framework and a self-assessment tool.

SUMMARY

- Runshaw used the Business Excellence Model as a guide to creating a quality management framework that earned it grade 1 in quality assurance in all of its inspections.
- If there is only one thing that colleges should do to improve their quality it would be to adopt this model.
- The model originated in Japan, was then developed in the US, and then completed by 14 European 'best practice' companies, which formed the EFQM.
- Its eight fundamental concepts act as a 'philosophy' for quality management, linking to all the leadership approaches described in previous chapters.
- Runshaw's approaches to 'customers' revolve around five key approaches: a stakeholder liaison structure, a customer-focused faculty management structure, a tier of middle management roles called heads of studies whose job was to act as the 'champion of the student', a central unit for student services and a systematic approach to finding out what students thought of the quality they receive in relation to the student charter.
- Runshaw developed a cross-college process-management structure of process improvement teams for its 13 key processes and these were used to formulate and implement its strategic plan.
- It invested heavily in the capacity to measure its quality through a quality unit.
- All staff met weekly in continuous (or curriculum) improvement teams. These acted as the bedrock supporting key processes like self-assessment.

10 CONCLUSION

- How did Runshaw make the breakthrough between 1993 and 1995?
- How did it sustain and improve on its level of excellence over the next decade?
- Is whatever it did transferable to other colleges?

This chapter aims to answer the questions asked in Chapter 1, to reflect upon what happened at Runshaw, to draw together the key messages in the previous chapters and to answer two additional questions:

- What are the core components of an improvement programme?
- What would a coherent, structured and sustained college improvement programme and implementation plan look like?

THE CORE COMPONENTS OF A COLLEGE IMPROVEMENT PLAN?

The need for a radical strategy

Runshaw became outstanding between 1993 and 1995 as a result of a conscious and deliberate rejection of traditional ways of leading a college – what is called 'transactional' leadership – and then an equally deliberate decision to introduce a culture-change programme and, with it, a new form of 'transformational' leadership. This was a recognition that the old ways were not working, that they could not cope with the new strains and pressures of the government's reform agenda and that they had run their course in 'tightening the screw'. As described in Chapter 2, the young man who castigated me in 1990 at his leaving ceremony for squeezing extra work out of staff had realised this, as had all those staff who loudly applauded him. It was not rocket science. It was obvious that things were not working and something different was needed. As Hopkins and Jackson (2003) said of the schools sector:

> *Reform strategies and leadership programmes can no longer take only an incremental approach to change. Such policies and strategies have to date not resulted in substantial changes . . . leadership now needs to be seen within a whole-school or system context to impact both on classroom practice and the work culture of the school . . . the implications of this perspective for school leadership are profound.*

What was needed was that leaders like myself should listen to staff, should take on board what was being said and should be determined to take radical action in response. In our case, we initially took the wrong action, thinking that a process management structure in itself would provide the solution. It was not until 1993 that we reassessed this decision, realised that it was making matters worse, and then took advice from best practice in the private sector to introduce a culture-change programme. That did transform the college – it was the start of a form of transformational leadership that prioritised culture management as the route to becoming 'outstanding'.

The whole process was started by Runshaw carrying out a 'health check', a kind of assessment, enabling us to identify the real issues, the most urgent priorities and an agenda for action. Out of this debate emerged an irresistible demand that the college and its leaders refocus on teaching and learning and the conditions that support it. In the book I have called this 'instructional' leadership and it was one of the key components of the transformational leadership approach that Runshaw adopted. Linked to this was a focus on 'right' and 'wrong' and the moral judgements that underpinned the emergence of a set of core values and their explicit translation into behaviours, policies and standards. We called this second element of transformational leadership 'moral leadership'. The third element we called 'dispersed leadership' because through the building of a professional learning community, everyone in the college effectively had a leadership role to achieve the high standards to which we had committed ourselves. All this changed the role of leaders significantly, shifting their energies from the corporate roles which incorporation had created back to those of the 'leading professional teacher'.

The core components of a model for college improvement are illustrated by Figure 10.1.

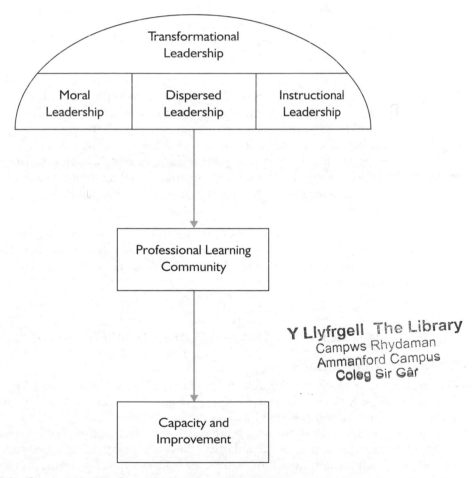

Figure 10.1   *Core components of a model for college improvement*

The first block encompasses the 'parent' overarching concept of 'transformational' leadership, replacing traditional 'transactional' leadership by focusing on the management of the culture of a college. Two forms of 'transformational' leadership are 'moral' and 'dispersed' leadership. As discussed earlier, the former generates moral authority and a strong sense of moral purpose from, for example, a process of defining and practising a college's core values. The second 'disperses' leadership to all staff, creating what I have called 'one united staff team', separating the notion of 'leader' and 'leadership' by reconceptualising the role of leader as facilitator, organiser and supporter of such dispersed leadership.

Hopkins (2003) is quoted in Chapter 1 as arguing that these forms of leadership are insufficient, that what is needed in an educational environment is what is called 'instructional' leadership, that is, a focus on teaching and learning and the conditions that improve teaching and learning. Harris *et al*. (2003), for example, argue: 'Successful school improvement projects focus specifically upon the teaching and learning processes and the "conditions" at school and classroom level that support and sustain school improvement.'

These conditions include an environment in which values drive behaviours, in which staff share in decision-making and in which a culture of high performance expectations is created, so 'instructional' leadership operates most effectively within the concept of transformational, moral and dispersed leadership.

All these forms of leadership, operating under the umbrella of transformational leadership, serve to create a 'professional learning community'. This is about the idea that a college should continuously grow its intellectual capital and its social cohesion by working collaboratively, learning by reflecting and sharing, all the time building its capabilities and capacity for improvement. It rejects the notion that there is only so much in the 'pot': it argues that the 'pot' of knowledge and capacity can become larger and larger, that a college can be a self-sustaining organism, feeding itself systemically, bringing knowledge in through its roots and passing them through its whole body, ever-enriching itself.

These core components are non-negotiable in the sense that they are what this whole approach is about – you either take this route to quality or you take another. That is the choice. Academic theorists in both the school and college sectors believe that most have not taken this route.

WHY HAVEN'T SCHOOLS AND COLLEGES ADOPTED THIS APPROACH?

'Profound' implications

The implications of such an approach are 'profound'. Schools and colleges have not been designed to cope with rapid change. Instead they have been designed to maintain a traditional culture in which hierarchy, departmental 'fiefdoms', isolation and individualism support the status quo. Moreover, the notion of dispersed leadership is alien and threatening to traditional authority roles. And many colleges are weak on what are called the 'foundation' conditions – they are 'turbulent, under strain, riven by conflicting pressures . . . others are rendered incoherent by the forces of external change, the reform agenda and the expectations of multiple accountabilities . . . inarticulate about shared values' (Hopkins and Jackson, 2003).

Most importantly, the management structures often impede culture change by the way in which senior management roles are distanced from the values of staff, by creating unclear and frustrated middle management roles, by preventing collaboration and liaison across college, by fragmenting decision-making about the student experience, and by creating weak lines of accountability and communications. Hopkins and Jackson (2003) argue:

> *schools are not currently structured in ways that facilitate the growth of leadership . . . currently leadership is locked into management structures . . . we must therefore redesign the internal social architecture of schools . . . it should involve a separation of management (maintenance) and leadership (learning and development). Organised routines and processes should also be redesigned to facilitate widespread leadership and knowledge-sharing . . . the most complex and difficult form of leadership for dispersed and capacity-building models is that which operates down through management systems, because it then becomes entwined with power relationships and role responsibilities.*

Connectiveness and networking

Hopkins and Jackson argued for the development of two related concepts, 'connectiveness' and 'networking':

> *opportunities for collaboration between those of different role and status levels need naturally to occur across and between what might otherwise be organisationally separate and balkanised cells or units. Organisationally, schools find this hard . . . they must adapt and reshape their practices in order to generate natural contexts for people to take responsibility in working with and through others. What is needed is the development of 'internal networks'.*

All of this describes the difficulties for schools in implementing a school improvement programme. The situation is significantly more complex and difficult for colleges because they need to overcome additional challenges. These include, firstly, that of size: that is, schools have fewer than 100 staff whereas colleges have many hundreds – over 800 in Runshaw's case. Secondly, colleges had a reduction of 30% in funding between 1993 and 1997, causing mass redundancies and very difficult industrial relations, and additional significant changes in funding are still being made. Thirdly, the conditions of service of college staff were significantly worsened, with the loss of six weeks' holiday, increased class contact hours and a longer working week, all without compensation. Fourthly, colleges are incorporated, funded directly by a central government agency and were removed from local authorities, so they lost the financial 'cushion' and support of services such as those of advisers. Fifthly, the funding per student is significantly lower in colleges than for students studying the same courses – for example, A-level – in schools. Colleges therefore have to employ a large number of part-time staff, have larger class sizes, pay lower salaries and require lecturers to work longer hours than teachers in schools. Sixthly, colleges are expected to 'widen participation' for students who have underachieved at school, who left school feeling disillusioned and disenchanted and who, after 11 years of compulsory education, lack basic skills. And, finally, if all this results in a college failing, it is not closed as a 'failing school' would be – instead, it usually 'withers on the vine' in a spiral of decline or a new principal has the task of reviving it with the existing managers and staff.

The need for colleges to develop 'connectedness' and 'networking' is, therefore, even more of an imperative.

HOW SHOULD COLLEGES IMPLEMENT THE CORE COMPONENTS OF A COLLEGE IMPROVEMENT PLAN?

An overview of Runshaw's plan

In broad terms, Runshaw's approach was to use its culture-change process to involve managers and staff in a prolonged exercise of dispersed leadership, with everyone participating in identifying the college's problems and in taking joint responsibility for solving them. The debate focused on values and behaviours, opening up a fundamental review of student behaviours – the 'foundation' conditions – and staff's new role in consistently implementing a 'New Beginning'. It also led to a reconceptualisation of the role of the manager, to a redefinition of management style and eventually to the identification of eight core competencies.

The engine that drove these debates and that gave the whole process coherence was the creation of 'one united management team', governed by a set of ground rules that included collective responsibility. When we came to apply this ground rule to middle managers, we found that it was first necessary to clarify their roles and remove structural barriers that impeded them. This contributed, along with the reassertion of the need for senior managers to focus on teaching and learning and the need to strengthen lines of communication, to a complete management restructuring, to the creation of what Hopkins and Jackson called 'internal networks' that facilitated collaboration and helped to create a community spirit.

We extended the concept of 'one united management team' to that of 'one united staff team' through the introduction of five 'stop-the-track' staff conferences each year. At the same time, we introduced new processes that improved communications, listening and recognition, and we developed a strategic approach to reducing staff workloads. We constructed a lavish and elaborate staff development and management development infrastructure, linking it to quality assurance and quality control processes like performance management, poor performance and lesson observation. As time went on, we began to revisit and review in an in-depth and unhurried way the core leadership approaches which had created the original transformation and we increasingly developed cross-college process management structures which enabled us to review and improve all of our key processes in a systematic and structured way. We became, in a quite literal way, a 'professional learning community'.

Developing the detailed implementation plan

An implementation plan needs to include four interconnected dimensions: that is, one dimension which clarifies the content of a plan; a second about how the plan will be conducted; a third about when each element could occur; and a fourth about who would be primarily responsible for formulating a specific plan for the implementation of each of the elements and for managing each element on an ongoing basis. The first two are interconnected because, for example, one of the things that a college will probably want to achieve will be to create 'one united management team' but the process for driving the whole plan forward will be by using such a team to reflect on and implement an 'agenda for action'. Nevertheless, it may be useful to make two separate lists that identify what a college may want to achieve and 'how' it could conduct the process of achieving it.

The content of the implementation plan

There are 15 elements in such a plan. They could be subdivided into seven clusters as shown in Figure 10.2.

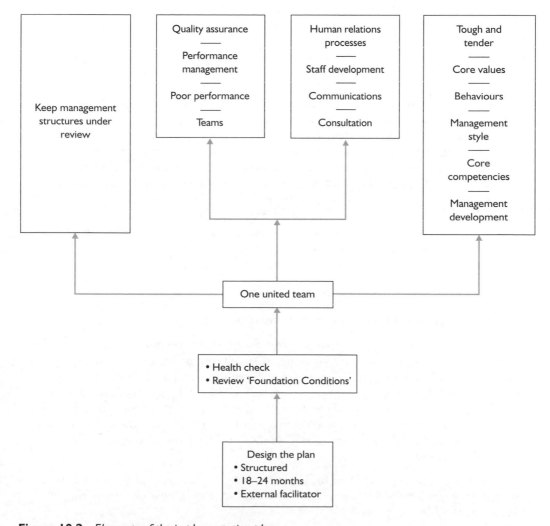

Figure 10.2 *Elements of the implementation plan*

The principal and senior managers should design the implementation plan:

1 Achieve full understanding of the concepts underlying a transformation project.
2 Develop a coherent and systematic implementation plan for 18 months to two years, including the employment of an external facilitator.
3 Conduct a health check and review the feedback from the surveys, identify priorities and develop responses, linking the criticisms made of leadership to the development of new forms of leadership.
4 Review the student culture and the 'foundation' conditions.
5 Review the management structures to ensure that the roles of senior managers are seen to be aligned with the values of staff, particularly those related to 'instructional' leadership, to ensure that lines of communication and accountability are strong, that middle managers are not impeded by structures in carrying out their roles and that 'internal networks' provide multiple opportunities for collaboration.
6 Create 'one united management team' with ground rules and a review of the feasibility for middle managers accepting collective responsibility.
7 Identify the college's core values and translate these into explicit behaviours – and the behaviours expected from staff and managers.
8 Review management styles, reflecting on the 'tough and tender' balance suggested by Runshaw's example, and identify the college's core competencies for managers.
9 Introduce processes that provide continuous feedback to managers on their behaviours as a form of management development – for example, regular staff surveys, 360-degree feedback or assessment centres.
10 Review and develop quality control and quality assurance processes, including process management, target-setting, performance measurement (for example, lesson observation, student surveys and data management), performance monitoring and assessment.
11 Introduce or develop processes for performance management and poor performance.
12 Review and develop continuous improvement teams.
13 Develop an effective infrastructure for staff development.
14 Review and develop human resources processes – for example, briefing, staff focus groups, recognition ceremonies, the staff newsletter.
15 Introduce processes that support whole-staff conferences.

These steps are now explained in more detail.

Developing an understanding and commitment

It is important that a college leadership makes an informed commitment to this whole approach, that it understands what is meant by such terms as 'transformational' leadership, that it realises that the approach will require a substantial investment of time and energy and that it will change people's roles – particularly those of leaders – and require new norms, attitudes and behaviours from people like themselves. Having said that, I do not think that there is a real option – that is, I believe that the continuance of traditional transactional leadership is unsustainable in the world of constant change in which colleges exist.

So the first practical step would be for the management team – certainly at least the senior management team – to learn about this new approach, possibly by inviting an external facilitator to explain it.

A coherent and systematic plan

Whilst writing this book, I have been working as a consultant with a number of colleges. Several of them have asked me to work with them over a long period – usually about 18 months to two years – coming for one day a month to work with various individuals and/or teams of managers. On a visit to one of these colleges, a particularly stimulating one in which I helped the senior management team to identify its core values and then begin to translate them into behaviours, policies and processes, the principal said to me, as we walked out of the college in the evening, that she was just beginning to understand fully the enormity of what she had taken on. She was inspired by the vision of transforming the college into an 'outstanding' one within two years, but she was just beginning to realise the fundamental nature of the changes that 'transformational', 'moral', 'dispersed' and 'instructional' leadership would mean for her, her management colleagues, her staff and for the students. She was not in the least deterred, but what she wanted, above all else, was a clear implementation strategy, a coherent, structured and sustainable college-improvement programme.

In asking for this, she reflected the conclusions of the International School Improvement Project (1982–6) which identified the need for a '. . . systematic, sustained effort aimed at changing the learning conditions and other related internal conditions' (quoted in Hopkins and Jackson, 2003).

Hence, it is clear that culture change, the introduction of new forms of leadership and the creation of capacity by establishing a 'professional learning community' cannot be achieved piecemeal or in an ad hoc way – it requires a planned, coherent and structured process to transform the way that a college is run and it needs to be carried out in a relatively short time period, probably about 18 months to two years.

External facilitation and coaching is, in my view, also essential. Apart from anything else, leaders in colleges are very busy, they do not always have the time to study theory or reflect and plan how to apply it, and they could be knocked off course by a thousand distractions. The whole process also benefits from the kind of facilitation that breaks down barriers by offering an independent and confidential channel for listening, for feeding back and for coaching. This encourages a level of openness and trust that is needed to create new relationships. In our case, we believed that 'a quality journey needed a map and a guide' so we used a consultant in 1993–4 to release all the pent-up frustrations and resentments that had acted as barriers to staff commitment. He helped us to make sense of them and to develop purposeful responses. He had experience and knowledge, a profound understanding of what was going on and the skills to facilitate action. Without him, we might have lumbered on, becoming increasingly depressed or producing responses which made matters worse.

Health check

Once a commitment is made, the college then needs to carry out a health check to identify staff's perceptions and to determine a hands-on agenda for action. Whilst this chapter argues that the overall approach – the new forms of leadership described above and the creation of a 'professional learning community' – is 'non-negotiable', the tools, mechanisms, structures, policies and processes that a college uses are all negotiable. That is, individual colleges could choose which of these to use, how to apply them, in what sequence, with what linkages and alignments, and so on. And where a college starts depends on the situation in which the individual college finds itself in terms of the kinds of issues that it faces and its state of readiness to develop. Colleges are at different levels of effectiveness and they have different contextual environments so they need different improvement strategies, customised to their specific needs, strengths, weaknesses and conditions.

It is therefore necessary to identify the 'real issues', the strength of staff satisfaction or dissatisfaction about the way the college is run and what responses should be made. Our consultant warned us about a 'perception gap', telling us that managers almost always think that they know what staff think but that they rarely do. We did not believe this was the case in our situation but he turned out to be right and we were wrong. Had we not carried out a health check, we would have wasted time and energy pursuing the wrong assumptions.

At Runshaw, after the initial culture-change programme – our version of the health check – we increasingly used the business excellence model in the way described in Chapter 9 to conduct our own health check (or self-assessment) for 'leadership and management'. Such an approach may not appeal to people in colleges which may already be struggling to cope with the requirements of the Learning Skills Council or Ofsted so a simple version could suffice. That is, the health check should measure the key 'results' or performance indicators like success rates, recruitment and finances, but equally important in the excellence model are high levels of student and staff satisfaction. Without staff commitment, for example, the excellence model argues that the other results would be weak.

Hence, a health check on the culture would probably start with a survey of staff, possibly subdivided into separate surveys of support staff, lecturing staff, middle managers and senior managers. The surveys would usually include questionnaires and focus groups. They would ask questions about the leadership of the college, about the way policy and strategy was made, about the way that staff were managed, about how external partnerships were developed, about how resources were managed, and about how key processes were identified, reviewed and continuously improved. These are what are called the 'enablers' in the Business Excellence Model, as described in Chapter 9.

With regard to 'leadership', for example, the survey would investigate whether leaders were value driven and whether they role model their values, whether they were visionary, whether the management system and structures supported the implementation of a high performance culture, whether leaders interacted appropriately with staff, students and other stakeholders, whether they were trusted and whether they managed change and improvement successfully. It would also ask questions about whether policy and strategy were imposed on staff or whether staff were involved in building a shared sense of direction. It would ask about the effectiveness of communications, listening and recognition, and about staff development. It would ask searching questions about quality management, particularly the way that performance was measured. All these questions would identify an 'agenda for action', prioritising those 'enablers' which needed most urgent attention.

Reviewing the 'foundation' conditions

When staff are asked about their concerns in a health check, it is almost inevitable that many of them will raise issues about student behaviour. This, therefore, provides an opportunity to ensure that the 'foundation conditions' are in place: that is, that the college is stable, orderly, that students are well behaved, that staff–student relationships are sound, and that, therefore, people will have the 'space' and the 'sheltered conditions' to enter into debates on values and beliefs in a relatively relaxed and unhurried way.

At Runshaw, once staff understood that culture change meant that everybody was being asked to share in setting an agenda for action, they placed at the top of that agenda all their concerns about student behaviours. In our case, this led to the creation of 'The New Beginning' in 1995 and 1996, which, in turn, led to a quantum-leap improvement in standards and student achievement.

So an implementation plan should include the opportunity for a college-wide debate about such matters. It is an opportunity to engage staff in taking joint responsibility for the formulation and implementation of college policy and strategy that will make an immediate impact on student achievement.

Review management structures.

In Chapter 5 it was explained that, in order to enable middle managers to engage fully in the ground-rule of collective responsibility as members of one united management team we first had to restructure the senior management team. The process of culture change had made us realise that, in our case, leadership really was 'locked into management structures' and that we needed to 'redesign the social architecture' to create 'internal networks' that would facilitate collaboration. Hence, Runshaw's management restructuring created a two-dimensional 'internal network' model, illustrated in Figure 10.3.

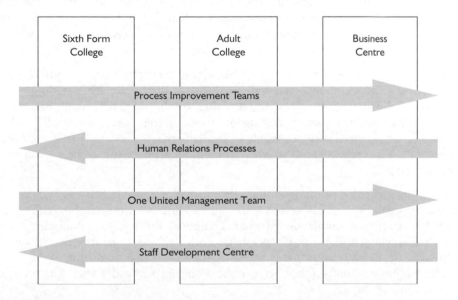

Figure 10.3 *Internal network model*

At its heart was the first dimension, a federal structure – 'three colleges in one' – with one of the 'colleges', the sixth-form centre, divided into two faculties, making a total of four faculties. These provided stability, a strong sense of identity, effective lines of communication and accountability, a student-centred focus linked to an equally strong focus on teaching and learning, and a solid and powerful infrastructure for continuous improvement and for what Hopkins and Jackson called 'maintenance'.

The second dimension had four elements, which acted as a basis for what Hopkins and Jackson called 'leadership (learning and development)':

- Cross-college structures of process improvement teams, centres of excellence, portfolio development groups and student services.
- A battery of human relations processes for communications, listening and recognition.
- The engine that did more than anything else to create a 'professional learning community' – the creation of 'one united management team', driving the creation of 'one united staff team' via 'stop-the-track' staff conferences, creating a shared sense of direction, shared values, shared vision and a consensus for college goals.
- Management development and staff development infrastructures.

Both dimensions enabled the new forms of transformational leadership to be enacted. They provided managers and staff with the wherewithal to take a corporate view and the capability to implement improvements effectively without being overcome by structural barriers to effective liaison, co-operation or collaboration or role conflicts.

Staff also wanted senior managers to refocus on teaching and learning. One of the strongest messages in the culture-change process of 1993–4 was that they felt that senior managers had lost sight of the importance of this, our key process. Research tells us that Runshaw's experience was typical of most colleges. That is, research about the college sector in the last decade has focused on concerns about 'managerialism' and about the fact that over 93% of senior management team structures have become orientated to 'corporate' roles, usually with only one senior manager linking decision-making at this level to faculty structures, lecturers and teaching and learning. When staff in Runshaw said in 1993–4 that 'resources have been misdirected from the classroom', they were pre-empting a complaint echoed in research about colleges in general.

In Runshaw's case, after 1995 all but one of our senior managers – the exception was the director of finance and resources – spent the majority of their time either leading research and development on teaching and learning, or observing teaching, or training teachers in teaching and learning, or talking and listening to teachers and students in structured and unstructured ways, or teaching students themselves. They role-modelled our concept of a 'great teacher' and they performed the primary role of being a 'leading professional teacher'.

Our strategic plan was also primarily about whom we would teach, how we would develop our approaches to teaching and learning, and how we would improve the conditions for effective teaching and learning. There was absolutely no doubt at Runshaw that 'teaching and learning was our first priority'. And I believe that it was this focus – 'instructional' leadership as it is called by theorists – that made one of the greatest contributions to our success. So all colleges need to consider what 'instructional' leadership means for them.

All this implies a set of challenging questions for a college in reviewing its management structures to determine whether they help or hinder culture management. These questions include the following:

- Does the composition of your senior management team include sufficient involvement of those most involved in directly managing teaching and learning and in most direct contact with students?
- Does that team provide sufficient capacity to line manage staff effectively, or does it locate line management of staff in the hands of a few, thereby creating the potential for a breakdown of communication and for blocking meaningful access to decision-making?
- Do your middle managers have clear staff management roles, properly supported from above, and are they equipped to manage high performance standards, challenging or confronting those who do not meet these standards?
- Do they have sufficient opportunities to liaise and implement decisions across the college through structured and supported 'internal networks'?
- Do they have meaningful roles in developing corporate policy and strategy and in communicating these to others?
- And are all these roles and structures sufficiently customer focused?

One united management team

In all the processes described above, a constant assumption has been made about the collective role of managers in developing them. This needs to be clarified. One of the central themes of this book is that a coherent, structured, managed culture-change process needs to be introduced and – as was argued in Chapter 5 – when a college community includes hundreds of staff, as most do, the potential for chaos in changing the culture is considerable. The key co-ordinating structure that provided a strong sense of coherence and that ensured that our approaches were fully and properly implemented was that of 'one united management team'. I would argue that this is absolutely essential in organisations the size of most colleges.

In practical terms, it can initially operate with whichever managers are deemed appropriate by the individual college but, eventually, it should ideally include all middle as well as senior managers. Like every other structure, it should have clear ground rules and the one that is likely to cause the most difficulty in gaining acceptance is that of collective responsibility. The concept of 'one united management team' needs to be used at the start of the implementation plan but there may not be the time then to make all the changes that will be necessary to gain full commitment from middle managers to the ground rules, so the ground rules could be developed as the occasion arises, building upon the creation of trust and mutual support within the team as it identifies its values, reviews student behaviour, receives feedback from staff focus groups and so on. In other words, the management team could be action-focused, developing its ethos through periodic reflection.

An acid test will occur in determining whether it is fair and reasonable to expect middle managers to accept collective responsibility – that is, whether they have the opportunities to participate in decision-making and are properly supported by the way the college is organised and structured to do their jobs properly. It is crucially important for the success of this whole approach that they can meaningfully accept collective responsibility and can fully participate in the concept of 'one united management team', but the situation in most colleges seems to be that they are not able to do so. Hence, this is a key issue that needs to be introduced by colleges, initially at least, early in the implementation programme and reflected upon at regular intervals.

'Tough and tender' leadership development: identifying the college's core values

The feedback from surveys and focus groups informs debates on values, management styles and competencies. At Runshaw we spent a great deal of time identifying all these and translating them very carefully into behaviours, policies and processes in the way described in Chapters 3 and 4. Those chapters also quote educational theorists in saying that 'all schools should identify their core values and translate them into explicit behaviours'. Doing so begins to shape a form of 'moral' leadership and to give a platform for people to assert what they think is 'right' and 'wrong'. In particular, it begins to put into place the conditions for reviewing the morality of the ways that colleges have traditionally tackled or not tackled issues related to poor performance.

Reviewing management style and core competencies

In Runshaw's case, we saw a direct link between the key concerns that staff identified in the 1993–4 surveys and the new forms of 'transformational', 'moral', 'dispersed' and 'instructional' leadership that we wanted to introduce. We then linked these to the core values, then to the management behaviours implied by these values and then to our core competencies, by which time we had articulated very clearly a distinctive new overarching approach which we called 'tough and tender'.

The linkages between all these were, in our case, made quite naturally. It was almost like an organic process in which one exercise of reflection grew into another. This made it relevant, practical, 'hands-on' and used the contextual language of Runshaw, so it made it immediate and concrete.

In summary, what this amounts to is that colleges should:

- first identify the 'real issues' – those perceived by staff to be the most significant barriers to obtaining their commitment to change and improvement
- then identify the college's core values
- then translate these into explicit behaviours
- use them to redefine the college's management styles and to identify its core competencies.

Every college should collectively articulate 'the way things are done around here' whatever those ways are. It should have a clear 'script' that enables everybody to know what is expected of them, what is regarded as 'right' and 'wrong' and what principles and criteria should be used to make decisions.

The method for producing all these would, I suggest, be through facilitated workshops, initially with the management team, and these should be informed by external sources like courses, books or consultancies on such matters as management styles. They should be organic, with clear linkages between workshops, and they should be unhurried, so time needs to be planned for people to meet and reflect, and preparations need to be made to ensure that this time is used properly and that tangible outcomes emerge.

Management development

In Runshaw's experience, all this naturally led to management development. The feedback processes were an intense form of management development through experiential learning. So too was the structured reflection on this feedback, along with the debates on values, beliefs, behaviours and styles. Collectively, they created a form of 'professional learning community' within the management team. And as we developed new additional approaches like regular staff surveys, 360-degree feedback and assessment centres to measure that 'we did what we said we would do', the additional flows of feedback created an increasing sense of self-realisation within managers of the need for further management development. In due course, we developed a rolling programme of management training modules linked to our values and core competencies.

I would, therefore, recommend that every college develop both feedback processes to managers and easy access for them to a modular programme of management training, particularly in interpersonal skills.

Quality assurance

Ultimately, the purpose of everything was to improve the college. Runshaw put into place a quality assurance infrastructure to support high quality standards by anticipating what could go wrong and acting to avoid it. This included investments in new forms of leadership, in staff development and in many other quality assurance strategies. Runshaw was also rigorous about monitoring quality. It operated quality control processes that enabled it to check, measure, monitor and review the implementation of all its standards. Its approaches included a process-management structure, the establishment of a quality unit, a monthly senior management team structure dedicated to monitoring an annualised schedule of 'performance results', an enormous investment in developing management information systems and a corporate intranet, the development of very high capability to produce a comprehensive range of data on a wide scope of measures, including the added-value performance of individual lecturers, a sophisticated student survey process and a significant investment in lesson observation.

It was all these approaches that contributed to accusations elsewhere of 'managerialism' but one of Runshaw's key achievements was to gain staff support for all these approaches, so that staff perceived them as mechanisms that helped continuous development of our service to students. Runshaw developed staff commitment to a truly professional way for the college to conduct itself.

Hence, whilst developing all the leadership strategies described above, most of which focus on raising staff morale and creating a community spirit, an implementation plan for culture change and transformation would also have to include quality assurance approaches similar to those developed at Runshaw.

Performance management and poor performance

One of our key quality assurance approaches was a performance management process that enabled individual staff and their respective line managers to set individual annual performance goals within the context of team and college goals. These were supported by individual training and development plans and coaching but they were also linked to appraisal. At Runshaw, we regarded this process as the 'backbone' of our approaches to managing the performance of staff. We linked it to job specifications, to lesson observation, to performance reviews of data and, of course, to staff development and management development. It applied to all staff so it is not about poor performance. In fact, it was a vehicle for recognition, for praising people and for saying 'thank-you'.

We operated a separate process for poor performance and we did not hesitate to use it when necessary. Challenging the few staff who were either lazy, or who treated students badly, or who were casually absent or late, was one of the most popular effects brought about by the culture-change process, driven as it was by clear values. The Hay Group points out that most colleges are weak at managing poor performance and that significant improvements in college standards would be achieved if this process was implemented properly. Hence, the introduction of these processes is an essential part of an implementation plan.

Development of continuous improvement teams

One of Runshaw's core structures was that of teams. They were not established at Runshaw as a result of the culture-change process so we tended to overlook their critical importance to the implementation at grass-root level of most of our policies and strategies. But we were concerned that, whilst many colleges operate similar teamwork structures, research shows that they can often be used to nurture mutually supportive teams of negative staff in criticising students, the curriculum, resources and the management in destructive ways.

Hence, we constantly reviewed teamwork, always seeking to clarify their purposes, how they should be led, how meetings should be chaired, how members should behave in meetings, their ground-rules, the frequency of meetings, and their linkages to other teams, structures and management roles. Whenever we did this it felt like opening a hornets' nest, such was the number and intensity of issues that emerged. So this is an important item to be reviewed in an implementation plan for college improvement.

An infrastructure for staff development

One of the key themes of this book is that, to create a 'professional learning community' and to engage staff in being committed to improvement, it is essential to establish a massive infrastructure for staff development. At Runshaw, this included the creation of a professional development centre, the establishment of professional tutor posts and the introduction of processes like 'best in class', which enabled hundreds of staff to visit other organisations, learning from others.

Most importantly, we recognised in principle that what would make a crucial difference to the quality and efficiency of everything that we did at Runshaw would be to focus on developing the capabilities of each individual member of staff. We did not pay lip-service to staff development: it was strategically central to our quality assurance approaches. In particular, we linked lesson observation to a rolling programme of modular training that was both accessible and of a very high quality – there was nothing more important to us than finding out what was going on the classroom and taking direct and immediate action to improve it. Mediocrity was not tolerated, but, for that condition to be acceptable in a culture based on trust, it had to be value driven, and enormous investment had to be made in support processes like coaching. It was also necessary to approach staff development as a positive opportunity for personal and professional growth. In summary, we committed an enormous amount of money, time and energy on staff development, so we would obviously see it as central to a college-improvement programme.

Human resources processes to make staff feel valued

Ultimately, the capacity of the college to be 'outstanding' depended on staff commitment. It would have been impossible to obtain that without the strategic approach explained in Chapter 7. We were purposely trying to develop a strong sense of social cohesion, a sense of coherence, openness, the building of social capital and the creation of emotionally intelligent relationships. We were trying to build trust, showing that we valued people, that we listened to them, that we liked them and that we respected them. We also tried to make them aware about external pressures and show them that Runshaw offered a relatively sheltered environment in which people could focus on what they valued most, that is, educating students.

Hence, an implementation plan should include strategies for managing four aspects of human relations. They are managing the culture, managing the staff, managing the work environment and managing change.

With regard to the first of these, this book has argued for a culture of openness, for a collaborative and consultative ethos in which staff are respected as responsible professionals, in which negotiation and consensus-building could take place and in which decisions could be made with the expectation everyone will abide with them. As already explained, core values should also be identified. Leaders should recognise achievement and contributions of staff, individually and in teams, informally and formally, and teams should be established to enable staff to work together productively.

With respect to the second aspect, that is, managing staff, this book has suggested every college should identify the equivalent of a 'Runshaw person', with a clear person specification linked to the values and vision of the college and alignment to the appointments and other processes. Once appointed, staff should be deployed properly, with clear job constructions, clear linkages to the roles of others, including their line managers, a clear strategy for using part-time staff, support staff and quasi-teaching staff for student support duties, and a clear policy on performance-related pay for the recruitment and retention of high-calibre staff.

The third aspect, managing the physical environment, is concerned with the physical working environment, policies for managing student behaviours, the promotion of work-like balances and with managers being concerned to reduce the intensification of workloads.

Finally, the management of change requires leaders to identify the benefits of initiatives for the college, to present these positively and carefully to staff, to align them with internal goals, to assess the scale of the impact on staff and their preparedness for it, to ensure that the change will be manageable and that staff are persuaded of the benefits to both themselves and the college, and that thorough evaluation is conducted during and after the change to shape future planning.

Stop-the-track staff conferences to create a shared sense of direction

The creation of a 'professional learning community' requires coherence, alignment, synergy, a process and a structure for pulling all the approaches described above together into a holistic strategy. An illustration of how the processes and structures involved in organising 'stop-the-track' days at Runshaw acted as a focal point for creating this kind of holistic synergy was the introduction of a new strategy in 2003 called the 'Hattie factors'. That is, in 2000 our professional tutor attended a course by a consultant, Geoff Pettie, who described the work of Professor John Hattie, a New Zealand education theorist who had scanned world-wide research to identify – in rank order – those teaching and learning methods that have the greatest impact on student achievement. She arranged for Geoff to provide a workshop for the senior management team at Runshaw and, following this, the senior managers went on an 'away-day' together to reflect on what they had learned. They then presented a set of proposals to the college management team, the structure that supported the concept of 'one united management team' and it enthusiastically supported further exploration of Hattie's ideas. On the basis of this, we then organised a series of similar workshops for curriculum middle managers and then for course and subject team leaders, all the time communicating with staff about all these developments through the staff update and briefing processes. All these meetings occurred in January and February 2003, so they naturally led into the preparations for the staff conference to be held on a 'stop-the-track' day in March. It was decided that we would focus on two themes at that conference: the 'Hattie factors' for teaching staff and a process management development for support staff. During the conference, each team of lecturers decided whether it wanted to commit itself to implement the 'Hattie factors' and, if so, what specific actions they planned to take, how they would monitor and evaluate their success, and whether they wanted to participate in any of the 20 college-wide action-research projects, which by then had spun out of the debate. The professional development centre then developed a new modular training programme to enable those who wanted to explore the concepts raised by the Hattie factors to do so. It also co-ordinated the action research projects, including organising dissemination of their outcomes.

In summary, a coherent, structured, inter-connected, cross-college, socially cohesive, relevant strategy which integrated and aligned many of the processes and structures described in this book created synergy and thereby had an extraordinary impact on improving the quality of education for students. This illustrates how Runshaw deployed its capacity to improve continuously, reaching out for new and higher levels of performance as an enjoyable and intellectually stimulating exercise in whole-college collaboration. And there were at least five such quantum-leap improvement projects every year. It was a real 'professional learning community' and it was very satisfying to be part of it.

THE IMPLEMENTATION PLAN

The guiding principles of the entire implementation process are those that underpin the concept of 'dispersed' leadership. That is, the role of leader is reconceptualised as that of facilitating, organising and supporting leadership for the many. Hence, when senior managers consider what to do, under this new approach they usually formulate (that is, they do not decide) a set of proposals that act as a hypothesis, a framework for further consideration by middle managers and then by the whole staff and, on some occasions like reviews of student conduct, by students and other stakeholders.

Having said that, the process needs coherence, so proposals should only be offered when they have been fully thought through after they have been tested for feasibility and after the resource implications have been properly provided for. There will also be a need for persuasion, for explanation, for communication and for detailed implementation, so the role of middle managers and possibly team leaders will be critical. Hence, the need to involve them in the formulation process, gaining increasing ownership as consultation occurs.

So the method or the process of an implementation plan will have seven elements:

- an external facilitator should guide and assist the process
- the principal needs to be the key player at all times, comfortable with the direction and pace of change and the overall capacity and capability of the college to absorb it without losing focus on other more immediate considerations
- the senior management team needs to be the driving force, generating ideas and formulating proposals, adapting approaches from elsewhere to the college's circumstances
- the whole 'united management team', consisting of senior and middle managers, needs to develop unhurried, careful implementation projects, probably through the kind of management development workshops held at Runshaw
- there may also be a role for team leaders in considering how a college-wide initiative could be applied in their respective areas
- a whole-staff conference, perhaps like those at Runshaw, would then equip academic board representatives with a mandate to recommend a decision to the principal and governors
- in some situations, students' parents, employers or other stakeholders may also be consulted and involved.

The specific implementation model which I use as a consultant is to visit a college for one day a month for about 18 months, initially obtaining the initial commitment by the principal and senior management team to a college-improvement programme like that described in this book, then conducting a health check, then feeding back to various groups the views of staff and others, helping them to identify core values, behaviours, management styles and core competencies. As part of this process, the concept of 'one united management team' begins to shake take shape as we begin to reflect on the ground rules. This specifically requires the facilitation of the removal of role conflicts that may exist for middle managers.

As this process unfolds, specific individuals or small groups can take on responsibility for introducing specific new approaches, like an equivalent to Runshaw's staff update or a staff survey mechanism. In due course, all managers will need to be trained in these processes, so management development workshops need to be arranged on a regular basis to support the introduction of specific processes like performance management or poor performance.

Essentially, the whole plan needs to be co-ordinated on a regular basis, maintaining momentum, coaching and providing frameworks for further progress. At the same time, there needs to be access to specific training in those processes that the college wishes to introduce and, once they have been thought through by a small group, they need to be cascaded to the whole management team and then to the whole staff for further consideration before detailed implementation. There will also need to be access for managers to a rolling programme of management development modules that support the development of core competencies like, for example, interpersonal skills.

The following, then, is a very approximate outline of when the 15 elements could be introduced. This is not intended as a strait-jacket and, to some extent, the pace and prioritisation will depend upon the needs of each individual college, its capacity for change, and how successfully initial elements are introduced. The times given are the times of introduction, not completion, and each element will need to be followed through properly to avoid creating a sense of 'false promises' or 'falsely raised expectations'.

Who is involved also depends on the particular situation in the college. What is clear is that this whole approach will demand a great deal of time and energy from the principal. It is important symbolically that such matters as a vision and values are seen to be developed from the top. The senior manager responsible for human relations management will also be a key player. To a lesser extent, so too will be the senior manager responsible for quality assurance and control. To an even lesser extent, the senior manager responsible for students or the curriculum will have an important role leading the review of the student culture and staff–student relationships. However, there is no reason why the various elements cannot be shared out more evenly, especially since many of those which involve staff or management development do not require specialist knowledge.

It should also be clarified that middle managers do not have to become 'expert' in these changes. They will need to develop expertise in those processes that they will directly manage, but these are relatively few. Specifically, the main ones are performance management, poor performance, briefing, staff absence (for example, 'return-to-work'), performance review and lesson observation.

Month 1–12: management level only.

Month 1: employ a consultant to provide a workshop for college managers to develop understanding and commitment.

Month 2: develop a coherent and systematic plan.

Month 3: health check to identify the real issues for senior managers, middle managers and staff, subdivided into teaching staff and support staff (led by the senior manager for human relations). Review the plan in the light of the feedback from the health check.

Month 4: start to review the 'foundation' conditions: for example

- student behaviours (led by the senior manager for students or the curriculum)
- expectations of staff (led by the senior manager for human relations)
- relationships and lines of communication/accountability (led by the principal and senior manager for human relations).

Month 5: start to review the management structures: for example, following up issues arising from the previous month's review of lines of communication and accountability (led by the principal). Reflect on the concept and practice of 'one united management team' (led by the principal).

Month 6: start to identify core values and behaviours, linked to the concept of transformational leadership, and to management styles and core competencies (led by the principal and by the senior manager responsible for senior human relations).

Month 7: introduce new approaches to feedback to managers and provide access to management training (led by the senior manager for human relations).

Month 8: review quality assurance processes (led by the senior manager responsible for quality assurance).

Month 9: introduce performance management and a review of poor performance processes (led by the senior manager responsible for human relations).

Month 10: review teamwork (led by the senior manager for human relations).

Month 11: review staff development (led by the manager for human relations).

Month 12: review page our processes: for example, communications (led by the senior manager for human relations).

Months 13–24: begin to introduce all the above to staff once they are properly thought through and resources are allocated for them. They would be introduced through staff conferences and the academic board to develop a shared vision and goals. Specialist courses could be provided to train managers in specific processes: for example, briefing, performance management, poor performance, lesson observation, surveying students, conducting student and staff focus groups, and 360-degree feedback. Specialist courses could also be provided for generic management development: for example, leading a team, interpersonal skills and strategic planning.

CONCLUSION

This chapter hopefully offers the reader the answers to the questions posed in the introduction and reassures him or her that the approaches at Runshaw are transferable. Hopefully, it also offers a practical tool – an agenda for action – to assist in such a transfer. It should be emphasised that what became known as the 'Runshaw way' did not, in fact, originate at Runshaw. We adopted it from Leyland Trucks and later came to recognise it as the way that the 14 leading European companies that founded the European Foundation for Quality Management and which created the Business Excellence Model conducted their businesses. Later still, we recognised it in the case study of a fictional Ontario school invented by Leithwood and others, and in the model for school improvement produced by Hopkins and Jackson for the National School Leadership Centre. It is a 'way' that many organisations in both the private sector and public sector, in schools and colleges, have implemented successfully. It does not depend upon the personality of any particular leader and, in fact, it argues that the 'great man' theory is an impediment to long-term sustained success.

The notion of a 'way' is useful though because it suggests two critically important dimensions about Runshaw's experience. Firstly, the concept of the 'way' does capture the importance of synergy and alignment, of the need to link all the approaches described in this book into a coherent whole. The case study used earlier in this chapter on the 'Hattie factors' illustrates the importance of synergy, alignment and of making connections. As Hadfield (2003) said:

> *Capacity-building requires leaders not only to look holistically at each area of their school but to develop an understanding of how to bring each of these areas together in a way that generates further capacity. This requires leaders to develop a deep understanding of what types of connections work best between certain areas, to create a synergy that guides which, when and how the connections are to made, and when certain connections need to be broken and replaced by others.*

The concept of a 'way' is also very apt because it captures the intangible and organic nature of the culture, emotions, feelings, relationships, norms, attitudes, values, beliefs and behaviours that characterised Runshaw. The phrase was first used formally at Runshaw in 2001 by an external researcher, Margaret Woods, who spent three months at Runshaw interviewing students and staff. Whenever she reported back to a steering committee that was tasked with overseeing the production of a manual on Runshaw's approaches, she used the phrase 'the Runshaw way' and, when challenged about its meaning, she said that there was something about the atmosphere in the college that motivated people to go 'the extra mile'. In her report she described the 'special blend of ingredients that contribute to the distinctiveness of the Runshaw way'. Those ingredients were described by her in the following terms (quoted in *The Runshaw Way: Values Drive Behaviours*):

> *Students appreciated the ready access to the right person at the right time and were impressed that tutors would always prioritise time to see them. Comments such as 'they are always offering help' and 'they help you out as much as they possibly can' were often used by students and typify the students statement on this issue. In these sorts of ways Runshaw was readily seen as student-centred . . .*

> *. . . it is staff's commitment and effort which have contributed so much to the current levels of student outcomes. Staff and students feel a great deal pride in belonging to the community of Runshaw College. This potent blend of pride, loyalty and commitment to its values, aims and purposes was a striking element of any discussions. The highly developed motivation to achieve excellence was another prominent feature of the discussions . . .*

> *Staff expressed pride in the relentless collective focus on improvement and standards as an important element in the success and excellent reputation of the college . . .*

I think we feel proud because of the caring nature of the people I work with, what they do and the commitment they've got and how close they are, you can feel that the student gets a lot from coming here . . .

. . . helpful, approachable readily accessible tutors who understand students and make students and their needs their first priority define much that is characteristic of the culture of this organisation . . .

Seeing one's role as a member of staff in terms of 'making a difference to people's lives' was a very powerful statement and an affirmation of the seriousness with which staff approached their roles and responsibilities. Central to this is the discretionary effort from staff who are willing to go that bit further for their students.

Several things stand out in these quotations. One is the constant focus on students. Another is the sense of pride felt by people at Runshaw. Another is the level of staff commitment to values, students and to each other. But what strikes me most strongly is the contrast between the kind of attitudes displayed here and those displayed at Runshaw in 1984 when low-achievers were described as 'dross', provision for adult students was described as 'Mickey Mouse' and when senior managers dismissed the views of what they called 'junior staff' with contempt. The worst of these attitudes had largely disappeared by 1993, when the culture-change programme was introduced, but there was not then a 'Runshaw way' to replace them. There was, instead, a vacuum, a sense of stumbling along trying to cope, a condition akin to being destabilised and debilitated by externally driven change.

After 1995, Runshaw was a completely different place. The 'Runshaw way' had been created and, with it, a culture in which people were the key focus of attention and in which systems, structures and strategies were used to support and to enact that focus, putting into practice the vision and values that motivated us. To quote Margaret Woods again: 'Whilst the college emphasises support and a caring and concerned approach for each student and his/her needs, this operates as part of a rigorous and robust academic framework.'

The 'quality journey' that started in 1993 was a journey of exploration and learning. This book may sound as though we knew what we were doing throughout it, that the whole thing was rational, logical, systematic, coherent and structured. I wish it had been and I am sure that, if we knew then what we know now, it would be a lot easier. But, essentially, the theme of this book is that a college needs to create the capacity to become outstanding and to sustain that level by being a 'professional learning community', that is, by continuously bringing knowledge in, by growing knowledge through structured reflection on people's experience, and by being prepared to experiment, explore, and to recognise the value of people's vision, intuition and instinct. One of the most commonly heard phrases at Runshaw was how staff had 'walked across the grass' when trying to find the 'right' way forward, how they had instinctively responded to a problem by treading a new path across uncharted territory. I was reminded of this phrase by the following:

All change is a hypothesis – a process of action, enquiry and experimentation to create intuitive and collective knowledge about what works and how it works from within. Engaging staff in this process is a means of reculturing. This change to the ways of working – the norms, values and relationships – is a process of restructuring . . . There are no clear solutions. Life is like a path you beat while you walk it. It is the walking that beats the path. It is not the path that makes the walk. (Fullan, 1998)

This describes what happened at Runshaw perfectly. It was an organic, socially cohesive and dynamic model of organisational development in which sharing, collaboration and reflection fed constant growth of intellectual and social capital and, with it, our capacity. The role of leaders was to facilitate, organise and support. And critical to that was trust. If I were to summarise the whole story of Runshaw's development in two simple phrases, they would be 'listening' and 'taking action'. That is, the two most important things that happened at Runshaw after 1993 were that other senior managers and I 'listened' to staff, and we did it again and again in structured and informal ways until it became embedded in the 'way that things work around here', the 'Runshaw way'. We also 'took action'. That is, we did not just consult and listen for the sake of it: it was a purposeful exercise that immediately produced tangible outcomes, sometimes radical and 'brave'.

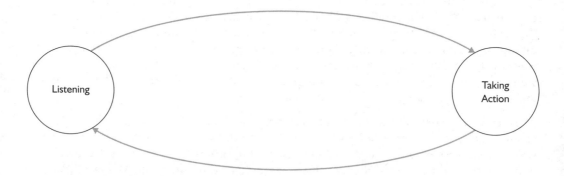

Figure 10.4 *Listening/action cycle*

This was the basis of trust. For staff to be fully committed, they needed to be convinced that senior managers genuinely wanted to listen, to learn, to collaborate, to share decision-making, and they needed to know that this was not empty rhetoric, that what they said would influence what happened and that action would be taken. 'Listening' and 'taking action' were the two behaviours that, above all else, characterised Runshaw's leadership after 1993. This is not to suggest that Runshaw's success was due to some kind of personality trait of its leaders: instead, it is to argue that these two simple attitudes and behaviour patterns can be adopted by anybody – that they are entirely transferable and that they are essential to any culture-change programme or to the implementation of transformational leadership.

At Runshaw, we listened in 1993 to what staff thought about the kind of leadership that existed then in the college. We listened to what leadership staff said they needed. We listened to what staff thought was 'right' and 'wrong' – their core values – and we acted upon what we heard by collaborating with them in translating those core values into explicit behaviours for ourselves, for staff and for students. It became a guiding principle for managers that we had to do what we say and that we should not raise false expectations or make false promises. We defined the concept of 'the great manager' in terms of behaviours like being student centred, setting high standards, supporting and coaching staff, following through, confronting non-compliance and poor performance with integrity, acting fairly on all occasions or, to put it simply, to 'putting our ethos into action'. This was the basis of trust that bound staff into a 'professional learning community'. It was a moral form of leadership that created a strong sense of moral conviction and purpose, the immediate outcome being that a new consensus emerged and, with it, an over-riding demand for consistency and high standards, thereby creating powerful 'dispersed' peer-group pressures for a culture of 'high performance expectations'.

It was this trust that defined the sense of community at Runshaw, which motivated people, and which, ultimately, created a college that served students exceptionally well. It became a good place in which to work and learn for students and staff, and that contributed significantly to the larger community of central Lancashire in which Runshaw was located. The quality journey was not finished, but Runshaw had come a very long way.

Summary

- This chapter aimed to identify the core components of a college-improvement programme and to describe a coherent, structured implementation plan.
- Runshaw's experience, in summary, identified four new forms of leadership as the basic core components. These created a 'professional learning community' and, with it, the capacity for sustained improvement.
- Most colleges do not use these core components because colleges are not designed in a way that makes their adoption possible.
- Colleges need to be redesigned to create connections and internal networks to facilitate collaboration and to support the concept of a 'community of learners'.
- A detailed implementation plan has various identifiable elements, listed here.
- There are seven steps in the process of implementing the plan. These put into practice the principles that underpin dispersed leadership.
- Essentially, a college should implement a plan over about 18 months, meeting monthly with a coach who facilitates the whole process and dipping into training modules on specific processes, cascading these to the whole management team and then to all staff once they have been properly understood and thought through by the managers responsible for their introduction.
- The concept of the 'Runshaw way' is explored and the special ingredients of that 'way' identified, using the perceptions of an independent researcher who interviewed staff and students at Runshaw over a period of three months.
- Trust is seen as the key ingredient.
- What happened at Runshaw is distilled into two key management behaviours, both completely transferable. They are 'listening' and 'taking action' in a continuous cycle.

BIBLIOGRAPHY

Ainley, P. and Bailey, B. (1997) *The Business of Learning*, Cassell, London.

Alexiadou, N. (2001) Management identities in transition: a case study from further education. *Sociological Review*, **49**(3): 412–35.

Audit Commission (1985) *Obtaining Better Value From Further Education*, HMSO, London.

Audit Commission/Ofsted (1993) *Unfinished Business: Full-time Educational Courses*, HMSO, London.

Barber, M. (2000) The very big picture. *Improving Schools*, **3**(2): 5–17.

Bass, B. and Avolio, B. (1994) *Improving Organisational Effectiveness through Transformational Leadership*, Sage, Thousand Oaks CA.

Bates, R.(1993) On knowing: cultural and critical approaches to educational administration. *Educational Management and Administration*, **21**(3): 171–6.

Bennett, N., Wise, C. and Woods, P. (2003) *Distributed Leadership*, National College for School Leadership, Nottingham.

Block, P. (1993) *Stewardship: Choosing Service over Self-Interest*, Berrett Koehler, San Francisco.

Bloomer, M. and Hodkinson, P. (1999) *College Life: the Voice of the Learner*, Further Education Development Agency, London.

Bridge, W. (1994) Change where contrasting cultures meet. *Coombe Lodge Report*, **24**: 189–98.

Briggs, A. (2001a) Academic middle managers in further education: reflections on leadership. *Research in Post-Compulsory Education*, **6**: 223–36.

Briggs, A. (2001b) Middle managers in further education: exploring the role. *Management in Education*, **15**(4): 12–15.

Briggs, A. (2002) Facilitating the role of managers in further education. *Research in Post-Compulsory Education*, **7**(1): 63–78.

Briggs, A. (2003) Finding the balance: exploring the organic and mechanical dimensions of middle manager roles in English further education colleges. *Educational Management and Administration*, **31**(4): 421–36.

Briggs, A. (2005) Middle managers in English further education colleges: understanding and modelling the role. *Educational Management Administration and Leadership*, **33**(1): 27–50.

Brooks, D. (2000) *BOBOS in Paradise*, Touchstone, New York.

Brotherton, B. (1998) Developing a culture and infrastructure to support research related activity in fFurther education institutions. *Research in Post-Compulsory Education*, **3**: 311–28.

Burns, J (1978) *Leadership*, Harper & Row, New York.

Burton, S. (1994) Factors affecting quality in the new FE – principals' views. *Coombe Lodge Report*, **24**: 349–439.

Bush, T. (2003) *Theories of Educational Leadership and Management*, 3rd edn, Paul Chapman, London.

Bush, T. and Glover, D. (2003) *School Leadership: Concepts and Evidence*, National College for School Leadership, Nottingham.

Campbell, A. and Nash, L. (1992) *A Sense of Mission: Defining Direction for the Large Corporation*, Addison-Wesley, New York.

Charlesworth, K., Cook, P. and Crozier, G. (2003) *Leading Change in the Public Sector, Making the Difference*, Chartered Management Institute, London.

Clarke, J. and Newman, J. (1997) *The Managerial State: Power, Politics and Ideology in the Remaking of Social Welfare*, Sage, London.

Cole, P. (2000) Men, women and changing management of further education. *Journal of Further and Higher Education,* **24**(2): 203–16.

Cunningham, J. (1999) Towards a college improvement movement. *Journal of Further and Higher Education,* **23**: 403–13.

Day, C., Harris, A., Hadfield, M., Tolley, H. and Beresford, J. (2000) *Leading School in Times of Change,* Open University Press, Milton Keynes.

Deem, R. and Johnson, R. (2000) Managerialism and university managers: building new academic communities or disrupting old ones? In: *Higher Education and its Communities* (ed. McNay, I.), Open University Press, Buckingham, pp. 65–84.

Department for Education and Skills (2002) *Time for Standards: Reforming the School Workforce,* DfES Publications, London.

Department for Education and Skills (2003) *Every Child Matters,* Stationery Office, London.

Department of Education and Science/Council of Local Education Authorities (1987) *Managing Colleges Efficiently,* DES, London.

Drodge, S. (2002) Managing under pressure: the management of vocational education in the British, Dutch and French Systems. *Research in Post-Compulsory Education,* **7**(1): 27–43.

Drodge, S. and Cooper, N. (1998) Strategy and management in the further education sector. In: *Educational Management: Strategy, Quality and Resources* (eds Preedy, M., Glatter, R. and Levacic, R.), Open University Press, Buckingham, pp. 205–17.

Drucker, P. (1993) *Post-Capitalist Society,* HarperCollins, New York.

Drucker, P. (1994) The age of social transformation. *Atlantic Monthly,* **27**: 53–80.

Earley, P. (1998) Middle management: the key to organisational success? In: *Strategic Management in Schools and Colleges* (eds Middlewood, D. and Lumby, J.), Chapman, London.

Elliott, G. (1996a) Educational management and the crisis of reform in further education. *Journal of Vocational Education and Training,* **48**: 5–24.

Elliott, G. (1996b) *Crisis and Change in Vocational Education and Training,* Jessica Kingsley, London.

Elliott, G. and Crossley, M. (1997) Contested values in further education: findings from a case study of the management of change. *Educational Management and Administration,* **25**: 79–92.

Elliott, G. and Hall, V. (1994) FE Inc. – business orientation in further education and the introduction of human resource management. *School Organisation,* **14**: 3–10.

Farnham, D. and Horton, S. (1993) *Managing the New Public Services,* Macmillan, Basingstoke.

Franks, D., Hartle, F., Hobby, R., Hyde, L., Lees, A. and Stanton, M. (2002) *Further Lessons of Leadership: How Does Leadership in Further Education Compare to Industry?* Hay Group, London.

Fullan, M. (1993) *Change Forces: Probing the Depths of Educational Reform,* Falmer, London.

Fullan, M. (1996). Leadership for change. In: *International Handbook of Educational Leadership and Administration* (eds Leithwood, K., Chapman, J., Corson, D., Hallinger, P. and Hart, A.), Kluwer, Dordrecht, pp. 701–22.

Fullan, M. (1998) Leadership for the twenty first century: breaking the bond of dependency. *Educational Leadership,* **55**(7): 6–10.

Fullan, M. (2001) *Leading in a Culture of Change,* Jossey-Bass, San Francisco.

Further Education Funding Council (FEFC) (1992a) *Establishment of the FEFC,* Circular 92/08, FEFC, Coventry.

Further Education Funding Council (FEFC) (1992b) *Funded Learning,* FEFC, Coventry.

Further Education Funding Council (FEFC) (1999) *Strategic Planning 2000 and Beyond: A Discussion Document,* Circular 99/11, FEFC, Coventry. Available at http://www.fefc.ac.uk. Accessed 14 March 2002.

Further Education Funding Council (FEFC) (2000) *Strategic Plans, Including Financial Forecasts and Accommodation Data,* Circular 00/18, FEFC, Coventry. Available at http://www.fefc.ac.uk. Accessed 14 March 2002.

Gewirtz, S. (2002) *The Managerial School: Post-Welfarism and Social Justice in Education,* Routledge, London.

Gibbons, C. (1998) An investigation into the effects of organisational change on occupational stress in further education lecturers. *Journal of Further and Higher Education,* 22(3): 315–28.

Glatter, R. and Kydd, B. (2003) 'Best practice' in educational leadership and management: can we identify it and learn from it? *Educational Management and Administration,* 31(3): 231–44.

Gleeson, D. (2001) Style and substance in education leadership: further education (FE) as a case in point. *Journal of Education Policy,* 16(3): 181–96.

Gleeson, D. and Shain, F. (1999a) Managing ambiguity between markets and managerialism: a case study of 'middle managers' in further education. *Sociological Review,* 47(3): 461–90.

Gleeson, D. and Shain, F. (1999b) Under new management: changing perceptions of teacher professionalism in the further education sector. *Journal of Education Policy,* 14(4): 445–62.

Gorringe, R. (1994) *Changing the Culture of Human Resource Development in Colleges.* In *Managing and Developing People* (ed. Brain, G.), The Staff College, Blagdon.

Goulding, J., Dominey, J. and Gray, M. (1998) *Hard-nosed Decisions: Planning Human Resources in Further Education,* Further Education Development Agency, London.

Grace, G. (1995) *School Leadership: Beyond Education Management,* Falmer, London.

Greenleaf, K. (1970) *Servant as Leader,* John Wiley, London.

Gronn, P. (1999) *The Making of Educational Leaders,* Cassell, London.

Gronn. P. (2000) Distributed properties: a new architecture of leadership. *Educational Management and Administration,* 28(3): 317–38.

Hadfield, M. (2003) Capacity-building, school improvement and school leaders. In: *Effective Leadership for School Improvement* (eds Harris, A., Day, C., Hopkins, D., Hadfield, M., Hargreaves, A. and Chapman, C.). Routledge Farmer, London.

Handy, C. (1999) *Understanding Organizations,* 4th edn, Penguin, Harmondsworth.

Hargreaves, A. (1994a) *Changing Teachers, Changing Times: Teachers' Work Culture in the Postmodern Age,* Teachers College Press, New York.

Hargreaves, A. (1994b) Individualism and individuality: understanding the teacher culture. In: *Changing Teachers, Changing Times* (ed. Hargreaves, A.), Cassell, London.

Hargreaves, D. (1995) School culture, school effectiveness and school improvement. *School Effectiveness and School Improvement,* 6(1): 23–46.

Hargreaves, D. (2001) A capital theory of school effectiveness and improvement. *British Educational Research Journal,* 27(4): 487–503.

Hargreaves, A. and Fullan, M. (1998) *What's Worth Fighting for Out There,* Teachers College Press, York.

Harper, H. (1997) *Management in Further Education: Theory and Practice,* David Fulton, London.

Harper, H. (2000) New college hierarchies: towards an examination of organisational structures in further education in England and Wales. *Educational Management and Administration,* 28: 433.

Harris, A. and Bennett, N. (eds) (2001) *School Effectiveness and School Improvement Alternative Perspectives,* Cassell, London.

Harris, A., Day, C., Hopkins, D., Hadfield, M., Hargreaves, A. and Chapman, C. (2003) *Effective Leadership for School Improvement,* Routledge Farmer, London.

Hartley, D. (1997) The new managerialism in education: a mission impossible? *Cambridge Journal of Education,* 27: 47–57.

Heifetz, R. A. (1994) *Leadership without Easy Answers*, Belknap Press, Cambridge MA.

Hellawell, D. and Hancock, N. (2001) A case study of the changing role of the academic middle manage in higher education: between hierarchical control and collegiality. *Research Papers in Education*, **126**(2): 183–97.

Hewitt, P. and Crawford, M. (1997) Introducing new contracts: managing change in the context of an enterprise culture. In: *Managing Change in Further Education* (eds Levacic, R. and Glatter, R.), FEDA, London.

Hodgkinson, C. (1991) *Educational Leadership: the Moral Art*, Albany State University of New York, New York.

Hoggett, P. (1996) New modes of control in the public service. *Public Administration*, **74**: 9–32.

Hopkins, D. (2001) *School Improvement for Real*, Routledge Falmer, London.

Hopkins, D. (2002) *Improving the Quality of Education for All*, 2nd edn, David Fulton, London.

Hopkins, D. (2003) Instructional leadership and school improvement. In: *Effective Leadership for School Improvement* (eds Harris, A., Day, C., Hopkins, D., Hadfield, M., Hargreaves, A. and Chapman, C.). Routledge Farmer, London.

Hopkins, D., Ainscow, M. and West, M. (1994) *School Improvement in an Era of Change*, Cassell, London.

Hopkins, D. and Harris, A. (2001) *Creating the Conditions for Teaching and Learning*, Fulton, London.

Hopkins, D., Harris, A. and Jackson, D. (1997) Understanding the school's capacity for development: growth states and strategies. *School Leadership and Management*, **17**(3): 401–11.

Hopkins, D. and Jackson, D. (2003) Building the capacity for leading and learning. In: *Effective Leadership for School Improvement* (eds Harris, A., Day, C., Hopkins, D., Hadfield, M., Hargreaves, A. and Chapman, C.), Routledge Farmer, London.

Hopkins, D. and Reynolds, D. (2001) *Improving Schools in Challenging Circumstances: A Review of the Literature*, DfES, London.

Jackson, P. and Stainsby, L. (2000) Managing public sector networked organisations. *Public Money and Management*, **20**(1): 11–16.

Jephcote, M., Salisbury, J., Fletcher, J., Graham, I. and Mitchell, G. (1996) Principals' responses to incorporation: a window on their cultures. *Journal of Further and Higher Education*, **20**(2): 34–48.

Kennedy, H. (1997) *Learning Works: Widening Participation in Further Education*, FEFC, Coventry.

Kerfoot, D. and Whitehead, S. (1998) Boys' own stuff: masculinity and the management of further education. *Sociological Review*, **46**(3): 436–57.

Learning and Skills Council (2001) *Planning: Strategic Plans, Including Financial Forecasts and Accommodation Data*, Circular 01/01, LSC, Coventry. Available at: http://www.lsc.gov.uk. Accessed 14 March 2002.

Leithwood, K. (1992) The move towards transformational leadership. *Educational Leadership*, **49**(5): 8–12.

Leithwood, K. (2001) School leadership in a context of accountability policies. *International Journal of Leadership in Education*, **4**(3): 217–35.

Leithwood, K., Jantzi, D. and Steinbach, R. (1999) *Changing Leadership for Changing Times*, Open University Press, Buckingham.

Leithwood, K. and Riehl. G. (2003) *What we Know about Successful School Leadership*, Laboratory for Student Success, Philadelphia. Available from www.cepa.gse.rutgersedu/whatweknow.pdf/

Lewis, N. (1994) Re-engineering the culture of a college. In: 'Factors Affecting Quality in the New FE – Principals' Views', Coombe Lodge Report, 24, pp. 349–439.

Lumby, J. (1999) Strategic planning in further education: the business of values. *Educational Management and Administration*, 27(1): 71–83.

Lumby, J. (2001) *Managing Further Education Colleges: Learning Enterprise*, Paul Chapman, London.

Lumby, J. (2003a) Culture change: the case of sixth form and general further education colleges. *Educational Management and Administration*, 31(2): 159–74.

Lumby, J. (2003b) Distributed leadership in colleges: leading or misleading? *Educational Management and Administration*, 31(3): 283–92.

Lumby, J. and Tomlinson, H. (2000) Principals speaking: managerialism and leadership in further education. *Research in Post-Compulsory Education*, 5(2): 139–51.

Morgan, G. (1997) *Images of Organization*, 2nd edn, Sage, London.

Nanus, B.(1992) *Visionary Leadership*, Jossey Bass, San Francisco CA..

National College for School Leadership (NCSL) (2001a) *Report of the Think Tank to the Governing Council*, NCSL, Nottingham.

National College for School Leadership (NCSL) (2001b) *Leadership for Transforming Learning*, Think Tank Report chaired by Professor David Hopkins, NCSL, Nottingham.

Office for Standards in Education (2003a) *Leadership and Management: What Inspection Tells Us*, HMI 1646, Ofsted, London.

Office for Standards in Education (2003b) *Leadership and Management. Managing the School Workforce*, HMI 1764, Ofsted, London.

Office of Public Services Reform (2002) *Reforming our Public Services*, Prime Minister's Office, London.

Patterson, M.G.,West, M.A.,Lathom, R. and Nickell, S. (1997) *Impact of People Management Practices on Business Performance*, Institute of Personnel and Development, London.

Peters, T. C. (1989) *Thriving on Chaos: Handbook for a Management Revolution*, Pan Macmillan, London.

Podsakoff, P.M., MacKenzie, S.B., Moorman, R.H. and Fetter, R. (1990) Transformational leaders' behaviours and their effects on followers' trust in leader, satisfaction, and organizational citizenship behaviours. *Leadership Quarterly*, 1(2): 107–42.

Pollitt, C. (1990) *Managerialism and the Public Services: Cuts or Cultural Change in the 1990s?* 2nd edn, Blackwell, Oxford.

Powell, L. (2001) 'It all goes wrong in the middle': a reassessment of the influence of college structures on middle managers. In: *Leadership Issues: Raising Achievement* (ed. Horsfall, C.), Learning and Skills Development Agency, London.

Preedy, M., Glatter, R. and Levacic, R. (1998) *Educational Management: Strategy, Quality and Resources*, Open University Press, Buckingham.

Preedy, M., Glatter, R. and Wise, C. (eds) (1997) *Strategic Leadership and Educational Improvement*, Paul Chapman, London.

Randle, K. and Brady, N. (1997) Managerialism and professionalism in the 'Cinderella Service'. *Journal of Vocational Education and Training*, 49(1): 121–39.

Randle, K. and Brady, N. (1997) Further education and the new managerialism. *Journal of Further and Higher Education*, 21: 229–39.

Schon, D. (1993) Generative metaphors and social policy. In: *Metaphor and Thought* (ed. Ortony, A.), 2nd edn, Cambridge University Press, Cambridge.

Senge, P. (1990) *The Fifth Discipline: The Art and Practice of the Learning Organization*, Doubleday, New York.

Sergiovanni. T. (1992) *Moral Leadership: Getting to the Heart of School Improvement,* Jossey-Bass, San Francisco.

Sergiovanni, T. (2000) *The Lifeworld of Leadership: Creating Culture, Community, and Personal Meaning in our Schools,* Jossey-Bass, San Francisco.

Sergiovanni, T. (2001) *Leadership,* Routledge Falmer, London.

Shain, F. and Gleeson, D. (1999) Under new management: changing conceptions of teacher professionalism and policy in further education. *Journal of Education Policy,* 14(4): 445–62.

Simkins, T. (2000) Education reform and managerialism: Comparing the experience of schools and colleges. *Journal of Education Policy,* 15(3): 317–32.

Simkins, T. and Lumby, J. (2002) Cultural transformation in further education: mapping the debate. *Researching Post-Compulsory Education,* 7(1): 9–25.

Somekh, B., Convery, A., Delaney, J., Fisher, R., Gray, J. Gunn, S., Henworth, A., Powell, L. (1999) *Improving College Effectiveness,* Further Education, London.

Stoll, L. (1999) Realising our potential: understanding and developing capacity for lasting improvement. *School Effectiveness and School Improvement,* 10(4): 503–32.

Tampoe, M. (1998) *Liberating Leadership,* The Industrial Society, London.

Tom, A. (1984) *Teaching as a Moral Craft,* Longman, New York.

Tschannen-Moran, M. and Hoy, W.K. (2000) A multidisciplinary analysis of the nature, meaning, and measurement of trust. *Review of Educational Research,* 70: 547–93.

INDEX